Error control coding
An introduction

Error control coding
An introduction

Peter Sweeney

Department of Electronic and Electrical Engineering
University of Surrey

Prentice Hall

New York   London   Toronto   Sydney   Tokyo   Singapore

AAX3381

First published 1991 by
Prentice Hall International (UK) Ltd
66 Wood End, Hemel Hempstead
Hertfordshire HP2 4RG
A division of
Simon & Schuster International Group

Typeset in 10/12 pt Times by Columns Design and
Production Services Ltd, Reading

Printed and bound in Great Britain
by Dotesios Printers Ltd, Trowbridge, Wiltshire.

Library of Congress Cataloging-in-Publication Data

Sweeney, Peter, 1950–
   Error control coding : an introduction / by Peter Sweeney.
     p. cm.
   Includes bibliographical references and index.
   ISBN (invalid) 0–13–248119–5
   1. Coding theory. 2. Error-correcting codes (Information theory)
I. Title
TK5102.5.S958   1991
629.8′315–dc20   90–7522
                                         CIP

British Library Cataloguing in Publication Data

Sweeney, Peter 1950–
   Error control coding : an introduction.
   1. Error-correcting codes
I. Title
005.72

   ISBN 0–13–284118–5
   ISBN 0–13–284126–6 pbk

---

1 2 3 4 5 95 94 93 92 91

Contents

List of figures   xi

Preface   xiii

1   The principles of coding   **1**

1.1	Error control schemes	1
1.2	Coding in communication systems	2
1.3	Measures of distance	6
1.4	Soft-decision metrics for a Gaussian channel	7
1.5	Example of block coding	9
1.6	Random error detection and correction capability of block codes	12
1.7	Output error rates using block codes	13
1.8	Code performance and coding gain	15
1.9	General considerations affecting coding gain	17
1.10	Information theory	18
1.11	Further reading	21
1.12	Exercises	21

2   Linear block codes   **23**

2.1	Introduction	23
2.2	Mathematics of binary codes	23
2.3	Linearity	24
2.4	Parity checks	26
2.5	Systematic codes	27
2.6	Minimum Hamming distance of a linear block code	27
2.7	How to encode – generator matrix	28
2.8	Encoding with the parity check matrix	29
2.9	Decoding with the parity check matrix	31
2.10	Decoding by standard array	33
2.11	Codec design for linear block codes	34

	2.12	Modifications to block codes	36
	2.13	Bounds on block codes	39
	2.14	Further reading	43
	2.15	Exercises	44

3　Cyclic codes　　　　　　　　　　　　　　　　　　　46

	3.1	Introduction	46
	3.2	Definition of a cyclic code	46
	3.3	Example of a cyclic code	47
	3.4	Polynomial representation	48
	3.5	Encoding by convolution	48
	3.6	Establishing the cyclic property	50
	3.7	Deducing the properties of a cyclic code	50
	3.8	Primitive polynomials	51
	3.9	Systematic encoding of cyclic codes	52
	3.10	Syndrome of a cyclic code	54
	3.11	Implementation of encoding	54
	3.12	Decoding	57
	3.13	Decoder operation	60
	3.14	Multiple error correction	61
	3.15	Example of multiple error correction	62
	3.16	Shortened cyclic codes	64
	3.17	Expurgated cyclic codes	65
	3.18	BCH codes	67
	3.19	Further reading	68
	3.20	Exercises	68

4　Block codes based on finite field arithmetic　　70

	4.1	Introduction	70
	4.2	Definition of a finite field	70
	4.3	Prime size finite field $GF(p)$	72
	4.4	Extensions to the binary field – finite field $GF(2^m)$	73
	4.5	Zech logarithms	75
	4.6	Implementation of finite field representation	75
	4.7	Properties of polynomials and finite field elements	77
	4.8	Specifying codes by roots	80
	4.9	Hamming codes	81
	4.10	BCH codes	81
	4.11	Fourier transform in a finite field	84
	4.12	Roots and spectral components	86
	4.13	BCH codes in the frequency domain	86
	4.14	BCH decoding and the BCH bound	87
	4.15	Decoding in the frequency domain	88

4.16 Encoding and decoding example 90
4.17 Further examples of Reed Solomon decoding 92
4.18 Decoding of binary BCH codes 95
4.19 Polynomial form of the key equation 96
4.20 Euclid's algorithm 97
4.21 The Berlekamp–Massey algorithm 99
4.22 Extended Reed Solomon codes 101
4.23 Erasure decoding of BCH codes 104
4.24 Example of erasure decoding of Reed Solomon codes 105
4.25 Further reading 107
4.26 Exercises 108

5 Convolutional codes 110

5.1 Introduction 110
5.2 General properties of convolutional codes 111
5.3 Generator polynomials 112
5.4 Terminology 112
5.5 Encoder state diagram 113
5.6 Distance structure of convolutional codes 114
5.7 Evaluating distance and weight structure 116
5.8 Catastrophic error propagation 117
5.9 Maximum likelihood decoding 118
5.10 The Viterbi algorithm 119
5.11 Example of Viterbi decoding 120
5.12 Applicability of convolutional codes 123
5.13 Performance of convolutional codes 125
5.14 Punctured convolutional codes 126
5.15 Sequential decoding 127
5.16 Syndrome decoding 129
5.17 Further reading 130
5.18 Exercises 131

6 Coding for bursty channels 133

6.1 Introduction 133
6.2 Description of bursty errors 134
6.3 Block codes for single-burst error correction 135
6.4 Fire codes 136
6.5 Convolutional codes for burst error correction 138
6.6 Phased-burst error correcting codes 139
6.7 Techniques for compound channels 140
6.8 Interleaving 141
6.9 Product codes 144

6.10   Further reading   148
6.11   Exercises   149

7   Concatenated codes   150

7.1   Introduction   150
7.2   General principle of concatenation   150
7.3   Concatenation using inner block code   152
7.4   Maximal length codes   152
7.5   Orthogonal codes   153
7.6   Reed Muller codes   153
7.7   Block codes with soft-decision decoding   154
7.8   Concatenation using inner convolutional code   155
7.9   Performance of concatenated codes   156
7.10   Further reading   157
7.11   Exercises   158

8   Coding for bandwidth-limited channels   159

8.1   Introduction   159
8.2   M-ary phase shift keying (MPSK)   160
8.3   Quadrature amplitude modulation   161
8.4   Ungerboeck codes   162
8.5   Set partitioning   162
8.6   Integration of coding with partitioning   165
8.7   Performance of Ungerboeck codes   166
8.8   Further reading   167
8.9   Exercises   168

9   Error detection methods   169

9.1   Introduction   169
9.2   Random error detection performance of block codes   170
9.3   Weight distributions   171
9.4   Worst case undetected error rate   173
9.5   Burst error detection   173
9.6   Examples of error detection codes   173
9.7   Synchronization using block codes   175
9.8   Automatic retransmission request   176
9.9   Stop-and-wait ARQ   177
9.10   Go-back-N ARQ   177
9.11   Selective repeat ARQ   179
9.12   ARQ in communications protocols   180
9.13   Hybrid ARQ/FEC   181

9.14 Error concealment   182
9.15 Further reading   183
9.16 Exercises   183

10 Selection of a coding scheme   185

10.1 Introduction   185
10.2 General considerations   186
10.3 Data structure   187
10.4 Information type   187
10.5 Data rate   188
10.6 Real-time processing   189
10.7 Power and bandwidth constraints   189
10.8 Channel error mechanisms   190
10.9 Cost   190
10.10 Applications   191

References   193

Index   196

List of figures

1.1	Coding system	2
1.2	Encoder	3
1.3	Binary symmetric channel	5
1.4	Soft decision detection thresholds	8
1.5	Performance curve for (255,191) block code	17
2.1	Encoder structure	35
2.2	Error correction for linear block code	36
3.1	Encoder for cyclic (7,4) Hamming code	55
3.2	Improved version of encoder for cyclic (7,4) Hamming code	56
3.3	General encoder for cyclic codes	56
3.4	Syndrome formation for shortened code	64
3.5	Syndrome formation for expurgated code	67
4.1	Shift register generation of transform of error locator polynomial	88
4.2	Frequency domain encoding and decoding of Reed Solomon codes	90
4.3	Shift register for recursive extension	91
4.4	Recursive extension with single error	93
4.5	Attempted recursive extension after triple error	94
4.6	Encoding of extended Reed Solomon code	102
4.7	Syndrome formation for extended Reed Solomon code	103
4.8	Recursive extension with one error and two erasures	107
5.1	Convolutional encoder	111
5.2	Encoder state diagram	114
5.3	Modified encoder state diagram	116
5.4	Code trellis	119
5.5	Survivor paths in Viterbi decoding	123
6.1	Error burst of length 10	134
6.2	End-around burst of length 6	135
6.3	Split syndrome formation for (105,94) Fire code	137
6.4	Block interleaving	142
6.5	Rate 1/2 convolutional encoder with interleaving to degree 3	143
6.6	Convolutional interleaving	143
6.7	Product code	144
6.8	Quadruple-error correcting product code with four errors	146
6.9	Product code after row decoding	146

6.10 Product code after decoding of two rows   146
6.11 Product code after row erasure   147
6.12 Cyclic ordering for product code   148
7.1   Code concatenation   151
8.1   Demodulator decision boundaries for MPSK   160
8.2   A 16-point QAM constellation   161
8.3   A 32-point QAM constellation   161
8.4   A 64-point constellation partitioned into two sets   163
8.5   Set A of a partitioned 64-point constellation   164
8.6   Set B of a partitioned 64-point constellation   164
8.7   A 64-point constellation partitioned twice   165
8.8   A 64-point constellation partitioned three times   165
8.9   Trellis for rate 1/2 code   167
8.10 Partitioned 8-PSK constellation   167
9.1   Syndrome calculation for synchronization   175
9.2   Go-back-5 ARQ   178
9.3   Selective repeat ARQ   179
9.4   Selective repeat ARQ with five-message buffer   180

Preface

All sciences and technologies contain subjects that are generally reckoned to be strictly for the *cognoscenti*, being both difficult and of marginal importance. In the early days of my exposure to the subject of error correcting codes, that was certainly the image that it presented to me. I was concerned that my efforts to understand would at best be useful for the one system on which I was working. Secretly I was afraid that whole subject might be beyond my mental capabilities. I went as far into the subject as was strictly necessary and no further. It was some years before the wider applicability became obvious and I was brave enough to delve a little deeper.

Having been closely concerned with the design and assessment of error control schemes for some seven years now, I can see that my image of the subject was completely wrong. Error control methods can deliver acceptable results more cheaply than can be achieved without them. Moderately successful attempts to teach at advanced undergraduate and postgraduate levels have shown that the subject is not even that difficult, even though some of the students are no more intelligent than I am! The old image dies hard, but good treatments of coding are starting to appear in the better text books on digital communications and there are at least four reference works from the 1980s that can play some part in making the subject more accessible.

The intention of this book is to help fill a gap in the middle market, providing a specialized text whose approach is designed for students and which is not beyond their pockets. Once the fundamentals have been grasped they can then make good use of the reference books and research papers to study particular matters in greater depth. This does not mean that there is no coverage of advanced material; such subjects as finite field arithmetic, Reed Solomon codes, the Berlekamp–Massey algorithm and the Viterbi algorithm are all treated in some detail, albeit through the medium of simple examples. Nor does it mean (I hope) that there is little of interest to the practicing engineer, since I have tried to point out the practical implications of the theory, including some that I have not seen treated elsewhere. Indeed I hope that the removal of certain specialist aspects will allow important principles to emerge more clearly.

The approach that I have adopted seems to work reasonably well for my own students. It has been tested out on several classes and has been improved in the process. In essence it is to start from simple examples and proceed from the particular to the general. Although my own difficulties with the subject are largely in the past, I can still remember what those difficulties were and I know that working through examples has helped me to understand more clearly. With the passage of time my own understanding has improved but my memory of the learning process has faded, so that in a few years time I am not sure that I will still be in touch with the needs of beginners. I hope I have captured roughly the right moment.

There is enough material in this book easily to fill thirty hours of lectures. I imagine that is more than enough for most courses on error control coding and some selection will have to be made. I have used the material to teach three different, although partially overlapping, courses to postgraduates and final-year undergraduates. I have tried to point out at the start of each chapter whether there are any prerequisites for its understanding. I have also occasionally included similar material in two different places to avoid too much cross-referencing. The example that comes to mind is that a simple description of Reed Solomon codes has been given in the chapter on burst error correction, even though they have been extensively described in an earlier chapter; that earlier treatment would not form a part of a good many courses.

Chapter 1 is intended to show in general terms the uses and benefits of coding and to convince through simple examples that error correction is possible. It would be possible to use this treatment at a relatively early stage of an undergraduate course, particularly if it was intended to take the subject further in a later year. From there the next step would be to cover some or all of Chapter 2 (on block codes) before covering cyclic codes in Chapter 3. Chapter 4 would be appropriate for an in-depth course on block codes including finite field arithmetic, transform techniques and algebraic decoding. If the course is aimed towards communications systems, then Chapter 5, covering convolutional codes and concentrating on Viterbi decoding, will be essential. Further chapters cover the various methods of coding for bursty channels, concatenated codes, coding for bandwidth limited channels (Ungerboeck codes), and methods not using forward error correction, particularly detecting errors and requesting retransmission. In the final chapter I have tried to approach the subject from the problem rather than the code, to meet the needs of the engineer who knows the nature of the problems faced and wants to know what solutions are worth considering. I am sure that this chapter could be a lot better than it is, but it is rare to have it at all and I think it does have something useful to say.

As well as defining the prerequisites, each chapter has suggestions for further reading at the end. The references are not intended to be exhaustive but should be seen as the initial directions along the paths of discovery. All but the last chapter have a selection of exercises at the end to test understanding. Some of the exercises are straightforward, some are more difficult and some are intended to make the reader think about issues that will arise later in the book. The ones marked with an asterisk are considered to be the most difficult, bearing in mind the stage of understanding that the student will have reached; often they are the ones intended to provoke thought about later issues. There is a teachers' manual too, intended to make sure that the exercises were sensible and that I could do all of them. I hope it will also help teachers to stay one step ahead of the class.

At this point I would like to record my gratitude to a number of people without whom this book might never have happened. Firstly, my initial learning of the subject relied heavily on the authors of books and papers mentioned at various points in the text; I have tried to give credit where it is due, although many of the approaches are so widely adopted that it is impossible to know the original source. My thanks to Bob Harris of ESTEC and Paddy Farrell of Manchester University who were instrumental in persuading me to look closely at coding in the first place, and to Barry Evans who let me use the students on our M.Sc. in Satellite Communication Engineering as guinea-pigs.

Many of the ideas in this book have come from, or been improved by, students here at the Department of Electronic and Electrical Engineering, University of Surrey. Toufic Bechnati, David Tran and Javed Mirza provided ideas on finite field arithmetic and algebraic decoding. John Jackson and Mun-Kein Chang improved my understanding of product codes. Rob Jeffrey and Maher Tarabah contributed to the treatment of convolutional codes. A lecture by Ray Hill of Salford University brought the Griesmer bound to my attention, and I have also adopted a suggestion made by Graham Norton of Bristol University regarding the treatment of linearity. Thanks also to the anonymous reviewers, conscripted by Prentice Hall, whose constructive criticisms have been so helpful. If I have forgotten anyone, as surely I must, my thanks and apologies go to them too.

Finally I want to thank members of my family for their patience and encouragement. My wife, Gillian, had to put up with my getting home late when my real work could not be reasonably accommodated with the preparation of the manuscript. My parents were not affected by such problems, nevertheless the book is a small testimony to their encouragement of my childhood studies. For all the work's deficiencies, however, the responsibility is mine.

Peter Sweeney

1
The principles of coding

1.1   Error control schemes

Error control coding is concerned with methods of delivering information from a source to a destination with a minimum of errors. As such it can be seen as a branch of information theory and certainly traces its origins to Shannon's work in the late 1940s. The early theoretical work indicates what is possible and provides some insights into the general principles of error control. On the other hand, the problems involved in finding and implementing codes have meant that the practical effects of employing coding are at present somewhat different from what was originally expected.

Shannon's work showed that any communication channel could be characterized by a capacity at which information could be reliably transmitted. At any rate of information transmission up to the channel capacity it should be possible to transfer information at error rates that can be reduced to any desired level. Error control can be provided by introducing redundancy into transmissions. This means that more symbols are included in the message than are strictly needed just to convey the information, with the result that only certain patterns at the receiver correspond to valid transmissions. Once an adequate degree of error control has been introduced, the error rates can be made as low as required by extending the length of the code, thus averaging the effects of noise over a longer period.

Experience has shown that to find good long codes is more easily said than done. Present-day practice is not to use codes as a way of obtaining the theoretical channel capacity but to concentrate on the improvements that can be obtained compared with uncoded communications. Thus the use of coding may increase the operational range of a communications system, reduce the error rates, reduce the transmitted power requirements or obtain a blend of all these benefits. Apart from the variety of codes that are available, there are several general techniques for the control of errors and the choice will depend on the nature of the data and the user's requirements for error-free reception. The most complex techniques fall into the category of forward error correction, where it is

1

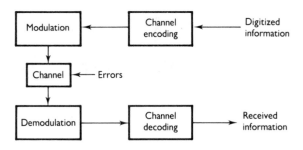

Figure 1.1 Coding system

assumed that errors will occur and a code capable of correcting the assumed errors is applied to the messages. Alternatives are to detect errors and request retransmission, which is known as retransmission error control, or to use inherent redundancy to process the erroneous data in a way that will make the errors subjectively unimportant. This latter technique of error concealment is essentially a signal-processing task and is not considered here. This book concentrates on forward error correction, but the performance of error detection codes and their use in conjunction with retransmission error control are considered in Chapter 9.

This chapter first looks at the place of coding within telecommunications systems. Sections 1.3 and 1.4 then address the question of what coding is in principle trying to achieve and the interface between the demodulator and the decoder; these sections may be omitted on first reading without seriously weakening the rest of the chapter. Next is found a simple example of a code, from a class known as block codes, which is used to show how error detection and correction may in principle be achieved. A number of general results for error detection and correction capabilities and output error rates are then obtained for block codes. Sections 1.8 and 1.9 introduce the concept of coding gain and explain many of the commonly found features of code performance. Finally the practical considerations are put into perspective by a summary of the results of information theory, which provide some insights into the possibilities for advancements in coded systems.

1.2   Coding in communication systems

A typical communication system incorporating coding is shown in Figure 1.1. The important elements of the system are as follows:

Source encoding

Information is given a digital representation, possibly in conjunction with techniques for removal of any inherent redundancy within the data. Such techniques, although an important subject in their own right, are not considered in this text. The most important point for our purposes is that the error control techniques to be described will all operate on a digital form of information.

Error control coding

The encoder is represented in Figure 1.2. The information is formed into frames to be presented to the encoder, each frame consisting of a fixed number of symbols. In most cases the symbols at the input of the encoder are bits; in a very few cases symbols consisting of several bits are required by the encoder. The term *symbol* will be used to maintain generality.

The symbols in the input frame, and possibly a number of previous frames, are used by the encoder to produce its output. The output generally contains more symbols than the input, i.e. redundancy has been added. A commonly used descriptor of a code is the *code rate* (R), which is the ratio of input to output symbols in one frame. A low code rate indicates a high degree of redundancy, which is likely to provide more effective error control than a higher rate at the expense of reducing the information throughput.

If the decoder uses only the current frame to produce its output, then the code is called a (n,k) block code, with the number of input symbols per frame designated k and the corresponding number of output symbols n. If the encoder remembers a number of previous frames and uses them in its algorithm, then the code is called a tree code and is usually a member of a subset known as convolutional codes. In this case the number of symbols in the input frame will be designated k_0 with n_0 symbols in the output frame.

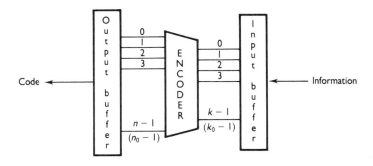

Figure 1.2 Encoder

In more complex systems the encoding may consist of more than one stage and may incorporate both block and convolutional codes and, possibly, a technique known as interleaving. Such systems will be considered in Chapters 6 and 7.

Modulation

The encoded information is used to modulate a carrier for transmission over the channel. The size of the symbols to be transmitted does not necessarily correspond to the size of the encoder's symbols. It is possible for a binary code to be used in conjunction with nonbinary signalling or for a nonbinary code to be used over a binary channel. In principle the error control coding and the modulation should be chosen together, although in practice the link between coding and modulation is often ignored. For conventional binary modulations this separation may be justifiable, although the tendency of methods such as differential phase-shift keying (DPSK) to produce pairs of bit errors must be taken into account. For nonbinary forms of modulation it is important to design the code and the modulation together, as explained in Chapter 8.

The channel

The transmission medium introduces a number of effects, such as attenuation, distortion, interference and noise, which make it uncertain whether the information will be received correctly. Although it is easiest to think in terms of the channel as introducing errors, it should be realized that it is the effects of the channel on the demodulator that produce the errors.

The way in which the transmitted symbols are corrupted may be described using the following terms:

- Memoryless channel – the probability of error is independent from one symbol to the next.

- Symmetric channel – the probability of a transmitted symbol value i being received as a value j is the same as that of a transmitted symbol value j being received as i, for all values of i and j. A commonly encountered example is the binary symmetric channel (BSC) with a probability p of bit error, as illustrated in Figure 1.3.

- Additive white Gaussian noise (AWGN) channel – a memoryless channel in which the transmitted signal suffers the addition of wide-band noise whose amplitude is a normally (Gaussian) distributed random variable.

- Bursty channel – the errors are characterized by periods of relatively high symbol error rate separated by periods of relatively low, or zero, error rate.

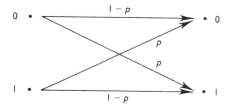

Figure 1.3 Binary symmetric channel

- Compound (or diffuse) channel – the errors consist of a mixture of bursts and random errors. In reality all channels exhibit some form of compound characteristics.

Demodulation

The demodulator attempts to decide on the values of the symbols that were transmitted and pass those decisions on to the next stage. In some cases the demodulator's decision will be easy, in other cases it will be difficult. In principle, if errors are to be corrected it is better for the demodulator to pass on the information about the certainty of its decisions because this might assist the decoder in pinpointing the positions of the likely errors; this is called soft-decision demodulation. Soft decision is only useful, however, if there is a practicable decoding algorithm that makes use of the confidence information. For this reason, the demodulator often provides only hard decisions, particularly when block codes are used.

Decoding

The job of the decoder is to decide what the transmitted information was. It is able to do this because only certain transmitted sequences, known as codewords, are possible and any errors are likely to result in reception of a noncode sequence. On a memoryless channel, the best strategy for the decoder is to compare the received sequence with all the codewords, taking into account the confidence in the received symbols, and select the codeword that is closest to the received sequence. The measure of difference between sequences is known as distance, and this method is called minimum distance decoding. The actual decoding method used is, however, often not a true minimum distance method because the amount of work in doing all the comparisons may make it impractical.

Regardless of the code and the decoding method, there are a number of common characteristics of coding systems. The first is that they aim to correct the most likely errors, but have to accept that less likely errors will not be handled correctly. The other main point is that when error correction is being carried out, if the decoder does not get it completely right, then it will make several errors and may well make things worse. This latter point will be seen in an example to be developed in Section 1.5.

1.3   Measures of distance

It was stated above that decoding should in principle be carried out by minimizing some measure of the difference, or distance, between the received sequence and a code sequence. It is instructive to see why this is so, and how we may choose a measure of distance for both hard-decision and soft-decision demodulation. The measure to be adopted will be called the *decoding metric*.

Suppose we receive a sequence of symbols **r** and wish to find the most likely transmitted sequence **v**. Thus we need to find the maximum value of $p(\mathbf{v}|\mathbf{r})$, the probability that **v** was the transmitted sequence given that **r** was received. But

$$p(\mathbf{v}|\mathbf{r}) = \frac{p(\mathbf{v},\mathbf{r})}{p(\mathbf{r})} = \frac{p(\mathbf{r}|\mathbf{v})\,p(\mathbf{v})}{p(\mathbf{r})} \tag{1.1}$$

where $p(\mathbf{v},\mathbf{r})$ is the probability that **v** is transmitted *and* **r** is received. Thus if the transmitted sequences are equiprobable, we are seeking to find the transmitted sequence that maximizes the probability of giving rise to the received sequence.

If the received sequence has n symbols and the symbol errors are independent, then

$$p(\mathbf{r}|\mathbf{v}) = \prod_{i=1}^{n} p(r_i|v_i)$$

$$\log p(\mathbf{r}|\mathbf{v}) = \sum_{i=1}^{n} \log p(r_i|v_i) \tag{1.2}$$

This logarithmic probability is negative and $p(\mathbf{r}|\mathbf{v})$ will thus be maximized whenever the magnitude of the sum on the right-hand side is minimized.

Let us now define a metric for any symbol, transmitted as i and received as j, as

$$m_{ij} = -A - B \log p(j|i) \tag{1.3}$$

The constants A and B do not affect the ranking of metrics for different paths of the same length, and can therefore be chosen to to have any convenient values. We therefore choose them to give a zero metric for a received symbol value the same as the transmitted symbol and a convenient range over other received symbol values. Over a binary symmetric channel, for example, we could make the metric be 0 for $i = j$ and 1 otherwise. If we now search over all possible transmitted sequences (codewords) for the minimum total metric value, we shall find the most likely transmitted sequence.

The implication of the above analysis is that minimization of distance is the optimum approach if symbol errors are independent (memoryless channel). In the case of hard decision, we can implement the decoding metric as a count of the instances where the received sequence and the code sequence differ, and minimum distance decoding will mean finding the code sequence that has the fewest differences from the received sequence. The soft-decision case is studied in the next section.

1.4   Soft-decision metrics for a Gaussian channel

If we wish to extend our concept of a metric to cover soft decision, then in principle we need to know the transition probabilities between the transmitted and received values. These probabilities, and thus the optimum metric, will vary according to the signal-to-noise ratio at the receiver. Nevertheless a fixed scheme will often provide an adequate compromise over a wide range of operating conditions.

Suppose we have binary transmissions over a symmetric channel and, in the absence of noise, we detect signal levels of $-\sqrt{E_s}$ for 0 and $\sqrt{E_s}$ for 1 (E_s is the received energy per symbol). If the noise has a Gaussian distribution with zero mean and variance $N_0/2$ (N_0 is the single-sided noise power spectral density), then the probability of a noise value between x and $x + dx$ is

$$p(x)\ dx = (\pi N_0)^{-\frac{1}{2}}\ e^{-(x^2/N_0)}\ dx \qquad (1.4)$$

In the presence of noise we would not normally have access to the analog detected signal, but we might quantize the output to several levels. In practice it is found that eight levels give an adequately good performance. We could therefore set the thresholds for our detected signal levels at intervals of $2\sqrt{E_s}/7$, as shown in Figure 1.4. The demodulator is here passing a 3-bit value to the decoder, ranging from 000 (high certainty of received value 0) to 111 (high certainty of received value 1). The demodulator chooses the value according to the range within which the detected signal falls. The question to be answered is the measure of distance to be attached when comparing one of these 3-bit values with a value 0 or 1 in a code sequence. We might assume that the received values 000, 001, 010, 011, 100, 101, 110, 111 should be given distances 0, 1, 2, 3, 4, 5, 6 and 7 from the code symbol 0. This turns out to be not quite right, but so close to the optimum that there is little point in doing anything else.

If the lower thresholds for outputs j and $j + 1$ are l_j and l_{j+1}, then

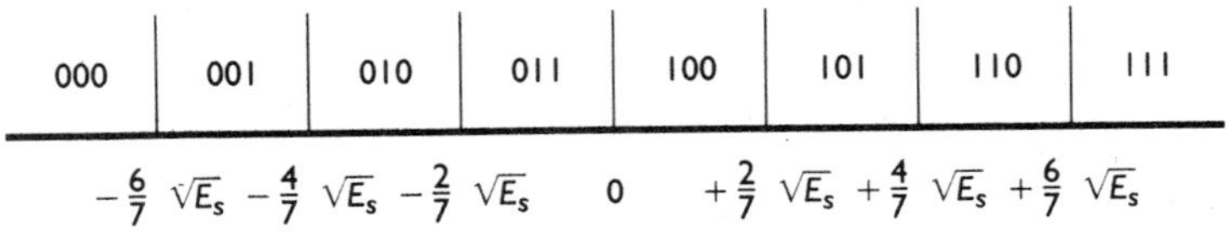

000	001	010	011	100	101	110	111

$$-\frac{6}{7}\sqrt{E_s} \quad -\frac{4}{7}\sqrt{E_s} \quad -\frac{2}{7}\sqrt{E_s} \quad 0 \quad +\frac{2}{7}\sqrt{E_s} \quad +\frac{4}{7}\sqrt{E_s} \quad +\frac{6}{7}\sqrt{E_s}$$

Figure 1.4 Soft decision detection thresholds

$$p(j|0) = (\pi N_0)^{-\frac{1}{2}} \int_{l_j}^{l_{j+1}} e^{-(x+\sqrt{E_s})^2/N_0} \, dx \qquad (1.5)$$

which gives values for eight-level quantization:

$$p(0|0) = 1.0 - 0.5 \, \text{erfc} \left(\frac{1}{7} \sqrt{E_s/N_0} \right)$$

$$p(j|0) = 0.5 \left[\text{erfc} \left(\frac{2j-1}{7} \sqrt{E_s/N_0} \right) - \text{erfc} \left(\frac{2j+1}{7} \sqrt{E_s/N_0} \right) \right], \qquad j = 1 - 6$$

$$p(7|0) = 0.5 \, \text{erfc} \left(\frac{13}{7} \sqrt{E_s/N_0} \right)$$

where

$$\text{erfc}(x) = \frac{2}{\sqrt{\pi}} \int_x^\infty e^{-t^2} \, dt$$

is the *complementary error function*.

From symmetry we can also say

$$p(7 - j|1) = p(j|0)$$

Evaluation of the optimum metrics is not easy, but the steps are explained by Clark and Cain (1981). For E_s/N_0 of 0 dB, they quote conveniently scaled values for the optimum metrics as 0, 1, 2, 3, 4, 5, 6 and 8.67. This is little different from the linear metric assumed above, the only discrepancy being that to receive a transmitted 0 as 111 (or transmitted 1 as 000) is slightly less likely than the linear metric would suggest. The linear metric works perfectly well in a wide range of practical cases. If for any case of interest a linear spacing of demodulation thresholds results in nonlinear metrics, the best solution might well be to adjust the thresholds rather than increase the complexity of the decoder's metric calculations.

1.5   **Example of block coding**

In order to see more clearly some of the effects of error control coding, an example of a binary block code is presented in Table 1.1. Encoding will be done by looking up the codeword that corresponds to the information. After introducing errors, decoding will be performed by comparing the received sequence with every codeword to find the one that is the least distance from the received sequence. In the hard decision case this boils down to a simple count of discrepancies, known as Hamming distance. Suppose we wish to transmit the information 1100. From Table 1.1, the codeword is 1100011. Note that the codeword consists of the information followed by some extra bits; these bits have in fact been calculated from the information in a manner that will be explained in Chapter 2. This construction of information symbols followed by further calculated symbols is common in block codes, the code being said to be *systematic*.

Table 1.1   Example of a block code

Information	Code
0 0 0 0	0 0 0 0 0 0 0
1 0 0 0	1 0 0 0 1 1 0
0 1 0 0	0 1 0 0 1 0 1
1 1 0 0	1 1 0 0 0 1 1
0 0 1 0	0 0 1 0 0 1 1
1 0 1 0	1 0 1 0 1 0 1
0 1 1 0	0 1 1 0 1 1 0
1 1 1 0	1 1 1 0 0 0 0
0 0 0 1	0 0 0 1 1 1 1
1 0 0 1	1 0 0 1 0 0 1
0 1 0 1	0 1 0 1 0 1 0
1 1 0 1	1 1 0 1 1 0 0
0 0 1 1	0 0 1 1 1 0 0
1 0 1 1	1 0 1 1 0 1 0
0 1 1 1	0 1 1 1 0 0 1
1 1 1 1	1 1 1 1 1 1 1

Let us now introduce a single error into the code sequence, assuming that the sequence 1000011 is received. We could now compare the received sequence with every codeword as shown in Table 1.2. There is only one codeword that has a single difference from the received sequence, and that is our originally transmitted sequence 1100011. The systematic construction then makes it easy to extract the information 1100.

Table 1.2 Example of single-error correction

Received	Codeword	Distance
1 0 0 0 0 1 1	0 0 0 0 0 0 0	3
1 0 0 0 0 1 1	1 0 0 0 1 1 0	2
1 0 0 0 0 1 1	0 1 0 0 1 0 1	4
1 0 0 0 0 1 1	1 1 0 0 0 1 1	1
1 0 0 0 0 1 1	0 0 1 0 0 1 1	2
1 0 0 0 0 1 1	1 0 1 0 1 0 1	3
1 0 0 0 0 1 1	0 1 1 0 1 1 0	5
1 0 0 0 0 1 1	1 1 1 0 0 0 0	4
1 0 0 0 0 1 1	0 0 0 1 1 1 1	3
1 0 0 0 0 1 1	1 0 0 1 0 0 1	2
1 0 0 0 0 1 1	0 1 0 1 0 1 0	4
1 0 0 0 0 1 1	1 1 0 1 1 0 0	5
1 0 0 0 0 1 1	0 0 1 1 1 0 0	6
1 0 0 0 0 1 1	1 0 1 1 0 1 0	3
1 0 0 0 0 1 1	0 1 1 1 0 0 1	5
1 0 0 0 0 1 1	1 1 1 1 1 1 1	4

Of course the error created for the above example was in one of the information bits, so it might be as well to check what happens if the error falls in one of the calculated bits. Suppose we start again from the codeword 1100011 but assume that 1100111 is received. We repeat the previous exercise with the results shown in Table 1.3. Again we have chosen the correct codeword. Further examples may be tried and it will be found that single-bit errors are always recovered.

Table 1.3 Second example of single-error correction

Received	Codeword	Distance
1 1 0 0 1 1 1	0 0 0 0 0 0 0	5
1 1 0 0 1 1 1	1 0 0 0 1 1 0	2
1 1 0 0 1 1 1	0 1 0 0 1 0 1	2
1 1 0 0 1 1 1	1 1 0 0 0 1 1	1
1 1 0 0 1 1 1	0 0 1 0 0 1 1	4
1 1 0 0 1 1 1	1 0 1 0 1 0 1	3
1 1 0 0 1 1 1	0 1 1 0 1 1 0	3
1 1 0 0 1 1 1	1 1 1 0 0 0 0	4
1 1 0 0 1 1 1	0 0 0 1 1 1 1	3
1 1 0 0 1 1 1	1 0 0 1 0 0 1	4
1 1 0 0 1 1 1	0 1 0 1 0 1 0	4
1 1 0 0 1 1 1	1 1 0 1 1 0 0	3
1 1 0 0 1 1 1	0 0 1 1 1 0 0	6
1 1 0 0 1 1 1	1 0 1 1 0 1 0	5
1 1 0 0 1 1 1	0 1 1 1 0 0 1	5
1 1 0 0 1 1 1	1 1 1 1 1 1 1	2

Finally, let us see what happens if two errors occur, corrupting the transmitted sequence 1100011 to 1101001 (see Table 1.4). In this case we choose the wrong codeword 1101001 and decode the information as 1101. The decoder has chosen a codeword that differs in three places from the transmitted codeword, adding one error to the two occurring on the channel. Two of those errors have followed through into the information, but that is purely chance; in other cases just one or even all three of the decoding errors could have occurred in the information bits.

Table 1.4   Example of attempted double-error correction

Received	Codeword	Distance
1 1 0 1 0 0 1	0 0 0 0 0 0 0	4
1 1 0 1 0 0 1	1 0 0 0 1 1 0	5
1 1 0 1 0 0 1	0 1 0 0 1 0 1	3
1 1 0 1 0 0 1	1 1 0 0 0 1 1	2
1 1 0 1 0 0 1	0 0 1 0 0 1 1	5
1 1 0 1 0 0 1	1 0 1 0 1 0 1	4
1 1 0 1 0 0 1	0 1 1 0 1 1 0	6
1 1 0 1 0 0 1	1 1 1 0 0 0 0	3
1 1 0 1 0 0 1	0 0 0 1 1 1 1	4
1 1 0 1 0 0 1	1 0 0 1 0 0 1	1
1 1 0 1 0 0 1	0 1 0 1 0 1 0	3
1 1 0 1 0 0 1	1 1 0 1 1 0 0	2
1 1 0 1 0 0 1	0 0 1 1 1 0 0	5
1 1 0 1 0 0 1	1 0 1 1 0 1 0	4
1 1 0 1 0 0 1	0 1 1 1 0 0 1	2
1 1 0 1 0 0 1	1 1 1 1 1 1 1	3

By trying further examples, the reader should soon be convinced that this is a code which can be guaranteed to correct single errors, but invariably fails if two or more errors occur. It will be seen shortly that the guaranteed correction is fairly easily predicted from the properties of the code, but the invariable choice of the wrong codeword if extra errors occur is slightly unusual; most codes have cases where a received sequence may fall at equal distance from two or more codewords, leaving the decoder unable to choose. In such cases it would be usual to declare a detected error but not to attempt correction. For example, in the simple code shown in Table 1.5 it can be seen that any single error will be corrected and some double errors (e.g. changing 01011 to 00001) will be miscorrected. Some double errors (e.g. changing 01011 to 10011) will, however, be uncorrectable because the received sequence differs in two places from two or more codewords.

Table 1.5

Information	Code
0 0	0 0 0 0 0
0 1	0 1 0 1 1
1 0	1 0 1 0 1
1 1	1 1 1 1 0

1.6   Random error detection and correction capability of block codes

If we try to analyze the reasons for the error correction performance of the block code in the previous section, we reach the conclusion that starting from any codeword we would have to change at least three bits to create another codeword. This least distance measure between codewords is important in determining the properties of the code and is called the *minimum distance*, d_{min}. If we change only one bit in a codeword, then we would have to change at least two more to reach another codeword, hence single-bit errors can be recovered. On the other hand two or more errors are likely (for this code certain) to leave us closer to another codeword than the original. We could instead aim merely to detect the presence of errors by detecting that the received sequence is not a codeword. In this case one or two errors must be detected, three or more errors might result in another codeword being received.

In general we can use block codes either for error detection alone, for error correction or for some combination of the two. Taking into account that we cannot correct an error that cannot be detected, we reach the following formula to determine the guaranteed error detection and correction properties, given the minimum distance of the code:

$$d_{min} > s + t \tag{1.6}$$

where s is the number of errors to be detected and t ($\leqslant s$) is the number of errors to be corrected. Assuming that the sum of s and t will be the maximum possible, then

$$d_{min} = s + t + 1$$

Thus if $d_{min} = 5$, the possibilities are

$$s = 4 \qquad t = 0$$
$$s = 3 \qquad t = 1$$
$$s = 2 \qquad t = 2$$

If we decided, for example, to go for single-error correction with triple-error detection, then the occurrence of four errors would be detected, but the likelihood is that the decoder would assume it was the result of a single error on a different codeword from the one transmitted.

If the code is to be used for correction of the maximum amount of errors, and if the value of minimum distance is odd, then setting $t = s$ gives

$$d_{\min} = 2t + 1 \qquad (1.7)$$

1.7   Output error rates using block codes

The use of error correcting codes does not produce error-free output, even when the channel error rates are accurately known. The design of any coding system must proceed from a definition of the acceptable output error rates. Some forms of data, such as speech or images, may contain a high degree of inherent redundancy, which means that bit error rates as high as 10^{-3} can be tolerated before the effects are subjectively significant. On the other hand, if the item of data to be transmitted is one from a fixed set of messages with every combination of bits representing a valid message, then message errors may result in completely the wrong information being transferred. In this case it will probably be the message error rate that is specified, with the requirement depending on the consequences of an error. The relative effects of coding on message and bit error rates are examined below and in Section 1.9.

For known channel characteristics and a given code it will always be possible to obtain an estimate of the output error rates, if necessary by simulation of the channel and the encoding/decoding. In many cases, however, the estimate can be obtained by calculation. This section shows how such an estimate may be achieved for a random error binary channel using block codes with hard-decision decoding, using the characteristics that we have already seen in our block coding example.

Suppose we are using a t-error correcting code and subjecting the decoder to a random bit error rate p. If we wish to work out the rate at which decoding errors occur, we usually assume that if more than t errors occur there will be a decoding error. This was true for our example system, but in general there will be some possibility of decoding beyond the guaranteed correction capability of the code or of detecting errors in such cases; it is therefore a pessimistic assumption.

If we use a binary code, then the code symbol error rate p_s will be the same as the channel bit error rate p. On the other hand, suppose our code uses symbols that consist of l bits. The symbol error rate over a binary channel will be given by

$$1 - p_s = (1 - p)^l$$

In other words, the probability of a symbol being correct is equal to the probability of all the bits being correct. Rearranging gives

$$p_s = 1 - (1 - p)^l \tag{1.8}$$

The probability $P(i)$ of i symbol errors out of n symbols is

$$P(i) = \left[\begin{array}{c} n \\ i \end{array} \right] p_s^i (1 - p_s)^{n-i} \tag{1.9}$$

where

$$\left[\begin{array}{c} n \\ i \end{array} \right] = \frac{n!}{i!(n-i)!}$$

The probability P_{de} of a block decoding error is just the sum of $P(i)$ for all values of i greater than t.

$$P_{de} = \sum_{i=t+1}^{n} P(i) = 1 - \sum_{i=0}^{t} P(i) \tag{1.10}$$

If a decoding error occurs, then we must decide whether we are interested in message or bit error rates. Message error rates P_{me} are the easier to calculate; if the message consists of m blocks, then it will be correct only if all m blocks are correct.

$$1 - P_{me} = (1 - P_{de})^m$$
$$P_{me} = 1 - (1 - P_{de})^m \tag{1.11}$$

If we want the output bit error rate, then we need to make a further assumption about the number $n_e(i)$ of additional errors output in a n-bit block when there is a decoding failure. At best the decoder will output d_{min} symbol errors, i.e. $d_{min} - i$ additional errors. At worst it will attempt to correct t errors and in so doing will add an extra t errors to those at the input.

$$d_{min} \leqslant n_e(i) \leqslant i + t \tag{1.12}$$

In practice the statistics will be dominated by the case when $i = t + 1$ and the upper and lower bounds on $n_e(i)$ are identical. Only at fairly high input bit error rates will there be an appreciable difference between using the upper and lower bounds.

Having chosen a suitable expression for $n_e(i)$, the output symbol error rate P_{se} will be

$$P_{se} = \frac{1}{n} \sum_{i=t+1}^{n} n_e(i)P(i) \tag{1.13}$$

If the code is binary, then this is the same as the output bit error rate p_o.

If the code uses l−bit symbols, then obtaining the output bit error rate is not straightforward. If we look at all possible symbol values, on average 50 percent of the bits would be wrong, a total of 2^{l-1} bit errors. One symbol value, however, does not represent an error, leaving $2^l - 1$ possible symbol error patterns over which to average. This, however, would give the bit error rate only for the additional symbol errors created by the decoder. For the symbol errors created on the channel the bit error rate is p/p_s. The overall output bit error rate is therefore

$$p_o = \frac{1}{n} \sum_{i=t+1}^{n} P(i) \left\{ \frac{ip}{p_s} + [n_e(i) - i] \frac{2^{l-1}}{2^l - 1} \right\} \tag{1.14}$$

1.8   Code performance and coding gain

It is often desired to represent code performance not in terms of the reduction in error rates but as a reduction in required signal to noise ratio for the same bit error rate. This immediately brings a problem of comparing like with like. Supposing we wish to use a half rate code, then the data rate must be reduced by half if the signalling rate is unchanged. If this reduction in data rate is acceptable, then there are methods other than coding that could improve the signal to noise ratio at the receiver. Merely reducing the transmission rate and reducing the bandwidth of the filters would give a 3 dB gain; the code must do better than this if it is to be worthwhile.

The answer to this problem is to assess the error performance of the link in terms of E_b/N_0, the ratio of energy per bit of information to noise power spectral density. Thus when coding is added, the number of bits of information is less than the number of transmitted bits, resulting in an increase in E_b/N_0. This increase acts as a penalty that the code must overcome if it is to provide real gains. The performance curve is built up in three stages as explained below.

As the first stage, the curve of bit error rate (BER) against E_b/N_0 is plotted for the modulation used. The value of E_b/N_0 is usually measured in decibels and the bit error rate is plotted as a logarithmic scale, normally covering several decades, e.g. from 10^{-1} to 10^{-6}. The curve could be a theoretical (ideal) curve for a Gaussian channel or may be measured performance. For example, using binary phase shift keying (PSK) modulation on an AWGN channel gives a theoretical bit error rate of

$$P_e = \frac{1}{2} \text{ erfc } \left(\frac{E_b}{N_0}\right)^{\frac{1}{2}} \qquad (1.15)$$

For large E_b/N_0 this becomes

$$Pe = \frac{e^{-(E_b/N_0)}}{2\left(\pi\frac{E_b}{N_0}\right)^{\frac{1}{2}}}$$

so that the bit error rate reduces approximately exponentially with E_b/N_0. This exponential dependence is also found with other modulations.

The second stage is the addition of coding without consideration of the changes to bit error rates. For a fixed number of transmitted bits, the number of information bits is reduced, thus increasing the value of E_b/N_0 by $10\log(1/R)$ dB. We can therefore plot a curve to the right of the uncoded plot that represents the performance on the uncoded link before error correction has taken place, i.e. the bit error rates represent the demodulator output on the coded channel.

The third stage is to consider the effect of coding on bit error rates. For a number of points on the second curve, obtain the change in bit error rates resulting from coding and use the results to plot performance of the coded channel. The change in bit error rates may be obtained by simulation or by calculation.

At any specified bit error rate, if the third curve is to the left of the first, then there is coding gain. Care should be taken when looking at quoted figures for coding gain; some authors do not apply the $10\log(1/R)$ dB penalty to the code, thus increasing the apparent gain!

It is also important to realize that in most cases the demodulator is not able to take advantage of the redundancy introduced by coding, and is thus working at a value of E_b/N_0 which is $10\log(1/R)$ dB lower than the value that gives the required error rate. If the curve for bit error rate on the uncoded channel is a theoretical one, then it ignores the degradations that occur as a result of synchronization problems at low values of E_b/N_0. These include carrier and clock recovery and, in extreme cases, bit slips resulting in framing errors on the symbols presented to the decoder. Thus synchronization problems may impose a lower limit to the values of E_b/N_0 that may be used, and this limit is higher than might be realized, particularly for low rate codes. If, for example, the demodulator requires an $E_b/N_0 \geqslant 1$ dB and a half rate code is used, then the coded channel must operate at $E_b/N_0 \geqslant 4$ dB.

An example performance curve for a block code of rate approximately 3/4 is shown in Figure 1.5. The code is a (255,191) code from a family known as binary BCH codes, and is capable of detecting and correcting eight errors per block. The performance has been simulated using calculations similar to those of Section 1.5. In comparison with the performance of uncoded binary PSK, the code is seen to give gains of approximately 2.5 dB at 10^{-3} BER and 3.5 dB at 10^{-5} BER.

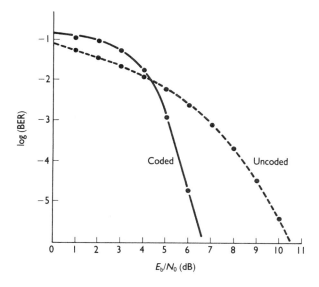

Figure 1.5 Performance curve for (255,191) block code

1.9 General considerations affecting coding gain

If the performance curves for a number of codes are studied, a number of common features are found. The first is that it is certainly possible for codes to make matters worse and for coding loss to be observed. This usually happens at relatively high bit error rates, with a crossover between the uncoded and coded curves somewhere between bit error rates of 10^{-1} and 10^{-2}.

If the distance between nearest codewords is d (convolutional codes use a measure called free distance, d_{free}, which is equivalent to the d_{min} of block codes), then the coding gain with soft-decision decoding approaches approximately $10\log(Rd)$ dB at low bit error rates. For hard decision, the gain approaches $10\log[R(d + 1)/2]$. These values are known as asymptotic coding gain. The maximum coding gain is thus in theory almost 3 dB higher for soft decision than hard decision, but in practice improvements of around 2.0 dB on the hard-decision figure are all that can be obtained.

It should be noted that, as in the example of Figure 1.5, the actual coding gain is a function of bit error rate, and some of the more complex block codes need extremely low bit error rates to achieve the asymptotic figure. Indeed, the example code should show an asymptotic coding gain of 9.5 dB, and it is obvious from Figure 1.5 that, even at bit error rates below 10^{-5}, the coding gain is still increasing as bit error rates reduce.

By looking at specific codes, it can be seen that longer codes are generally superior to shorter ones as a result of noise averaging being performed for longer periods. There are, however, problems in producing efficient long codes, as mentioned in the next section. Increased redundancy, producing low rate codes, is not always a good thing. For example a (63,57) code with $d = 3$ has an asymptotic coding gain of 2.6 dB (hard decision) or 4.3 dB (soft decision). For the corresponding (63,36) code with $d = 11$ the gains have risen to 5.3 and 8.0 dB respectively. To increase the distance to 15, a (63,24) code is needed, giving asymptotic coding gains of 4.8 dB (hard decision) or 7.6 dB (soft decision). The best rate to maximize coding gain depends on the type of code being used (convolutional codes can go to lower rates than block codes) and whether the demodulation employs coherent detection (coherent demodulation gives higher coding gains and better results with low rate codes). These considerations, along with the synchronization problems mentioned in the previous section, mean that codes with rates lower than 0.5 are rarely encountered.

It is worth noting some reasons why coding gain as conventionally defined may not be the best way to show the benefits of coding. For one thing, bit error rate is usually difficult to relate to the quality of service experienced by the users. In many cases different bits will have different significance, so looking only at bit error rates must rest on an assumption that errors affect all bits with equal likelihood. More seriously, it is often message error rates that are important, the receiver caring little whether a message error contains one bit error or many. Coding has an additional benefit here in that, for a given bit error rate, it tends to produce fewer message errors than would be found on an uncoded channel because each message error will contain a larger number of bit errors. For example, out of 100 messages sent, an uncoded channel might result in 10 message errors with one bit wrong in each. A coded channel might produce only one message error but 10 bit errors within that message. The bit error rates are the same but the message error rate is better on the coded channel.

Published performance curves almost always pertain to the AWGN channel. This is because bursty channels often do not conform to any straightforward theoretical model. In principle, higher gains can be achieved on a bursty channel, although one has to be sceptical about the assumed demodulator performance. Bursty channels may exhibit a lower limit to bit error rate that cannot be improved upon without coding, regardless of the value of E_b/N_0. If coding allows a lower error rate to be obtained, then the coding gain is infinite!

1.10   Information theory

We have now seen the sort of benefits that coding provides in present-day practice. It is worth making a comparison with the results obtained from Shannon's work on information theory, to show that in some respects coded systems have still a long way to go. There are many ways in which we still do not know how to achieve the performance that in theory is available.

The starting point for calculation of rates of information transfer is to have a definition of information. Shannon's definition was that the correct transfer of a message, whose probability of transmission is p, constitutes a transfer of $-\log_2 p$ bits of information. Thus if a message consists of n transmitted bits and all permutations are equally probable, n bits of information are transferred when the message is correctly received. The use of the term *bits* for the unit of information may cause slight confusion with the normal concept of a bit, but the use of terms such as *information bits* and *transmitted bits* may help to clarify the meaning. The addition of redundancy through coding immediately creates a difference between information and transmitted bits, as does any difference in probability of different messages. Here it will generally be assumed that messages are equiprobable, so that the only difference between information and transmitted bits will be that resulting from the redundancy of the code. The assumption of equiprobable messages is also built into the concept of minimum distance decoding.

Information theory shows that, using an average of all possible codes of length n, the error rate over the channel is characterized by a probability of message error

$$P_{me} \leqslant e^{-nE(R_I)} \tag{1.16}$$

where E, which is a function of the information rate, is called the random coding error exponent, and R_I is the rate of information transmission. Any specific code will have its own error exponent, and the greater the error exponent, the better the code, but there are calculable upper and lower bounds to the achievable value of E. In particular, a positive error exponent is achievable provided R_I, the rate of information transfer, is less than some calculable figure called the channel capacity. Provided a positive error exponent can be obtained, the way to achieve lower error probabilities is to increase the length of the code.

As was seen in Section 1.9, codes show an asymptotic coding gain and thus the bit error rate reduces exponentially with E_b/N_0, as it does in the uncoded case. Thus the error exponent is proportional to E_b/N_0. The difficulty with known codes is maintaining the error exponent while the length is increased. All known codes produced by a single stage of encoding can hold their value of error exponent only by reducing the rate to zero as the code length increases towards infinity. For example, orthogonal signalling, which can be achieved by frequency shift keying (FSK) or by means of a block code, is often quoted as approaching the theoretical capacity on an AWGN channel as the signal set is expanded to infinity. Unfortunately the bandwidth efficiency or the code rate reduces exponentially at the same time. This can be overcome by the use of multiple-stage encoding, known as concatenation, although even then the error exponents are less than the theoretically attainable value, the fraction reducing to zero as the channel capacity is approached. Nevertheless, concatenation represents the closest practicable approach to the predictions of information theory, and as such is likely to be a technique of increasing importance for the future. It is treated in more detail in Chapter 7.

Since the most widely available performance figures for error correcting codes are for the AWGN channel, it is interesting to look at the theoretical capacity of such a channel. The channel rate is given by the Shannon–Hartley theorem:

$$C = B \log_2 \left(1 + \frac{S}{N} \right) \tag{1.17}$$

where B is bandwidth, S is signal power and N is noise power within the bandwidth. This result behaves roughly as one might expect, the channel capacity increasing with increased bandwidth and signal-to-noise ratio. It is interesting to note, however, that in the absence of noise the channel capacity is not bandwidth limited. Any two signals of finite duration are bound to show differences falling within the system bandwidth, and in the absence of noise those differences will be detectable.

Using the fact that $\log_2(x) = \ln(x)/\ln(2)$ gives

$$C = 1.44B \ln \left(1 + \frac{S}{N} \right)$$

Let $N = BN_0$ and $S = R_I E_b$ (N_0 is the single-sided noise power spectral density, R_I is the rate of information transmission ($\leqslant C$) and E_b is energy per bit of information), then

$$C = 1.44B \ln \left(1 + \frac{R_I E_b}{BN_0} \right)$$

As the bandwidth approaches infinity, the channel capacity is given by

$$C = 1.44R_I \frac{E_b}{N_0}$$

For transmission at the channel capacity ($R_I = C$)

$$\frac{E_b}{N_0} = 1/1.44 = -1.6 \, \text{dB} \tag{1.18}$$

This means that we should be able to achieve reliable communications at the channel capacity with values of E_b/N_0 as low as -1.6 dB. The channel capacity is, however, proportional to the information rate; increasing the rate for a fixed value of E_b/N_0 increases the signal power and therefore the channel capacity. Thus at -1.6 dB we should be able to achieve reliable communications at any rate over an AWGN channel.

It must be stressed that Shannon merely proved that it was possible by coding to obtain reliable communications at this rate; as explained above, known implementable codes do not achieve the theoretically-attainable performance.

1.11 Further reading

Many books on digital communications will give information on the place of coding in communication systems as well as models of channel noise and the performance of different modulations in the presence of noise. Particular recommendations are Bhargava *et al*. (1981), Proakis (1983), Haykin (1988) and Sklar (1988). The introductory chapter of Michelson and Levesque (1985) also covers this material well.

Most of the subjects in this chapter are treated in more detail by Clark and Cain (1981). In particular they have better coverage of performance calculations, and coding metrics. They also show the way that different levels of soft-decision quantization affect the error exponent and thus the coding gain.

Information theory is a large subject covering all the aspects of representing and conveying information digitally. Any reader willing to grapple with the mathematics involved may turn to Blahut (1987) for a comprehensive treatment. Most of the results of particular relevance are, of course, to be found in publications by earlier authors including Gallager (1968) and Shannon (1948, 1949).

1.12 Exercises

1* A channel has a bit error rate of 10^{-2}. Would you expect the errors to be easier or more difficult to control if they occur in bursts rather than randomly throughout the messages?

2 Which item of a forward error correction system would you expect to be more expensive – the encoder or the decoder? Would your answer change for error detection coding?

3 Using Table 1.1, encode the information 0101, introduce a single error into the middle bit and decode the result.

4 Use Table 1.1 to decode the sequences 0110110, 0111101 and 1110101.

5 Using Table 1.1, encode the information 0010, introduce two errors – one in the first bit and one in the last. Decode the result.

6 A binary block code has a minimum distance of 8; what is the maximum number of bit errors per block that can be reliably detected and corrected? If the decoder

attempts correction only on single or double bit errors, how many bit errors could be detected and not corrected?

7* In a system using the code of Exercise 6, the demodulator is unable to decide the value of one of the bits in a block. This occurrence is called an erasure. By considering the principle of minimum distance decoding, decide how many additional errors in the block can now be guaranteed to be detectable. Hence derive a general formula for the error detecting and correcting properties of a code in the presence of e erasures.

8 A (15,11) binary code has $d_{min} = 3$. Estimate the output bit error rates for random channel bit error rates of 10^{-1} and 10^{-2}.

9 A (31,21) binary code has $d_{min} = 5$. Estimate the output bit error rates for random channel bit error rates of 10^{-1} and 10^{-2}.

10 A (15,11) code, with symbols consisting of 4 bits, has $d_{min} = 5$. Estimate the output bit error rates for random channel bit error rates of 10^{-1} and 10^{-2}.

11 Nine-bit blocks of information are to be transmitted either using a (15,9) block code with $d_{min} = 4$, or uncoded. If the code is used to provide error correction, compare the coded and uncoded cases in respect of (a) the probability of an information block being correctly received and (b) the probability of an information block having undetected errors, for channel bit error probabilities of 10^{-1}, 10^{-2} and 10^{-3}. What assumptions do you need to make for the calculations?

12 A PSK channel is encoded using a rate 1/2 code. It is found that for a channel bit error rate of 10^{-2}, the bit error rate from the decoder is 10^{-5}. Estimate the coding gain at 10^{-5} BER.

13 The performance of a coded channel is assessed theoretically and it is calculated that for bit error rates of 10^{-4} and 10^{-6}, the required values of E_b/N_0 are 9.5 and 11 dB uncoded, and 6.5 and 7.5 dB with a rate 1/2 code. It is found, however, that the demodulator follows the theoretical performance only when its operating E_b/N_0 is above 4 dB and that the bit error rate rises very rapidly below that figure. What is the effect of demodulator performance on the usable coding gains at 10^{-4} and 10^{-6} BER?

14 Estimate the asymptotic coding gains to be achieved with the codes of Exercises 8 and 9 using both hard- and soft-decision decoding. Compare the hard-decision results with the actual coding gains achieved at the bit error rates previously calculated as corresponding to a channel bit error rate of 10^{-2}. Assume binary PSK modulation.

2
Linear block codes

2.1   Introduction

This chapter presents the most important aspects of linear block codes. Block codes were defined in Section 1.2 and an example of a block code was used extensively in the first chapter. Almost all useful block codes possess the property of linearity, which will be defined in Section 2.3. The topics to be covered in this chapter include the ways in which codes can be defined, the uses of linearity in the encoding and (hard-decision) decoding operations, minimum distance and the bounds on distance that apply to block codes. It is largely assumed that forward error correction is required because the detection of errors is achieved as the first step of error correction and thus is included in the techniques described.

It is assumed that the reader is familiar with the material of Sections 1.1, 1.2, 1.5 and 1.6. Anyone wishing to know how the minimum distances obtainable relate to output error rates in the presence of random errors will also need to read Section 1.7. Only binary codes are treated in this chapter, enabling the mathematics of nonbinary codes to be left until Chapter 4. The special techniques associated with the subset of linear block codes known as cyclic codes will be covered in Chapter 3.

2.2   Mathematics of binary codes

The mathematics of coding can be rather complicated if all classes of codes are to be studied. By restricting ourselves, for the moment, to simple codes we can employ simple mathematics to gain familiarity with the subject before attempting the more difficult codes. As a result this chapter will require nothing more difficult than an understanding of matrix representation of equations and the application of simple logical functions.

The main reason that the mathematics of coding can appear complicated is that we need to be able to carry out arithmetic in what is called a *finite field*. Any code consists of a number of symbols which can take only certain values, the simplest example of a symbol being a bit, which can take only two values, although other symbols with more levels can be devised. It is necessary to define our arithmetic operations in a way that only valid symbol values can be produced. A finite field is a defined set of values plus two defined operations and their inverses which can yield only values within the set.

The operations to be carried out on the defined finite set of values are called addition and multiplication, and their inverses may be thought of as subtraction and division. The operations themselves will not, however, correspond to our normal understanding of those terms. For nonbinary fields the definition of the appropriate arithmetic is necessary before the encoding and decoding can be explained.

Fortunately there is only one important family of nonbinary codes, namely the Reed Solomon codes, although for a proper understanding of some other codes a finite field approach is valuable. Nevertheless we can get a long way dealing only with binary fields, for which the appropriate arithmetic is simply modulo 2.

$$0 + 0 = 0$$
$$0 + 1 = 1$$
$$1 + 1 = 0$$

$$0 \times 0 = 0$$
$$0 \times 1 = 0$$
$$1 \times 1 = 1$$

The inverse of addition (subtraction) is equivalent to addition, division by zero is not allowed and division by 1 is equivalent to multiplication by 1. Our finite field arithmetic will therefore be rather easy, with the only matter of note being the modulo 2 addition, corresponding to the exclusive-OR function of Boolean logic.

2.3   Linearity

Linearity is usually defined in coding theory in a way that is related to the geometry of n-dimensional space. This mathematical definition is likely to leave nonmathematicians rather cold, and so a definition in terms of the usual concepts of a linear system is often to be preferred. There is a difference between the definitions of linearity obtained by these two approaches, but the intention is to use the properties of linearity so that encoding and decoding can be simplified through the use of linear systems. As a result the difference will be of no practical significance.

The proper definition of a linear system is one to which the principles of superposition and scaling apply; if we add together two signals at the input we expect the output to be the sum of the two individual corresponding outputs, and if we multiply the input by a scalar factor we expect the output to be similarly scaled. Thus given two input signals x_1, x_2 and the corresponding outputs y_1, y_2, applying the sum of the two inputs $x_1 + x_2$ to the system will result in the sum of the two outputs $y_1 + y_2$.

$$y_1 = f(x_1)$$
$$y_2 = f(x_2)$$
$$y_1 + y_2 = f(x_1 + x_2)$$

Multiplying input x_1 by a scalar factor c results in output cy_1

$$cy_1 = f(cx_1)$$

We can apply this idea to coding systems in a similar way. If we take two information sequences and add them together, symbol by symbol, before they go into a linear encoder, the resulting codeword should be the sum of the two codewords that correspond to the individual information sequences. Similarly if we scale some input by any valid symbol value, the codeword output should consist of the original codeword similarly scaled. (Since the only binary symbol values are 0 and 1, the scaling property is not important for binary codes, but may be important in the nonbinary case.)

Let us take as an example the case where a code is defined by Table 2.1. The information word 11 could be produced by addition of 10 and 01. Adding the corresponding codewords gives $10101 + 01011 = 11110$, which is the correct codeword for 11.

Table 2.1 Linear code

Information	Code
0 0	0 0 0 0 0
0 1	0 1 0 1 1
1 0	1 0 1 0 1
1 1	1 1 1 1 0

This definition of linearity is in fact rather tighter than the mathematical definition of a linear code. The mathematical definition is directly equivalent to saying that the sum of two codewords, or a codeword multiplied by a scalar factor, must yield a result that is itself a codeword. It is not necessary for the result to correspond to the sum of the two original information sequences. Thus if we modified the code of Table 2.1 as shown in Table 2.2, we would still have a linear code according to the mathematical definition. The codewords are the same as before and thus the sum of two codewords will always yield a codeword result as before. All that has changed is the mapping between information and codewords, which is not taken into account by the mathematical definition. The two codes produced by Tables 2.1 and 2.2 are said to be *equivalent*, and if we use a linear system to produce a linear code the difference between the two definitions will never bother us.

Table 2.2 Linear code (mathematical definition)

Information	Code
0 0	1 1 1 1 0
0 1	0 1 0 1 1
1 0	0 0 0 0 0
1 1	1 0 1 0 1

One important consequence of linearity is that the all-zero word is always a codeword. This is because if we add a codeword to itself we obtain a string of zeros.

2.4   Parity checks

To obtain an insight into how a linear code might be produced, let us take a simple example in which a codeword is produced from the information by letting the information flow directly through into the codeword and then following it with a single bit calculated from all the information bits. We shall consider two methods of calculating this final bit: (i) the final bit is set such that the modulo 2 sum of all the bits in the codeword is 1 (ii) the final bit is set such that the modulo 2 sum of all the bits in the codeword is 0.

In the first case the codeword is said to have odd parity, i.e. there is an odd number of ones in the codeword. In the second case there is an even number of ones in the codeword, which therefore has even parity. The extra bit is called a parity check bit and may be called an odd parity or even parity check as appropriate.

The odd and even parity codes are shown in Tables 2.3 and 2.4 respectively for the case in which there are three information bits. We note that the code of

Table 2.3 Odd parity code

Information	Code
0 0 0	0 0 0 1
0 0 1	0 0 1 0
0 1 0	0 1 0 0
0 1 1	0 1 1 1
1 0 0	1 0 0 0
1 0 1	1 0 1 1
1 1 0	1 1 0 1
1 1 1	1 1 1 0

Table 2.3 does not contain the all-zero sequence which must be part of a linear code. Thus the odd parity check produces a nonlinear code. On the other hand, the code of Table 2.4 is linear; systems that produce even parity checks on some or all of the bits result in a linear code. Note that in this case the parity check bit is the modulo 2 sum of the bits from which it is calculated. Thus the parity for the information sequence 101 is the modulo 2 sum of 1, 0 and 1, i.e. 0.

Table 2.4 Even parity code

Information	Code
0 0 0	0 0 0 0
0 0 1	0 0 1 1
0 1 0	0 1 0 1
0 1 1	0 1 1 0
1 0 0	1 0 0 1
1 0 1	1 0 1 0
1 1 0	1 1 0 0
1 1 1	1 1 1 1

2.5   Systematic codes

Many of the above examples have the property that the information bits appear in the codeword unchanged with some parity bits added. A particularly common arrangement is that the information appears at the start of the codeword and is followed by the parity check bits. In this case the code is said to be systematic. Any linear block code can be put into systematic form and at worst is only trivially different from a systematic arrangement. A linear block code can always be considered as *equivalent* to a systematic code.

Consider, for example, the code of Table 2.2. It is not systematic, but by rearranging the mapping from information to code we can produce the code of Table 2.1, which is systematic. Systematic codes will always obey the 'linear systems' definition of linearity given in Section 2.3.

2.6   Minimum Hamming distance of a linear block code

A consequence of linearity is that the distance structure of the code appears the same regardless of which code word it is viewed from. If **u**, **v** and **w** are codewords and **d(u,v)** signifies the distance between **u** and **v**, then

$$\mathbf{d(u,v)} = \mathbf{d(u + w,v + w)} \tag{2.1}$$

The sequences **u** + **w** and **v** + **w** are codewords and so the relationship between **u** and $\mathbf{v}$ is repeated at other points in the code. In particular we can set $\mathbf{w} = \mathbf{v}$ to give

$$d(\mathbf{u},\mathbf{v}) = d(\mathbf{u} + \mathbf{v}, \mathbf{0}) \qquad (2.2)$$

Thus we can say that the distance between any pair of codewords is the same as the distance between some codeword and the all-zero sequence. We can therefore reach the following conclusion:

> *The minimum distance of a linear block code is equal to the minimum number of nonzero symbols occurring in any codeword (excluding the all-zero codeword).*

The number of nonzero symbols in a sequence is called the weight of the sequence, and so the minimum distance of a linear block code is equal to the weight of the minimum weight codeword.

2.7   How to encode – generator matrix

In the previous examples of codes, we have used a table to hold all the codewords and looked up the appropriate codeword for the required information sequence. We can, however, create codewords by addition of other codewords, which means that there is no need to hold every codeword in a table. If there are k bits of information, all we need is to hold k linearly independent codewords, i.e. a set of k codewords none of which can be produced by linear combinations of two or more codewords in the set. The easiest way to find k linearly independent codewords is to choose those which have 1 in just one of the first k positions and are 0 in the other $k - 1$ of the first k positions. Using, for example, the example (7,4) code of Chapter 1, we need just the following four codewords:

$$1000110$$
$$0100101$$
$$0010011$$
$$0001111$$

If we wish, for example, to obtain the codeword for 1011, we add together the first, third and fourth codewords in the list to give 1011010.

The process of encoding by addition can be represented in matrix form by

$$\mathbf{v} = \mathbf{u}\,\mathbf{G} \qquad (2.3)$$

where $\mathbf{u}$ is the information block, $\mathbf{v}$ the codeword and $\mathbf{G}$ the generator matrix.

Taking the above example, we can represent the code by the following generator matrix:

$$\mathbf{G} = \begin{bmatrix} 1\,0\,0\,0\,1\,1\,0 \\ 0\,1\,0\,0\,1\,0\,1 \\ 0\,0\,1\,0\,0\,1\,1 \\ 0\,0\,0\,1\,1\,1\,1 \end{bmatrix}$$

If, as before, we wish to encode the sequence 1011 we obtain

$$\mathbf{v} = [1\ 0\ 1\ 1] \begin{bmatrix} 1\,0\,0\,0\,1\,1\,0 \\ 0\,1\,0\,0\,1\,0\,1 \\ 0\,0\,1\,0\,0\,1\,1 \\ 0\,0\,0\,1\,1\,1\,1 \end{bmatrix}$$

$$\mathbf{v} = [1\ 0\ 1\ 1\ 0\ 1\ 0]$$

Note that the generator is a $k \times n$ matrix where k is the dimension of the code (number of information bits) and n is the length of any codeword. In this case the generator has a special form corresponding to a systematic code. It consists of a $k \times k$ unit matrix followed by a $k \times (n - k)$ matrix of parity check bits.

If we were going to use the generator matrix approach to encoding of a systematic code, there would be no point in storing that part of the codewords that corresponds to the information. We therefore need only to store $k \times (n - k)$ bits in some form of read-only memory (ROM), and let the information bits determine which of the $(n - k)$-bit sequences are to be modulo 2 added to form the parity checks of the codeword.

2.8   Encoding with the parity check matrix

In Section 2.4 we introduced the idea of a parity check and deduced that even parity checks corresponded to a linear encoding operation. It should therefore be possible to define a code in terms of groups of bits which must be of even parity, i.e. their modulo 2 sum must be zero. For example, we may choose to calculate three parity check bits from four information bits as shown below. The leftmost bit is considered to be bit 6 and the rightmost bit 0, so that the information corresponds to bits 6–3 and the parity checks are bits 2–0.

$$\text{bit } 2 = \text{bit } 6 + \text{bit } 5 + \text{bit } 3$$
$$\text{bit } 1 = \text{bit } 6 + \text{bit } 4 + \text{bit } 3$$
$$\text{bit } 0 = \text{bit } 5 + \text{bit } 4 + \text{bit } 3$$

In other words, bits 6, 5, 3 and 2 form an even parity group, as do bits 6, 4, 3 and 1 and bits 5, 4, 3 and 0. If the information is 1011, then

$$\text{bit } 6 = 1 \quad \text{bit } 5 = 0 \quad \text{bit } 4 = 1 \quad \text{bit } 3 = 1$$

from which we can calculate

$$\text{bit } 2 = 0 \quad \text{bit } 1 = 1 \quad \text{bit } 0 = 0$$

The codeword is therefore 1011010, as was the case for the example in Section 2.7. A check of the codewords forming the rows of the generator matrix in that section will confirm that this system of parity checks in fact generates the same code. The way in which a code specified by a generator matrix can be transformed to an equivalent system of parity checks will shortly become apparent.

The system of parity checks can be put into the following matrix representation:

$$\mathbf{H} = \begin{bmatrix} 1\ 1\ 0\ 1\ 1\ 0\ 0 \\ 1\ 0\ 1\ 1\ 0\ 1\ 0 \\ 0\ 1\ 1\ 1\ 0\ 0\ 1 \end{bmatrix}$$

The matrix $\mathbf{H}$ is called the parity check matrix and each row represents an even parity group with ones in the positions of the bits that comprise the group.

Since the rows of the parity check matrix correspond to even parity groups, the scalar product of any codeword with any row will be zero. The generator matrix has rows which are themselves codewords. Thus if we form the scalar product of any row of the generator matrix with any row of the parity check matrix the result will be zero. Matrix multiplication is carried out, however, by forming scalar products of the rows of the first matrix with columns of the second. We can therefore write

$$\mathbf{GH}^{\mathrm{T}} = 0 \tag{2.5}$$

We can now see how to form the parity check matrix and thus how to formulate a code in terms of parity checks. It is a $(n - k) \times n$ matrix constructed in such a way that equation (2.5) is satisfied. Starting from the generator matrix, separate the $k \times (n - k)$ section corresponding to the parity checks

$$\begin{bmatrix} 1\ 1\ 0 \\ 1\ 0\ 1 \\ 0\ 1\ 1 \\ 1\ 1\ 1 \end{bmatrix}$$

transpose it

$$\begin{bmatrix} 1\ 1\ 0\ 1 \\ 1\ 0\ 1\ 1 \\ 0\ 1\ 1\ 1 \end{bmatrix}$$

and follow it with a $(n - k) \times (n - k)$ unit matrix

$$\mathbf{H} = \begin{bmatrix} 1\,1\,0\,1\,1\,0\,0 \\ 1\,0\,1\,1\,0\,1\,0 \\ 0\,1\,1\,1\,0\,0\,1 \end{bmatrix}$$

this form again assumes a systematic code.

This particular parity check matrix has one further feature of note. Looking at the columns of the matrix we see that all possible 3-bit patterns of ones and zeros are to be found, with the exception of the all-zero pattern. This feature is characteristic of the family of codes to which this code belongs, namely the Hamming codes. We can construct Hamming codes with any number of parity check bits by making a matrix with $n - k$ rows and with the columns consisting of all the $2^{n-k} - 1$ possible patterns of $n - k$ bits which exclude the all-zero pattern. For example, the parity check matrix

$$\mathbf{H} = \begin{bmatrix} 1\,1\,0\,1\,0\,0\,1\,1\,1\,0\,1\,1\,0\,0\,0 \\ 1\,0\,1\,0\,1\,0\,1\,1\,0\,1\,1\,0\,1\,0\,0 \\ 0\,1\,1\,0\,0\,1\,1\,0\,1\,1\,1\,0\,0\,1\,0 \\ 0\,0\,0\,1\,1\,1\,0\,1\,1\,1\,1\,0\,0\,0\,1 \end{bmatrix}$$

defines a (15,11) Hamming code. The order of the columns is immaterial as far as the definition of a Hamming code is concerned, although we may wish to preserve the unit matrix on the right corresponding to the systematic form.

The form of the parity check matrix gives the Hamming code some special decoding properties that will be seen in the next section.

2.9   Decoding with the parity check matrix

Decoding generally consists of two stages. The first is to check whether the sequence corresponds to a codeword. If only error detection is required, then this completes the decoding process. If error correction is required, then there must be an attempt to identify the error pattern. This second stage is likely to be much more complex than the first and its implementation will normally be the major factor in the overall complexity, speed and cost of the encoder/decoder (codec).

Error detection involves deciding whether all the even parity checks are satisfied in the received sequence. If we perform modulo 2 addition on all the even parity groups, the result will be zero for those that are satisfied and one for those that are not. The resulting $(n - k)$-bit result is called the *syndrome*. An alternative, but equivalent definition of syndrome is that it is the sequence formed by modulo 2 adding the received parity bits to the parity bits recalculated from the received information. If the received sequence is $\mathbf{v}'$, then the syndrome can also be regarded as a vector $\mathbf{s}$ where

$$\mathbf{s} = \mathbf{v}'\mathbf{H}^{\mathrm{T}} \tag{2.6}$$

An all-zero syndrome indicates that the sequence is correct. Any other syndrome indicates the presence of errors. Because of the linear properties of the code, any received sequence can be considered to be the sum of a codeword and an error pattern and the syndrome is likewise the sum of that for the codeword (i.e. zero) and that for the error pattern. This leads to the result that *the syndrome value depends only on the errors, not on the transmitted codeword.*

The equivalence of the above three definitions of syndrome can be verified by taking an example. Suppose we receive a sequence 1000101, calculating the syndrome by each of the three methods gives the following:

1.
$$\text{bit } 6 + \text{bit } 5 + \text{bit } 3 + \text{bit } 2 = 0$$
$$\text{bit } 6 + \text{bit } 4 + \text{bit } 3 + \text{bit } 1 = 1$$
$$\text{bit } 5 + \text{bit } 4 + \text{bit } 3 + \text{bit } 0 = 1$$

2.
$$\text{received information} = 1000$$
$$\text{recalculated parity} = 110$$
$$\text{received parity} = 101$$
$$\text{syndrome} = 011$$

3.
$$\mathbf{s} = [1\,0\,0\,0\,1\,0\,1]\begin{bmatrix} 1 & 1 & 0 \\ 1 & 0 & 1 \\ 0 & 1 & 1 \\ 1 & 1 & 1 \\ 1 & 0 & 0 \\ 0 & 1 & 0 \\ 0 & 0 & 1 \end{bmatrix} = [0\,1\,1]$$

We need also to be able to relate the syndrome to the errors that have occurred. The columns of the parity check matrix have an important interpretation which will in the case of a Hamming code enable this to be done. The first column is the syndrome of an error in the first bit; likewise any column m contains the syndrome of an error in position m. Because for a Hamming code the columns contain all the nonzero syndromes, we can relate any syndrome to a single bit error. Thus if the syndrome is 011, as in this case, we know that the error is in bit 4 and we can correct the received sequence 1000101 to 1010101, which is indeed a codeword.

To design a decoder, we could use combinational logic to look for the syndromes corresponding to each position to tell us which bit was in error. Alternatively we could store a number of error patterns ordered according to their syndrome, and merely select the appropriate pattern once the syndrome has been formed.

What happens if two bits are in error? Supposing bits 3 and 2 were wrong, the syndrome would be $111 + 100 = 011$. This would be interpreted in the decoder as an error in bit 4. Because all the syndromes are contained in the parity check matrix, the decoder will always think that it knows what has occurred, even when it is wrong. The Hamming code is good for detecting and correcting single errors per block (minimum distance = 3), but any more errors will always cause a decoding error. Of course we do not expect a decoder to be able to cope with errors beyond half the minimum distance, but the fact that it always fails is a special property of Hamming codes.

2.10   Decoding by standard array

Another way to look at the decoding process is to list all the received sequences in sets, each set containing just one codeword that should be the decoder output for any of the sequences in the set. For a binary code there are 2^k codewords and 2^n possible received sequences. The received sequences are therefore partitioned into sets of 2^{n-k}, each set containing one codeword and each sequence in the set having a different syndrome. If the sets are arranged in columns with the codeword at the top, and with all the sequences at a given position in every set having the same syndrome, then the result is an array known as the *standard array*.

Let us consider the example of a (5,2) code from Section 2.3. The standard array could be

00000	01011	10101	11110
10000	11011	00101	01110
01000	00011	11101	10110
00100	01111	10001	11010
00010	01001	10111	11100
00001	01010	10100	11111
11000	10011	01101	00110
10010	11001	00111	01100

The way in which this was constructed is as follows. The top row consists of all the codewords. The code has minimum distance of 3, so we expect to detect and correct all single-bit errors, a total of five error patterns. The second row consists, therefore, of all the patterns with an error in the first bit, the third row has an error in the second bit, etc. By the end of the sixth row, we have used all the single bit error patterns, but we still have eight sequences that have not been written into the array. An arbitrary choice of one is made to head row 7 and is used as an error pattern to generate the rest of that row. Then one of the remaining four patterns is chosen to head the last row, and using it as an error pattern the final row is completed.

The error patterns that make up the last two rows of the standard array in our example would not normally be considered to be correctable errors. The decoder may therefore be designed merely to detect such errors and not attempt correction. Decoding is then said to be incomplete because not all received sequences are decoded. In this respect codes in general will differ from Hamming codes which do not have any sequences falling more than one bit different from a code sequence, and for which error correction will always involve complete decoding.

Note that because the first sequence in each row is treated as an error pattern and applied to every column, the same syndrome will be obtained for every sequence in the row. When we receive a sequence we only need to know the row in which it falls and the error pattern which heads that row. The elements of a row are called a coset, and the error pattern is called the coset leader. To carry out decoding the syndrome acts as an indicator of the coset in which the received sequence falls.

For the code in question

$$\mathbf{G} = \begin{bmatrix} 1 & 0 & 1 & 0 & 1 \\ 0 & 1 & 0 & 1 & 1 \end{bmatrix}$$

$$\mathbf{H} = \begin{bmatrix} 1 & 0 & 1 & 0 & 0 \\ 0 & 1 & 0 & 1 & 0 \\ 1 & 1 & 0 & 0 & 1 \end{bmatrix}$$

We can therefore construct the syndromes for the coset leaders, treating each in turn as a received sequence. For example, the syndrome of 10000 is the leftmost column of the parity check matrix, i.e. 101; the syndrome of 11000 is the sum of the two leftmost columns, i.e. 110. We find that the syndromes of the coset leaders are 000, 101, 011, 100, 010, 001, 110, 111 respectively.

For any code, the number of syndromes cannot be less than the number of correctable error patterns. This gives us an expression for a binary code which can detect and correct t errors

$$2^{n-k} \geqslant \sum_{m=0}^{t} \begin{bmatrix} n \\ m \end{bmatrix} \tag{2.7}$$

This is called the Hamming bound, and any code that meets it with equality is called a perfect code because decoding up to the limits imposed by minimum distance produces a complete decoder. The only known perfect codes are the Hamming codes and the Golay code, which has $n = 23$, $k = 12$, $d_{min} = 7$.

2.11   Codec design for linear block codes

We have now seen all the principles that can be used to design practical encoders and decoders for short block codes. Our codec design will focus on fairly short and simple block codes to keep the complexity to a minimum. It will become clear that technological limitations on complexity will limit the usefulness of the approach.

Although minimizing complexity is obviously desirable, defining it is more difficult. The amount of hardware needed is one measure, the length of time to complete the calculations is another. In general there will be trade-offs between these two components and a common measure of decoder complexity (usually far more complex than the encoder) is the product of *hardware complexity* and *decoding delay*. The decoder designs considered here are aimed primarily at minimizing decoding delay. Later chapters will discuss codes whose structures are different, allowing different decoding methods and reduced hardware complexity at the expense of increased delay.

The encoder requires storage for k sequences of $n - k$ parity bits, an addressing mechanism to select the appropriate sequences, a register $n - $ k bits wide and associated logic to compute the parity checks and possibly some buffering for the information bits prior to encoding. In the case of a systematic code it may be possible to dispense with the buffering by transmitting each bit at the same time as it triggers the encoding logic and then sending the parity bits immediately following the information. There is, however, a need to balance the rate of arrival of information with the transmitted bit rate, which is higher because of the extra redundant bits. This will usually entail some sort of buffering in the system.

A possible encoder arrangement is illustrated in Figure 2.1. The k parity sequences are held in the first k locations of a ROM, and it is assumed that the ROM can allow access to $n - k$ bits at once. The addressing is done by means of a counter which counts from 0 to $k - 1$, the increment being triggered by the arrival of a bit of information. The read enable of the ROM is considered to be

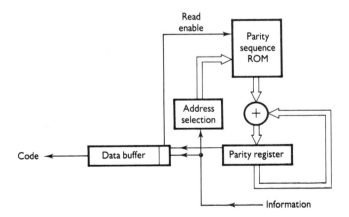

Figure 2.1 Encoder structure

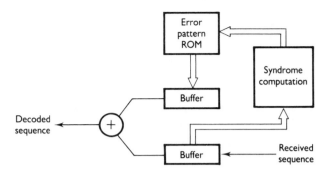

Figure 2.2 Error correction for linear block code

positive. The register in which the final parity check sequence is computed must allow an incoming sequence to be bit-by-bit exclusive-ORed with the contents of the register and it must be possible to clear the register at the start of each new word.

The decoder will contain some elements that are virtually identical to the encoder. The formation of the syndrome will be by a slight modification of the encoder in which the final stage is to exclusive-OR the recalculated parity bits with the received parity bits. Buffering of the received sequence will certainly be required while the decoding is carried out. The final stage will be to use the syndrome to access a stored error pattern. At worst we shall need 2^{n-k} locations for error patterns, each of n bits, although things may be simplified if conditions such as error-free reception or uncorrectable errors are detected and handled separately. A schematic diagram for the error correction stage is shown in Figure 2.2.

These implementations are not, of course, the only possible ones. It would be possible, for example, to construct the parity check matrix in a way that allows the error pattern to be defined relatively easily from the syndrome. It is also possible to do encoding and syndrome formation by means of buffering and a large number of hard-wired exclusive-OR gates. Note, however, that the complexity of the decoder is going to increase as codes get longer (increasing number and size of correctable error patterns for a given value of t), and as the error correcting capability (t) of the code increases (increasing number of correctable error patterns). Because ROM is relatively cheap, the more complex codes are likely to be implemented with a minimum of logic and a maximum of memory.

2.12   Modifications to block codes

To confine our attention to Hamming codes would rather limit our coding capabilities. For one thing they are only single-error correcting. Secondly, they have only a limited range of values of length n and dimension k, and the available values may not suit the system. These problems may be overcome by looking to other types of codes, but the ones worth considering will best be left to the next chapter. There are also simple modifications that may be carried out to Hamming codes (and to other block codes). In particular, reduced values of k may be used in the codes, and it is possible to create codes with $d_{min} = 4$, i.e. single-error correcting, double-error detecting (SECDED) codes. SECDED codes are commonly used in computer memory protection schemes.

Expanded codes

Expanding a code means adding extra parity checks to it, i.e. increasing n while keeping k the same. In particular if we add one overall parity check to a code of odd minimum distance, then the minimum distance is increased by 1.

Considering the (7,4) Hamming code, there is one codeword of weight 0 (as always in linear codes), seven of weight 3, seven of weight 4 and one of weight 7. If we add an overall parity check to create a (8,4) code, then all codewords must become even weight sequences. The 16 codewords will thus become one of weight 0, 14 of weight 4 and one of weight 8. The minimum distance of the expanded code is therefore 4. Some thought about this process will show that this increase in minimum distance will always occur when d_{min} has an odd value.

Shortened codes

Shortening a code means reducing the number of information bits, keeping the number of parity checks the same. The length n and the dimension k are thus reduced by the same amount. The way in which this is done is to set one of the information bits permanently to zero and then remove that bit from the code.

Suppose we take as our example the (7,4) Hamming code for which

$$\mathbf{G} = \begin{bmatrix} 1 & 0 & 0 & 0 & 1 & 1 & 0 \\ 0 & 1 & 0 & 0 & 1 & 0 & 1 \\ 0 & 0 & 1 & 0 & 0 & 1 & 1 \\ 0 & 0 & 0 & 1 & 1 & 1 & 1 \end{bmatrix}$$

and

$$\mathbf{H} = \begin{bmatrix} 1 & 1 & 0 & 1 & 1 & 0 & 0 \\ 1 & 0 & 1 & 1 & 0 & 1 & 0 \\ 0 & 1 & 1 & 1 & 0 & 0 & 1 \end{bmatrix}$$

The effect of setting to zero, say, the third bit of information would be to remove the third row from consideration in the generator matrix

$$\mathbf{G} = \begin{bmatrix} 1 & 0 & 0 & 0 & 1 & 1 & 0 \\ 0 & 1 & 0 & 0 & 1 & 0 & 1 \\ 0 & 0 & 0 & 1 & 1 & 1 & 1 \end{bmatrix}$$

and then to delete that bit, delete the third column

$$\mathbf{G} = \begin{bmatrix} 1 & 0 & 0 & 1 & 1 & 0 \\ 0 & 1 & 0 & 1 & 0 & 1 \\ 0 & 0 & 1 & 1 & 1 & 1 \end{bmatrix}$$

The parity checks at the end of the deleted row of the generator matrix appear as the third column of the parity check matrix, and so in the parity check matrix the third column should be deleted

$$\mathbf{H} = \begin{bmatrix} 1 & 1 & 1 & 1 & 0 & 0 \\ 1 & 0 & 1 & 0 & 1 & 0 \\ 0 & 1 & 1 & 0 & 0 & 1 \end{bmatrix}$$

We have now created a (6,3) code; the important question is whether we have altered the minimum distance. A simple argument suffices to show that the minimum distance is not reduced; by forcing one of the information bits to zero we have reduced the number of codewords, but all the remaining codewords are still part of the original code. Minimum distance, therefore, cannot have been reduced and may have been increased by the removal of certain codewords. Neither can the deletion of one bit have had any effect on distance, because it was a zero that was deleted.

Increasing minimum distance by shortening

Supposing we took the (7,4) Hamming code and shortened it by deleting all the odd weight codewords. We would then have created a code with even d_{min}; in fact d_{min} would be 4 because we would be left with the weight 4 codewords. This could be achieved fairly easily by removing all the information bits that generate an even number of parity checks. This is equivalent to removing all the even weight columns of the parity check matrix. Thus we change

$$\mathbf{H} = \begin{bmatrix} 1 & 1 & 0 & 1 & 1 & 0 & 0 \\ 1 & 0 & 1 & 1 & 0 & 1 & 0 \\ 0 & 1 & 1 & 1 & 0 & 0 & 1 \end{bmatrix}$$

to

$$\mathbf{H} = \begin{bmatrix} 1 & 1 & 0 & 0 \\ 1 & 0 & 1 & 0 \\ 1 & 0 & 0 & 1 \end{bmatrix}$$

This is now a (4,1) code; the information bit is repeated three times to make up the four bits of the code. Although this is a trivial example, the technique can be applied to other Hamming codes, or to other families of codes with an odd value of d_{min}, to create new codes of genuine interest.

As a second example, consider the (15,11) Hamming code created in Section 2.8, for which the parity check matrix was

$$\mathbf{H} = \begin{bmatrix} 1 & 1 & 0 & 1 & 0 & 0 & 1 & 1 & 1 & 0 & 1 & 1 & 0 & 0 & 0 \\ 1 & 0 & 10 & 1 & 0 & 1 & 1 & 0 & 1 & 1 & 0 & 1 & 0 & 0 \\ 0 & 1 & 1 & 0 & 0 & 1 & 1 & 0 & 1 & 1 & 1 & 0 & 0 & 1 & 0 \\ 0 & 0 & 0 & 1 & 1 & 1 & 0 & 1 & 1 & 1 & 1 & 0 & 0 & 0 & 1 \end{bmatrix}$$

Removing all the even weight columns gives

$$\mathbf{H} = \begin{bmatrix} 1 & 1 & 1 & 0 & 1 & 0 & 0 & 0 \\ 1 & 1 & 0 & 1 & 0 & 1 & 0 & 0 \\ 1 & 0 & 1 & 1 & 0 & 0 & 1 & 0 \\ 0 & 1 & 1 & 1 & 0 & 0 & 0 & 1 \end{bmatrix}$$

leaving us with a (8,4) code with $d_{min} = 4$.

It may also be possible to shorten further the codes created, deleting columns from the parity check matrix, in a way that will minimize the logic required for decoding. This is achieved by minimizing the number of ones in the matrix and having as nearly as possible the same number of ones in each row. Codes created in this way are known as Hsaio codes and are discussed in more detail by Lin and Costello (1983).

2.13   Bounds on block codes

This section examines the question of the relationship between the values of n and k and the amount of error correction that is possible. Common sense tells us that for given values of n and k there must be a limit to the minimum distance that can be obtained, but is there any way of knowing exactly what the value of minimum distance or the number of correctable errors is? It is found that there is no fixed relationship, but there are a number of upper bounds applying to minimum distance or error correction (Hamming bound, Plotkin bound, Griesmer bound and Singleton bound) and one lower bound which tells us a value of minimum distance that we should be able to achieve.

Although in this chapter we have been dealing only with binary codes, the forms of these bounds for multilevel codes may be derived without the need to employ anything other than straightforward mathematics. For the sake of completeness, therefore, the multilevel forms of these bounds are given as well as the binary forms.

Hamming bound

We have already met the Hamming bound, which states that the number of syndromes is at least equal to the number of correctable error patterns. For a q-ary symbol, any error can have $q - 1$ possible values, and the formula becomes

$$q^{n-k} \geqslant 1 + n(q - 1) + \frac{n(n - 1)}{2} (q - 1)^2 + \frac{n(n - 1)(n - 2)}{3} (q - 1)^3 + \cdots$$

$$q^{n-k} \geqslant \sum_{i=0}^{t} \begin{bmatrix} n \\ i \end{bmatrix} (q - 1)^i \tag{2.8}$$

Plotkin bound

The Plotkin bound is similar to the Hamming bound in that it sets an upper limit to d_{min} for fixed values of n and k. It tends, however, to set a tighter bound for low rate codes, the Hamming bound being tighter for higher rates.

The Plotkin bound applies to linear codes and states that the minimum distance is at most equal to the average weight of all nonzero codewords. For a q-ary code with n symbols, the chance over the whole set of codewords of any symbol being nonzero is $(q - 1)/q$ (provided the code is linear) and there are q^k codewords in the whole set. The number of nonzero codewords is $q^k - 1$ and so the average weight of a codeword is

$$\frac{n \dfrac{q - 1}{q} q^k}{q^k - 1}$$

The minimum distance cannot be greater than this, so

$$d_{min} \leqslant \frac{n(q - 1)q^{k-1}}{q^k - 1} \tag{2.9}$$

For a binary code this becomes

$$d_{min} \leqslant \frac{n 2^{k-1}}{2^k - 1} \tag{2.10}$$

It is not easy to find the maximum value of k for a given n and d_{min}, but it can be shown from the above result that

$$k \leqslant n - \frac{q d_{min} - 1}{q - 1} + 1 + \log_q d_{min} \tag{2.11}$$

or for a binary code

$$k \leqslant n - 2d_{\min} + 2 + \log_2 d_{\min} \tag{2.12}$$

Griesmer bound

The Griesmer bound is often tighter than the Plotkin bound, and its derivation leads to methods of constructing good codes. Let $N(k,d)$ represent the lowest possible value of length n for a linear code C of dimension k and minimum distance d. Without loss of generality, the generator matrix can be taken to have a first row consisting of d ones followed by $N(k,d) - d$ zeros.

$$\mathbf{G} = \begin{bmatrix} 111 \ldots 1 & 000 \ldots 0 \\ \mathbf{G}_1 & \mathbf{G}_2 \end{bmatrix}$$

The matrix $\mathbf{G}_2$ generates a $(N(k,d) - d, \ k - 1)$ code of minimum distance d_1, called the residual code. If $\mathbf{u}$ is a codeword of the residual code which when concatenated with a sequence $\mathbf{v}$ of length d produces a codeword of C, then we can say

$$d_1 + \text{weight } (\mathbf{v}) \geqslant d$$

However, $\mathbf{u}$ concatenated with the complement of $\mathbf{v}$ is also a codeword

$$d_1 + d - \text{weight } (\mathbf{v}) \geqslant d$$

Therefore $2d_1 \geqslant d$, or $d \geqslant \lceil d/2 \rceil$. (The symbol $\lceil d/2 \rceil$ represents the integer that is not less than $d/2$.) Since the code generated by $\mathbf{G}_2$ is of length $N(k,d) - d$, we can say

$$N(k,d) = N(k - 1, \lceil d/2 \rceil) + d$$

Applying this result iteratively gives

$$N(k,d) = \sum_{i=0}^{k-1} \left\lceil \frac{d}{2^i} \right\rceil$$

This is the lowest possible value of length, so the general statement of the Griesmer bound for binary codes is

$$n \geqslant \sum_{i=0}^{k-1} \left\lceil \frac{d}{2^i} \right\rceil$$

For q-ary codes, the argument generalizes to give

$$n \geq \sum_{i=0}^{k-1} \left\lceil \frac{d}{q^i} \right\rceil$$

Singleton bound

If we change one of the information symbols in a block code, the best we can hope for in terms of distance between codewords is that all the parity symbols will also change. In this case the distance between the two codewords will be $n - k + 1$. This sets an upper bound to minimum distance of

$$d_{\min} \leq n - k + 1 \qquad (2.13)$$

The only binary codes that achieve this bound with equality are simple $(n,1)$ repetition codes; other upper bounds are usually tighter for binary codes. On the other hand, Reed Solomon codes, which are multilevel codes, do have a minimum distance which is the maximum permitted by this bound. Reed Solomon codes will be treated in Chapter 5.

Gilbert–Varsharmov bound

The Gilbert–Varsharmov bound shows that for a given value of n and k a certain value of minimum distance should be achievable by a linear block code. It does not necessarily mean that the code or codes that achieve this distance are known or have practicable implementations, merely that they exist.

Consider a code that has minimum distance d. The syndrome of an error pattern containing $d - 1$ errors may be the same as that of a single error, but no syndrome of an error pattern of weight $d - 2$ or less may be the same as a single error syndrome. From this observation, we look at how we can make up the columns of the parity check matrix, which are just the syndromes of single symbol errors, such that no column can be made from linear combinations of $d - 2$ or fewer other columns.

Each column of the parity check matrix contains $n - k$ symbols and for a q-ary code there are q^{n-k} possible columns. As we make up the columns, certain values are not allowed if we are to ensure that the column we are creating cannot be made from linear combinations of up to $d - 2$ previous columns. The problem of finding suitable columns becomes more acute as we fill the matrix, and the last column (the nth) will be the most difficult. At this stage the prohibited combinations will be as follows:

- All zeros (one possibility).

- Any of the $q - 1$ nonzero multiples of any of the $n - 1$ previous columns $[(n - 1)(q - 1)$ possibilities].

- A linear combination of nonzero multiples of i of the previous $n - 1$ columns $\{[^n_i^{-1}](q - 1)^i$ possibilities for each value of i from 2 to $d - 2\}$.

Hence we obtain

$$\sum_{i=0}^{d-2}\begin{bmatrix} n \\ i \end{bmatrix} (q - 1)^i < q^{n-k} \tag{2.14}$$

We are, however, allowed to choose values that are linear combinations of the possibilities up to $d - 1$ of the previous $n - 1$ columns, which gives us the full form of the Gilbert–Varsharmov bound

$$\sum_{i=0}^{d-2}\begin{bmatrix} n \\ i \end{bmatrix} (q - 1)^i < q^{n-k} \leqslant \sum_{i=0}^{d-1}\begin{bmatrix} n \\ i \end{bmatrix} (q - 1)^i \tag{2.15}$$

In this form, one can use the bound either to determine the maximum value of minimum distance that is sure to be available with a given set of q, n and k, or to set an upper limit to the value of $n - k$ that is needed to provide a desired minimum distance with a q-ary code of length n.

2.14   Further reading

As much of this chapter represents the basics of the subject, the treatment has been a fairly full one, and alternative treatments can be found in any book on coding. Clark and Cain (1981) use the term *group codes* to describe linear block codes.

    One subject that has not been treated here concerns the manipulations that can be carried out to generator or parity check matrices to create equivalent codes. Any row of a generator matrix may be altered by adding one or more of the other rows and this obviously affects the columns of the parity check matrix. Moreover adding a row of the parity check matrix onto another row does not alter the codewords produced at all. To understand the reasons for these phenomena, it is recommended that the appropriate chapter of Lin and Costello (1983) is studied while at the same time thinking about the physical effects of the matrix manipulations. A reasonable goal for the reader would be to understand how to obtain the parity check matrix from the generator matrix (or vice versa) in a nonsystematic form.

    Another area that has been glossed over here is the reason why any linear block code can be put into a systematic form, which is related to the existence of

k linearly independent codewords and the properties of linear codes in n-dimensional space. This topic is treated fairly succinctly by Blahut (1983).

The bounds described here are ones that are fairly easy to prove. MacWilliams and Sloane (1977) describe methods of constructing codes which come close to the Griesmer bound. Many of the bounds described in the literature relate to the best value of d_{min}/n that can be obtained for a given code rate. The Gilbert–Varsharmov lower bound can be put into this form, as can another upper bound, the Elias bound, described by Blahut (1983). The tightest known upper bound is that of McEliece *et al.* (1977).

2.15   Exercises

1   An 8-bit byte is constructed by taking seven information bits and adding a parity check to produce an odd number of ones in the byte (odd parity). Is this a linear code? What are the values of n, k and minimum distance?

2   Below is given a generator matrix in systematic form. What are the values of n and k for the code? What is the parity check matrix?

$$\begin{bmatrix} 1\,0\,0\,0\,0\,0\,1\,0\,1\,1 \\ 0\,1\,0\,0\,0\,0\,0\,1\,0\,1 \\ 0\,0\,1\,0\,0\,0\,1\,1\,1\,1 \\ 0\,0\,0\,1\,0\,0\,1\,1\,1\,0 \\ 0\,0\,0\,0\,1\,0\,1\,0\,1\,0 \\ 0\,0\,0\,0\,0\,1\,0\,1\,1\,1 \end{bmatrix}$$

3   For the parity check matrix below, explain how to encode and form the syndrome of the received sequence. Obtain the generator matrix. What are the values of n and k for this code? What is the syndrome of the error patterns 110001100 and 001010010?

$$\begin{bmatrix} 0\,1\,1\,0\,1\,1\,0\,0\,0 \\ 1\,0\,1\,1\,0\,0\,1\,0\,0 \\ 1\,1\,1\,0\,1\,0\,0\,1\,0 \\ 0\,0\,0\,1\,1\,0\,0\,0\,1 \end{bmatrix}$$

4   A (6,3) linear code is constructed as follows:

bit 2 is a parity check on bits 5 and 4
bit 1 is a parity check on bits 4 and 3
bit 0 is a parity check on bits 5 and 3

Find the generator and parity check matrices and the minimum distance for the code.

Construct a standard array for the code. Determine the syndromes of the coset leaders. For each bit of any 6-bit sequence, determine a logical function of the syndrome that will indicate whether that bit is in error. Assume complete decoding by your standard array.

5* A (16,9) linear code is constructed as follows. The information is held in bits 0, 1, 2, 4, 5, 6, 8, 9 and 10. Bit 3 is a parity check on bits 0–2, bit 7 checks bits 4–6 and bit 11 checks bits 8–10. Bit 12 is a parity check on bits 0, 4 and 8, bit 13 checks bits 1, 5 and 9, bit 14 checks bits 2, 6 and 10, bit 15 checks bits 3, 7 and 11. Obtain the parity check matrix and show that the code would be unchanged if bit 15 were calculated as a parity check on bits 12–14.

Show that the code can be represented as a 4 × 4 array with information in a 3 × 3 array and parity checks on each row and column. Hence deduce an approach to decoding single errors. Find the minimum distance of the code.

6* You are given 15 coins which should be of equal weight, but you are told that there may be one that is different from the others. You also have a balance on which to compare the weights of different coins or sets of coins. Devise a scheme using four balance checks to determine which coin, if any, has the wrong weight.

7 What is the longest SECDED code that can be created by shortening a (31,26) Hamming code? What is its parity check matrix?

8* Write down a parity check matrix for a (7,4) Hamming code. Construct the parity check matrix of the expanded code by appending a zero to each row and creating an extra row representing the action of the overall parity check. Now construct the generator matrix for the original code, append an overall parity check to each row and hence obtain the parity check matrix for the expanded code. Reconcile the two forms of the parity check matrix.

9* Could the (8,4) code created by expanding a (7,4) Hamming code also be created by shortening a longer Hamming code?

10 Are the following binary codes possible?

$$
\begin{aligned}
n &= 7, & k &= 2, & d_{min} &= 5 \\
n &= 63, & k &= 31, & t &= 17 \\
n &= 63, & k &= 45, & d_{min} &= 7 \\
n &= 127, & k &= 109, & d_{min} &= 7
\end{aligned}
$$

3
Cyclic codes

3.1   Introduction

Chapter 2 showed that the properties of linearity could be used to simplify the tasks of encoding and decoding linear block codes. There are many other ways in which the structure of a code can be used to assist its implementation, and for block codes the most common structure to be encountered belongs to the subclass known as cyclic codes. Their popularity is partly because their structural properties provide protection against bursty errors in addition to simplifying the logic required for encoding and decoding, although the simplified decoding may be achieved at the expense of speed.

To obtain the best understanding of this chapter, the reader should first be familiar with the material of Sections 1.1, 1.2, 1.5, 1.6 and 2.1–2.6. In addition the concept of a syndrome defined in Section 2.9 and the ability to modify block codes as in Section 2.12 will also reappear and, although they will be explained fully in this chapter, familiarity with the appropriate material from Chapter 2 will no doubt help.

This chapter draws attention to the parallel between the polynomials that are commonly used to represent cyclic code sequences and the z-transform used in digital signal processing for the representation of sampled signals and digital filters. It would be of considerable advantage to the reader to be familiar with the idea of the z-transform and, in particular, the representation of convolution. Almost any book on digital signal processing will have the necessary material, one good example being Oppenheim and Schafer (1975).

3.2   Definition of a cyclic code

Cyclic codes are a subset of linear block codes, that is to say that we are still dealing with block codes and all the properties of linearity and the associated techniques apply equally to cyclic codes. The cyclic property is an additional property that may be of use in many circumstances.

The structure of a cyclic code is such that if any codeword is shifted cyclically, the result is also a codeword. This does not mean that all codewords can be produced by shifting a single codeword; it does, however, mean that all codewords can be generated from a single sequence by the processes of shifting (from the cyclic property) and addition (from the property of linearity).

3.3   Example of a cyclic code

The properties of the sequences that can be used to generate cyclic codes will be stated in the next section, but for the purposes of an example we shall use a particular result, namely that it is possible to generate a cyclic code of length 7 from a generator sequence of 0001011. Bearing in mind that the all-zero sequence is always a codeword of a linear code, we may construct all the codewords as follows

1	all zero	0000000
2	generator sequence	0001011
3	shift generator left	0010110
4	2nd shift	0101100
5	3rd shift	1011000
6	4th shift	0110001
7	5th shift	1100010
8	6th shift	1000101
9	sequences 2 + 3	0011101
10	shift sequence 9	0111010
11	2nd shift	1110100
12	3rd shift	1101001
13	4th shift	1010011
14	5th shift	0100111
15	6th shift	1001110
16	sequences 2 + 11	1111111

What we have done here is to start from the generator sequence and shift it cyclically left until all seven positions have been registered. We then find two of those sequences which add together to give a new sequence, and then shift cyclically left again until a further seven sequences have been generated. It is then found that there are two sequences that add to form 1111111, which remains the same if shifts are applied. Further shifts and additions will not create any more code sequences.

As there are 16 codewords in the above code we have 4 bits of information, and thus a (7,4) code. The minimum distance can be seen to be 3 because the minimum weight nonzero codeword has weight 3. The code has the same properties as the example code from Chapters 1 and 2 and is indeed another example of a Hamming code, this time in cyclic form (there are both cyclic and noncyclic versions of Hamming codes, depending on the ordering of the columns in the parity check matrix).

3.4   Polynomial representation

The special methods of encoding and decoding that apply to cyclic codes are best understood through the use of an algebra in which a polynomial is used to represent sequences. In the polynomial representation, a multiplication by X represents a shift to the left, i.e. to one position earlier in the sequence. For those familiar with z-transforms of digital signals, there is a direct parallel with the way in which the z operator represents a unit advance in time.

The terms in a polynomial represent the positions of the 1 in the sequence, the rightmost position being the X^0 position, the next left the X^1 position, the next the X^2 position, etc. The generator sequence for the above code is therefore

$$g(X) = X^3 + X + 1$$

We could have taken any of the shifted positions of this basic sequence as the generator for our code, but conventionally we always take the case where the generator is shifted as far to the low powers of X as possible.

3.5   Encoding by convolution

If we take the generator sequence and its first $k - 1$ left shifts, we find that we have k linearly independent sequences, that is to say that none of them can be produced by addition of two or more of the others. For our example code, we could therefore use the properties of linearity to produce any codeword by additions of sequences selected from 1011000, 0101100, 0010110 and 0001011. This would mean the code having a generator matrix (see Section 2.7) of

$$\mathbf{G} = \begin{bmatrix} 1\,0\,1\,1\,0\,0\,0 \\ 0\,1\,0\,1\,1\,0\,0 \\ 0\,0\,1\,0\,1\,1\,0 \\ 0\,0\,0\,1\,0\,1\,1 \end{bmatrix}$$

The sequences used to generate the code, when put into polynomial form, are all multiples of the generator sequence. Any codeword can therefore be considered to be the product of the generator and some polynomial, this polynomial representing the information content of the codeword.

$$c(X) = g(X)i(X)$$

The information is a k-bit quantity which means that $i(X)$ has as its highest possible power of X a term in X^{k-1}. The polynomial is thus said to be of *degree* $k - 1$. As $c(X)$ is of degree $n - 1$, the degree of $g(X)$ must be $n - k$.

Another equivalent view of the code generation may be obtained from the analogy between the polynomial representation and the z-transform. It is found that multiplying two z-transforms is equivalent to *convolution* of the equivalent sequences. We can therefore view the encoding as a convolution of the information with the generator sequence. Discrete convolution is written $c(j) = a(j) \circledast b(j)$ and defined by

$$c(j) = \sum_{i=0}^{j} a(i)\, b(j - i) \qquad (3.1)$$

where j represents the position in the sequence. Both $a(j)$ and $b(j)$ are of the same length, being padded with leading zeros to the total length of the convolution. We shall see from the following example what length that should be.

Example

Consider the case where $b(j)$ is the generator sequence 1011 (with the zero-order term on the right) and $a(j)$ is the information sequence 1010. The convolution is carried out as follows:

$$
\begin{aligned}
j = 0 \quad & a(0)b(0) = 0 \\
j = 1 \quad & a(0)b(1) + a(1)b(0) = 0 \times 1 + 1 \times 1 = 1 \\
j = 2 \quad & a(0)b(2) + a(1)b(1) + a(2)b(0) = 0 \times 0 + 1 \times 1 + 0 \times 1 = 1 \\
j = 3 \quad & a(0)b(3) + a(1)b(2) + a(2)b(1) + a(3)b(0) = 0 \times 1 + 1 \times 0 + 0 \\
& \qquad\qquad\qquad\qquad\qquad\qquad\qquad\qquad \times 1 + 1 \times 1 = 1 \\
j = 4 \quad & a(1)b(3) + a(2)b(2) + a(3)b(1) = 1 \times 1 + 0 \times 0 + 1 \times 1 = 0 \\
j = 5 \quad & a(2)b(3) + a(3)b(2) = 0 \times 1 + 1 \times 0 = 0 \\
j = 6 \quad & a(3)b(3) = 1 \times 1 = 1
\end{aligned}
$$

For $j = 7$ or more it is seen that the sequences cannot overlap in the convolution and so the result must be 0. The length of the convolution is therefore 7 and the codeword is 1001110, which is the same as adding the first and third rows of the generator matrix above.

It is found that convolution is commutative, i.e. $a(j) \circledast b(j) = b(j) \circledast a(j)$, and that if one sequence is of length l and the other of length m, then the length of the convolution is $l + m - 1$. Thus an information sequence of length k can be convolved with a generator sequence of length $n - k + 1$ to give a code sequence of length n.

3.6   Establishing the cyclic property

If we take the generator and shift it k times, the cyclic property means that the leftmost bit now wraps around into the right position. To achieve the wrap around, every time we get a term in X^n we must add $X^n + 1$ to move the leftmost 1 into the right-hand position. We find that this can only produce a codeword if $X^n + 1$ is a multiple of the generator.

We can formulate the problem mathematically and obtain the same result as follows:

$$g(X) X^k + X^n + 1 = g^{(k)}(X)$$

where $g^{(k)}(X)$ is the polynomial obtained by cyclically shifting the generator by k places. As this is a codeword we have

$$g(X) X^k + X^n + 1 = a(X) g(X)$$
$$X^n + 1 = [a(X) + X^k] \, g(X)$$

where $a(X)$ is some polynomial.

Thus the generator polynomial of a (n,k) cyclic code must be a factor of $X^n + 1$.

3.7   Deducing the properties of a cyclic code

We have seen from the above two sections that to generate a (n,k) cyclic code, the generator must satisfy two properties.

 1. The generator polynomial is a factor of $X^n + 1$.

 2. The degree of the generator polynomial is $n - k$.

We may also, given a generator polynomial, wish to know the properties of the code generated. It is easy to obtain the number of parity check bits from the degree of the generator, but obtaining the length is more difficult. To be able to tackle this problem, we shall need to master the art of long division in modulo 2 arithmetic. The objective is to divide the sequence 1000 . . . 0 by the generator polynomial until the remainder is 1; we then know that if the final 0 were changed to a 1 the remainder would have been 0 and the problem is solved.

Example

Consider the generator sequence 1011 from our previous examples. We shall carry out a long division recording only the remainders, giving the results below

```
1011  |1000000000000
      1011
        1100
        1011
          1110
          1011
            1010
            1011
               1
```

The modulo 2 arithmetic means that addition and subtraction are the same. It is therefore perfectly valid to subtract 1011 from sequences such as 1000, all that matters is having a 1 on the left of the subtrahend so that the degree of the remainder is reduced.

From the above example we see that the sequence 10000001 will divide exactly by 1011, i.e. $X^7 + 1$ divides by $X^3 + X + 1$. Thus the length of the code generated is 7, confirming our original assumption in Section 3.2

Farrell and Campello de Souza (1982) have shown that it is also possible to deduce the minimum distance of the code from the above procedure. The sequence 10000001 is a multiple of 1011 and therefore the remainder after every subtraction in the long division is also a multiple of 1011. As these remainders are also of degree $n - 1$ or less they are codewords. The process of long division has therefore produced the codewords 0110001, 0011101 and 0001011. Of these the minimum weight is 3 and so the minimum distance cannot be greater than 3. In practice, the maximum value of minimum distance obtained by this approach will almost always give the actual minimum distance and so provides a very useful way of simultaneously finding the length and minimum distance of the code generated by an unfamiliar polynomial.

There is one valid objection to the procedure above for finding the length of a cyclic code, namely that it finds the smallest value of n although others may be possible. For example, $X^3 + X + 1$ is also a factor of $X^{14} + 1$ and so could generate a code of length 14. Such a code, although possible, would not be very practical; the sequence $X^7 + 1$, which has weight 2, would be a codeword and thus the code would have a minimum distance of only 2. In practice, therefore, one would wish to impose another condition on any generator polynomial, namely that it is not a factor of $X^j + 1$ for any lower value of j than the desired value of n. As a result the objection raised is of no practical significance.

3.8   Primitive polynomials

If n is the lowest possible value such that $X^n + 1$ is a multiple of some polynomial $g(X)$ and $n = 2^{n-k} - 1$ where $n - k$ is the degree of $g(X)$, then the polynomial $g(X)$ is a generator for a Hamming code in cyclic form. The Hamming code polynomials are of wider importance in the theory of block codes and are called primitive polynomials.

Degree	Polynomial
2	$X^2 + X + 1$
3	$X^3 + X + 1$
4	$X^4 + X + 1$
5	$X^5 + X^2 + 1$
	$X^5 + X^4 + X^3 + X^2 + 1$
	$X^5 + X^4 + X^2 + X + 1$
6	$X^6 + X + 1$
	$X^6 + X^5 + X^2 + X + 1$
	$X^6 + X^5 + X^3 + X^2 + 1$
7	$X^7 + X^3 + 1$
	$X^7 + X^3 + X^2 + X + 1$
	$X^7 + X^4 + X^3 + X^2 + 1$
	$X^7 + X^6 + X^5 + X^4 + X^2 + X + 1$
	$X^7 + X^5 + X^4 + X^3 + X^2 + X + 1$
	$X^7 + X^6 + X^4 + X^2 + 1$
	$X^7 + X + 1$
	$X^7 + X^6 + X^3 + X + 1$
	$X^7 + X^6 + X^5 + X^2 + 1$
8	$X^8 + X^4 + X^3 + X^2 + 1$
	$X^8 + X^6 + X^5 + X^3 + 1$
	$X^8 + X^7 + X^6 + X^5 + X^2 + X + 1$
	$X^8 + X^5 + X^3 + X + 1$
	$X^8 + X^6 + X^5 + X^2 + 1$
	$X^8 + X^6 + X^5 + X + 1$
	$X^8 + X^6 + X^4 + X^3 + X^2 + X + 1$
	$X^8 + X^7 + X^6 + X + 1$

Table 3.1   Primitive polynomials

Table 3.1 lists primitive polynomials of degree 8 or less. For every polynomial listed here, the polynomial representing the same bit pattern in reverse is also primitive. For example $X^4 + X + 1$ represents the pattern 10011, which means that 11001 or $X^4 + X^3 + 1$ is also primitive. The patterns with the lowest weights are the easiest to implement and thus are usually chosen for error control applications.

3.9   Systematic encoding of cyclic codes

Although we have seen that encoding may be carried out by a process of convolution of the information with the generator sequence, this may not be the most convenient method because the code produced is not in systematic form, which can make it difficult to extract the information when decoding. We therefore wish to know whether there is a convenient method of generating cyclic codes in systematic form. It is found that there is such a method, that it is based on modulo 2 long division of sequences as encountered in Section 3.7 and that it can be conveniently implemented using shift registers with feedback.

A code in systematic form consists of the information followed by parity check bits. Applying the polynomial notation, we can shift the information into the leftmost bits by multiplying by X^{n-k}, leaving a codeword of the form

$$c(X) = i(X)X^{n-k} + p(X)$$

or (remembering that addition and subtraction are the same)

$$c(X) + p(X) = i(X)X^{n-k}$$

where $i(X)$ represents the information and $p(X)$ is a sequence of parity check bits.

If we take each side modulo $g(X)$, i.e. divide by $g(X)$ and find the remainder, then since $c(X)$ is a multiple of $g(X)$ and $p(X)$ is of lower degree than $g(X)$, we obtain

$$p(X) = i(X)X^{n-k} \bmod g(X) \tag{3.2}$$

To encode in systematic form we therefore take $i(X)$ shifted left by $n - k$ places, divide by $g(X)$ and use the remainder as the parity checks.

Example

Consider the encoding of the sequence of 1010 using 1011 as the generator sequence. We must carry out long division of the sequence 1010000 by 1011 as follows:

$$
\begin{array}{r}
1011 \quad \overline{|1010000} \\
\underline{1011} \\
1000 \\
\underline{1011} \\
011
\end{array}
$$

The remainder is 011, which means that the codeword is 1010011. This is indeed one of the codewords generated in Section 3.3.

3.10   Syndrome of a cyclic code

It is fairly easy to show that if we divide a sequence by the generator and take the remainder, the result is the syndrome. To do this, consider the received sequence $r(X)$ as consisting of the sum of the code sequence $c(X)$ and an error pattern $e(X)$:

$$r(X) = c(X) + e(X)$$

Splitting both the code and the error polynomials into the information and parity positions gives

$$r(X) = i(X)X^{n-k} + p(X) + e_i(X)X^{n-k} + e_p(X)$$

where $e_i(X)X^{n-k}$ represents the error pattern in the information bits and $e^p(X)$ the errors in the parity bits.

Taking the received sequence modulo $g(X)$

$$r(X)\bmod g(X) = \{[i(X) + e_i(X)]X^{n-k}\}\bmod g(X) + p(X) + e_p(X)$$

In other words, the remainder is the same as the parity bits recalculated from the received information plus the received parity bits. It therefore corresponds to our definition of syndrome from Section 2.9.

Example

Suppose the received sequence is 1010110. The parity sequence corresponding to information 1010 was calculated in the previous section as 011. Comparing with the received parity of 110 we see that the syndrome is 101. This can be checked by long division as follows:

$$
\begin{array}{r}
1011 \quad \overline{)1010110} \\
\underline{1011} \\
1110 \\
\underline{1011} \\
101
\end{array}
$$

The syndrome obtained is therefore 101, as expected.

3.11   Implementation of encoding

The fundamental operation of encoding and forming a syndrome is that of division by the generator polynomial and taking the remainder. A circuit to

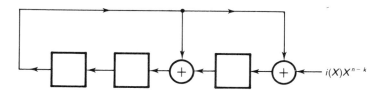

Figure 3.1 Encoder for cyclic (7.4) Hamming code

achieve this uses an arrangement of shift register stages with feedback as shown in Figure 3.1 for the Hamming code example mentioned previously. The way that this works is to look for bits of value 1 shifted out of the left side of the registers and then to add the pattern 011 in the next three positions. This is exactly what will happen if the encoding is carried out by long division.

To see the way the circuit works, let us consider the encoding of the information 1010. The information is shifted into the registers and an extra $n - k$ shifts applied. With every incoming bit the contents of the registers is shifted left and the value shifted from the leftmost stage is modulo 2 added to the bits flowing between stages at the positions shown. At the end of this process the contents of the registers form the parity bits. The stages in the encoding are shown in Table 3.2, and the codeword is therefore 1010011, as expected.

Table 3.2

Input	Register contents
–	000
1	001
0	010
1	101
0	001
0	010
0	100
0	011

Another way of viewing this process is to consider that the information is shifted into the registers subject to the repeated setting of $g(X) = 0$. This means that only the remainder will be left at the end of the operation. For the example given

$$X^3 + X + 1 = 0$$

$$X^3 = X + 1$$

Every time an X^2 term is shifted left out of the registers it becomes X^3 and is set equal to $X + 1$.

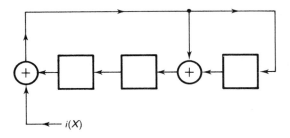

Figure 3.2 Improved version of encoder for cyclic (7.4) Hamming code

The problem with the circuit of Figure 3.1 is that after the information has been entered a further $n - k$ shifts are required before the syndrome is formed. The extra shifts can be dispensed with if the sequence is shifted into the left of the registers as shown in Figure 3.2. In this case the encoding of the information 1010 will proceed as shown in Table 3.3. The codeword is therefore 1010011, as before.

Table 3.3

Input	Register contents
–	000
1	011
0	110
1	100
0	011

A general form of this type of circuit is shown in Figure 3.3. To determine the exact form for any given polynomial the circuit should have the same number of stages as the degree of the polynomial and the appropriate feedback connections should be made. If the shift register stages are considered as

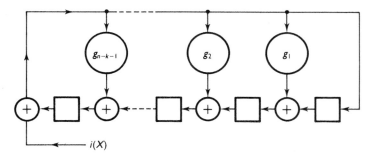

Figure 3.3 General encoder for cyclic codes

representing, from the left, the terms X^{n-k-1} down to X^0 then the positions of the connections are to the right of the stages corresponding to the terms in the polynomial. Note that it is the flow out of the leftmost (X^{n-k-1}) stage which corresponds to the highest power term in the polynomial.

3.12   Decoding

The syndrome of any received sequence can be formed by shifting it into the encoder circuit of the type shown in Figure 3.1. Combinational logic or a look-up table could then be used to find the error pattern as for ordinary linear block codes. The logic can, however, be simplified by using the cyclic nature of the code, albeit at the expense of speed.

Suppose we form the syndrome $s(X)$ of a received sequence $r(X)$ and then apply one further shift to the registers to produce $Xs(X) \bmod g(X)$. It is found that this is the same as if we had cyclically shifted the received sequence by one place and then formed the syndrome.

The syndrome depends only on the error pattern, not on the transmitted codeword, and so can be found by taking the error pattern modulo $g(x)$. Hence the error pattern is the sum of the syndrome and some multiple of the generator. Thus

$$e(X) = a(X)g(X) + s(X)$$

where $e(X)$ is the error polynomial and $a(X)$ is some arbitrary polynomial. If the coefficient of X^{n-1} in $e(X)$ is e_{n-1}, then the shifted error pattern is

$$e^{(1)}(X) = Xe(X) + e_{n-1}(X^n + 1)$$
$$= Xa(X)g(X) + e_{n-1}(X^n + 1) + Xs(X)$$

Taking the above expression modulo $g(X)$ gives the syndrome of the shifted error pattern and, since $X^n + 1$ is a multiple of $g(X)$, the remainder is just $Xs(X) \bmod g(X)$. This is the same as applying a single shift to the $s(X)$ in the syndrome registers as explained above. The result is therefore proved.

The practical significance of this result is that if we are just looking for a single error we can keep on shifting until the error reaches a chosen position (say bit $n - 1$), detect the appropriate syndrome and use the number of shifts to determine the original location of the error. Any decoder using this principle is called a Meggit decoder.

If we take our example code and create a table of the syndromes corresponding to the possible error positions, the result is as shown in Table 3.4.

Table 3.4

Error position	Syndrome
6	101
5	111
4	110
3	011
2	100
1	010
0	001

If we start from 001 and shift the registers with feedback, the result is as shown in Table 3.5. The expected relationship is apparent; if the error is in bit 2, for example, then a further four shifts will change the syndrome into the value associated with an error in bit 6. If the error is in bit 5, then only one extra shift is needed.

Table 3.5

Shifts	Register contents
0	001
1	010
2	100
3	011
4	110
5	111
6	101

One does not with this method get the virtually instantaneous decoding that could be obtained using a method based purely on combinational logic or a look-up table because a number of shifts have to be applied. There is, however, a maximum to the number of shifts before the patterns start to repeat (at most $n - 1$ shifts are needed after formation of the syndrome).

Let us look at some examples of this principle in operation. Suppose the transmitted codeword is 1010011 but that bit 6 is received incorrectly, making the received sequence 0010011. The codeword corresponding to the received information 0010 is 0010110 (from Section 3.3), making a syndrome of 101. This can be checked either by long division or by considering the operation of the circuit of Figure 3.1. The latter is shown in Table 3.6; the former is left to the reader.

Table 3.6

Input	Register contents
–	000
0	000
0	000
1	001
0	010
0	100
1	010
1	101

If, instead, bit 5 is in error, the received sequence is 1110011, **the codeword with information** 1110 is 1110100 and the syndrome is 111. Alternatively, **looking** at the operation of the circuit, we obtain the result shown in **Table 3.7.**

Table 3.7

Input	Register contents
–	000
1	001
1	011
1	111
0	101
0	001
1	011
1	111

If we apply a further shift with 0 at the input, the result will **be 101, which is** the same as the syndrome when bit 6 was in error. Thus the fact **that one extra** shift was required to reach the desired syndrome tells us that the error is in bit $6 - 1$, i.e. **bit 5.**

An interesting effect occurs if we use the circuit of Figure 3.2 or 3.3 for forming the syndrome. We have seen from the encoding example that using this type of circuit is equivalent to applying an extra $n - k$ shifts compared with the circuit of Figure 3.1. If bit $n - 1$ of the received sequence is in error, the effect is to form the syndrome of an error shifted left by $n - k$ positions, i.e. to position $n - k - 1$. If this is the only error, the syndrome thus formed will be 1 followed by $n - k - 1$ zeros. The combinational logic required to detect a single-bit error in the first position thus becomes particularly simple.

For our example of the received sequence 0010011 which has an error in bit 6, the syndrome formation using Figure 3.2 proceeds as shown in **Table 3.8, which** is the expected result. If the received sequence is 1110011 (error **in bit 5) then the** process is as shown in Table 3.9 and one further shift will give 100 as expected.

Table 3.8

Input	Register contents
–	000
0	000
0	000
1	011
0	110
0	111
1	110
1	100

Table 3.9

Input	Register contents
–	000
1	011
1	101
1	010
0	100
0	011
1	101
1	010

Note that although the syndrome calculated in this way is not the same as the previous definitions of syndrome, it carries the same information and therefore the term syndrome is still applied. This form of the syndrome is so common, because of its convenience, that a special term referring to it would be useful. Unfortunately there is no established term to describe it, and I shall use the symbology s^{n-k} or $s^{n-k}(X)$ to distinguish it, depending on whether it is treated as a vector or a polynomial.

3.13   Decoder operation

The operation of a Meggit decoder is based around the syndrome circuit of Figure 3.3. A pseudocode representation of the way in which the error detection and correction may be achieved is given below. The syntax of the pseudocode is based upon the *Pascal* programming language. The code is appropriate to single-error correction, but can be extended to other cases. It includes detection of uncorrectable errors, which is not required for perfect codes such as Hamming codes but is needed in all other cases.

```
begin
shift received sequence into syndrome circuit;
```

```
if syndrome zero then no errors
else
    begin
    i: = n - 1;
    while syndrome <> 10 . . . 0 and i > 0 do
        begin
        i: = i - 1;
        shift syndrome register;
        end;
    if syndrome = 10 . . . 0 then error in bit i
    else uncorrectable error;
    end;
end.
```

In a practical implementation, buffering of the received sequence is required while the syndrome is formed, and at that stage it will be known whether bit $n - 1$ is in error. Bit $n - 1$ can therefore be shifted out of the buffer, corrected if necessary, and at the same time a further shift applied to the syndrome circuit to decide whether the next bit ($n - 2$) requires correction. In this way the data can then be shifted out of the buffer at the same time as the further shifts are applied to syndrome circuit and no buffering of the error pattern is required.

3.14   Multiple error correction

Many cyclic codes are capable of correcting multiple errors. One example is the Golay code which is a perfect (23,12) code with $d_{min} = 7$. The generator polynomial is either

$$g(X) = X^{11} + X^{10} + X^6 + X^5 + X^4 + X^2 + 1$$

or

$$g(X) = X^{11} + X^9 + X^7 + X^6 + X^5 + X + 1$$

There are several methods of decoding such a code, but all are based on the Meggit decoder and a straightforward implementation would be to use the circuit of Figure 3.3 and an extension of the decoding logic as follows:

1. Form the syndrome of the received sequence.

2. Look for syndromes corresponding to any correctable error patterns which include an error in bit $n - 1$.

3. If we detect such a pattern after i additional shifts, this tells us that bit $n - (i + 1)$ was in error, and so that bit can be corrected.

4. The contribution to the syndrome of any bit that has just been corrected will be a 1 in the leftmost place. The first bit in the syndrome registers is therefore inverted when any bit is corrected so that the remaining value in the syndrome registers represents the errors in the uncorrected bits.

5. Continue until the remaining value in the syndrome registers is 0 or all n bits of the received sequence have been assessed.

Strictly speaking, step 4 is not necessary, but it helps in deciding when all errors have been found and in detecting conditions where uncorrectable errors have occurred.

3.15   Example of multiple error correction

The polynomial

$$g(X) = X^8 + X^4 + X^2 + X + 1$$

generates a (15,7) double-error correcting code. If an encoder of the type shown in Figure 3.3 is used to form a syndrome, an error in position 14 will have a syndrome 10000000 and the syndromes of all the other single-bit errors can be found by shifting through the syndrome registers. The complete sequence is shown in Table 3.10.

Table 3.10

Error position	Syndrome
0	00010111
1	00101110
2	01011100
3	10111000
4	01100111
5	11001110
6	10001011
7	00000001
8	00000010
9	00000100
10	00001000
11	00010000
12	00100000
13	01000000
14	10000000

The syndromes to look for are those resulting from an error in bit 14, either on its own or in combination with one other bit. This gives rise to the list shown in Table 3.11.

Table 3.11

Error positions	Syndrome
14,0	10010111
14,1	10101110
14,2	11011100
14,3	00111000
14,4	11100111
14,5	01001110
14,6	00001011
14,7	10000001
14,8	10000010
14,9	10000100
14,10	10001000
14,11	10010000
14,12	10100000
14,13	11000000
14	10000000

Now suppose that the errors are in positions 12 and 5. By adding the syndromes of those single errors we get a syndrome value 11101110 as being computed by the encoder. This does not appear on our list of syndromes that the encoder will try to detect, so shift once to give 11001011 and once again to give 10000001. This is on the list, the two shifts needed to reach this state indicating that bit 12 was in error. We therefore correct bit 12 and invert the leftmost bit of the syndrome to leave 00000001. A further seven shifts, making nine in all, will produce the pattern 10000000, indicating another correctable error in bit 5. Correcting this error and inverting the leftmost bit of the syndrome leaves 0, showing that the error correction is finished.

Suppose the errors are in bits 12 and 10. The syndrome calculated by using the encoder will be 00101000. Two shifts will bring this to 10100000. We correct bit 12 and invert the first bit of the syndrome, leaving 00100000. Two further shifts produce the syndrome 10000000, indicating an error in bit 10. If we did not bother to amend the syndrome after correcting the first error, those two further shifts would produce syndromes 01010111 and 10101110. This second value is also on our list of corrections, so we would correct the error in bit 10. The only drawbacks are that if we had a more powerful code to correct three or more errors, it would be difficult to know when the process had come to an end, and that after checking for errors in every bit we would not know whether all errors had been found or an uncorrectable pattern had occurred.

3.16   **Shortened cyclic codes**

In common with all linear block codes, cyclic codes may be adapted to system parameters by shortening, which is the removal of a number of bits of information. In the case of cyclic codes, the most convenient method to shorten a code is to set the first few bits to zero and then not transmit those bits. The resulting codes are not, strictly speaking, cyclic, but they can be encoded and decoded using the same methods as cyclic codes because the leading zeros that have been omitted would have no effect on the formation of parity bits or of syndromes. Care must be taken, however, with the bit count when decoding because the Meggit decoder will start off looking for errors in bits that have been omitted from the code. Clearly if it thinks it has found errors in any of those bits, then an uncorrectable error pattern has occurred. Alternatively, the arrangement of shift registers with feedback may be modified in such a way that the syndrome is effectively preshifted by the appropriate number of places so that searching for correctable errors can begin immediately.

Suppose we have a (n, k) cyclic code shortened to $(n - i, k - i)$. We receive a sequence $r(X)$ and wish to compute the syndrome of $X^j r(X)$, where j is the sum of i (number of bits removed) and $n - k$ (the usual amount by which the syndrome is preshifted). If $s_1(X)$ is the syndrome of $r(X)$ and $s_2(X)$ is the syndrome of X^j, then the required syndrome is $s_1(X)s_2(X) \bmod g(X)$. We therefore multiply the received sequence by $s_2(X) \bmod g(X)$ by feeding it into the appropriate points of the shift registers.

Consider, for example, the $(15,11)$ code generated by $X^4 + X + 1$, shortened to $(12,8)$. First we compute $X^7 \bmod g(X)$, which is found to be $X^3 + X + 1$. Now we arrange the feeding of the received sequence into the shift registers as shown in Figure 3.4, such that there is a feed into the X^3, X and 1 registers. If a sequence 100000000000 is fed into this arrangement, the sequence of register contents is as shown in Table 3.12. Thus the expected result is obtained, with the registers containing the syndrome 1000. If the first transmitted bit is in error, that fact will therefore be indicated immediately. Any other

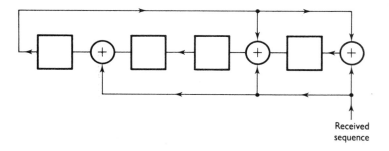

Figure 3.4 Syndrome formation for shortened code

syndrome will indicate a need to shift until 1000 is obtained or the error is found to be uncorrectable.

Table 3.12

Input	Register contents
–	0000
1	1011
0	0101
0	1010
0	0111
0	1110
0	1111
0	1101
0	1001
0	0001
0	0010
0	0100
0	1000

As is the case with other linear block codes, the process of shortening cannot reduce the minimum distance and may indeed increase it. The strategies of Section 2.12 for increasing the minimum distance by shortening are not, however, appropriate for implementation using the circuits designed for cyclic codes.

3.17   **Expurgated cyclic codes**

Expurgation is the conversion of information bits to parity bits, i.e. keeping the length n the same, the dimension k is reduced and the number of parity symbols $n - k$ increased.

If a cyclic code has an odd value of minimum distance, multiplying the generator by $X + 1$ has the effect of expurgating the code and increasing d_{min} by 1. For example:

$$g(X) = X^3 + X + 1$$

$$g(X)(X + 1) = X^4 + X^3 + X^2 + 1$$

The degree of the new generator is increased by 1, increasing the number of parity bits; however, $X + 1$ is a factor of $X^n + 1$ for any value of n, so that the new generator is still a factor of $X^n + 1$ for the original value of n, and hence the code length is unchanged.

Any codeword of the new code consists of a codeword of the original code multiplied by $X + 1$, i.e. shifted left and added to itself. The result is bound to be of even weight because the two sequences being added are of the same weight and modulo 2 addition cannot convert even overall parity into odd. For example, taking the code sequence 1000101 from Section 3.3, shifting left and adding to itself gives

$$1000101 + 0001011 = 1001110$$

Each of the sequences being added was of weight 3, but addition has caused cancellation of two of the 1s leaving a codeword of weight 4.

Assuming that the original code had an odd value of minimum distance, and therefore contained odd weight codewords, the codewords of the expurgated code are just the even weight codewords of the original code. The term *expurgation* arises from the removal of all the odd weight codewords. The result is to increase the minimum distance to some even value.

In the example case where the generator $X^3 + X + 1$ was expurgated to $X^4 + X + 1$, the new generator is of weight 4 so it is obvious that the new $d_{\min}$ cannot be greater than 4. Since the minimum distance must have increased to an even value from its original value of 3, it must now be exactly 4. In other cases of expurgated Hamming codes, the generator may be of higher weight, but it can still be shown that the code contains codewords of weight 4 so that after expurgation $d_{\min} = 4$.

Proof

Let a code be generated by a polynomial $g(X)$ which is primitive of degree c. We choose three distinct integers p, q and r all less than $2^c - 1$ such that $X^p + X^q + X^r$ is not a codeword. If we divide this sequence by $g(X)$ we obtain a remainder $s(X)$ which, because $g(X)$ generates a perfect single-error correcting code, must be able to be interpreted as the syndrome of a single-bit error X^s. Thus there is a sequence $X^p + X^q + X^r + X^s$ which is a codeword. Moreover, the integer s cannot be equal to p, q or r because that would imply the existence of a codeword of weight 2 and a minimum distance of 2. Therefore any cyclic code generated by a primitive polynomial has codewords of weight 4.

The expurgated code could be decoded in the usual way based on the new generator, but because the codewords are also codewords of the original Hamming code, we can form two syndromes based on division by the original Hamming code generator and a separate division by $X + 1$, as shown for our example case in Figure 3.5. If both syndromes are zero there are no errors. If both are nonzero we assume a single-bit error and attempt to correct using the Hamming syndrome circuit in the usual way. If one syndrome is zero and the other nonzero we have an uncorrectable error. This method is advantageous in the detection of uncorrectable errors.

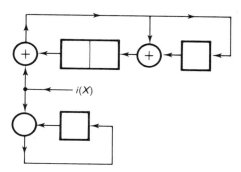

Figure 3.5 Syndrome formation for expurgated code

Example

The sequence 0111010 is a codeword of the (7,3) expurgated code generated by $g(X) = X^4 + X^3 + X^2 + 1$. The following events give rise to the syndromes shown if the circuit of Figure 3.5 is used:

received sequence 0110010 (single error), syndromes are 101 and 1 (correctable error);

received sequence 0110011 (double error), syndromes are 110 and 0 (uncorrectable error);

received sequence 1011000 (triple error), syndromes are 000 and 1 (uncorrectable error).

In the first case, shifting the first syndrome gives 001, 010, 100, showing that the error is in bit 3.

3.18   BCH codes

Many of the most important block codes for random error correction fall into the family of BCH codes, named after their discoverers Bose, Chaudhuri and Hocquenghem. BCH codes include Hamming codes as a special case. There are binary and multilevel BCH codes, although only binary codes will be considered at the moment. For a full understanding of BCH codes, including the construction of the generator polynomial, it is necessary to have an understanding of the construction of finite fields, which will be treated in a later chapter. Nevertheless, the generator polynomials are to be found in most textbooks and it is easy to look them up.

The construction of a t-error correcting binary BCH code starts with an appropriate choice of length:

$$n = 2^m - 1 \qquad (m \text{ is an integer } \geq 3)$$

The values of k and d_{min} cannot be known for sure until the code is constructed, but one can say that

$$n - k \leq mt \qquad (\text{equality holds for small } t)$$

and

$$d_{min} \geq 2t + 1$$

where t is the design value of the number of errors to be detected and corrected. The actual code may exceed this expected value of minimum distance.

BCH codes are generally decoded by algebraic means in which the syndrome is used to form an error-locator polynomial whose roots give the positions of the errors. A further explanation of the codes and the methods of construction and decoding can be found in Chapter 4.

3.19   Further reading

Before delving into other books the reader should be warned that the convention adopted here with high order terms (i.e. first bits transmitted) on the left is reversed by many other authors. This is so that the circuit diagrams can be drawn conventionally with inputs on the left and outputs on the right. Blahut (1983) adopts the same convention as found here. Clark and Cain (1981) and Lin and Costello (1983) adopt the reverse order. Once the order reversal has been mastered, the reader will probably find that Lin and Costello is the best complementary source; they show more details of circuit implementation, including an alternative for codes of rate less than 1/2. This has not been treated here because of the limited value of low rate codes.

3.20   Exercises

1   The primitive polynomial $X^4 + X + 1$ is used to generate a cyclic code. Encode the sequences 10011101001 and 01010000111.

2   Using the code of Exercise 1, form the syndromes of the sequences 000111001110011 and 100111111110011.

3   Find the length and minimum distance of the code generated by the polynomial $X^5 + X^3 + X^2 + X + 1$.

4   Use the division method to confirm the length and minimum distance of the binary Golay code produced by the generator polynomial
$g(X) = X^{11} + X^9 + X^7 + X^6 + X^5 + X + 1$.

5   Show that the polynomial $X^4 + X^2 + 1$ can be used to generate a code of length 12. Find the minimum distance and comment on the result.

6*   Prove that an error in bit $n - 1$ of a received sequence results in a syndrome $s(X) = [g(X) + 1]/X$.

7   If the circuit of Figure 3.2 is used to form a syndrome s^{n-k} for the sequences in Exercise 2, what will be the results? Hence determine the errors.

8   The binary polynomial $X^5 + X^2 + 1$ generates a Hamming code. What are the values of n and k? Design a Meggit decoder for the code and explain how it works.

9   Show that the polynomial $g(X) = X^8 + X^7 + X^6 + X^4 + 1$ generates a double-error correcting code of length 15. Find the syndromes $s^8(X)$ corresponding to correctable errors including an error in bit 14. Decode the sequence 100010110010001.

10   A (15,11) cyclic Hamming code is shortened by removal of five information bits. What are the values of length, dimension and minimum distance for the shortened code? If the generator polynomial is $g(X) = X^4 + X + 1$, encode the sequence 110001 and, using the encoder circuit to calculate syndrome, show how the decoding works if the second received bit is in error. Modify the syndrome former to premultiply by the appropriate amount and repeat the decoding process.

11   Determine the result of using the circuit of Figure 3.5 to form syndromes when there are errors

(a) in bit 0
(b) in bits 6 and 0.

12   The binary polynomial $X^7 + X^3 + 1$ is primitive. Show that the polynomial $X^8 + X^7 + X^4 + X^3 + X + 1$ generates a (127,119) code with $d_{min} = 4$. Design a Meggit decoder for the code and explain how it works.

13   Which of the following codes appear to be consistent with the rules for BCH codes?

$$(31,21)\ d_{min} = 5$$
$$(63,45)\ d_{min} = 7$$
$$(63,36)\ d_{min} = 11$$
$$(127,103)\ d_{min} = 7$$

4
Block codes based on finite field arithmetic

4.1   Introduction

So far we have confined our attention to binary arithmetic when operating on block codes. It was pointed out in Chapter 2 that binary arithmetic is a special example of the arithmetic of a finite field, and this chapter sets out to explain the general approach to finite field arithmetic.

Many books on coding seek to introduce the reader to finite field methods at a much earlier stage than I have attempted. Finite field arithmetic is not inherently difficult and there are certainly a number of results that may be obtained through finite field arithmetic that have already been seen in a different way in the earlier chapters of this book. In my experience, however, it is best for the reader to be familiar with the material of Chapters 2 and 3 before attempting this chapter, because the revisiting of certain results should help to establish some confidence in the topic. This is particularly useful because the subject can seem very abstract until one has seen examples of its applicability.

There is an interesting analogy between finite field arithmetic and the more familiar topic of complex numbers which may also be of help the reader. It is found that there is an interesting and useful relationship between the binary field and larger fields derived from it, similar to that between real and complex numbers. Any irreducible binary polynomial will factorize in the appropriate larger field, just as complex numbers allow one to factorize any polynomial with real coefficients. Moreover the analogy with complex numbers will allow us to define a Fourier transform over a finite field, which is useful for the encoding and decoding of certain cyclic codes.

4.2   Definition of a finite field

A finite field consists of a set of values plus some defined arithmetic operations such that, when the arithmetic operations are carried out on values in the field, the result is itself always a member of the field. It might be thought that this would mean finding sets of real values that can be used in familiar operations so that the rules are satisfied. In reality, the values of the elements in the set are defined in rather an abstract way and the problem of finite field arithmetic boils down to defining the allowed operations.

A finite field is also often known as a Galois field. A Galois field in which the elements can take q different values is referred to as GF(q). The properties of a finite field are as follows:

1. There are two defined operations, namely addition and multiplication.

2. The result of adding or multiplying two elements from the field is always an element in the field.

3. One element of the field is the element zero, such that $a + 0 = a$ for any element a in the field.

4. One element of the field is unity, such that $a \times 1 = a$ for any element a in the field.

5. For every element a in the field, there is an additive inverse element $-a$, such that $a + (-a) = 0$. This allows the operation of subtraction to be defined as addition of the inverse.

6. For every nonzero element a in the field there is a multiplicative inverse element a^{-1}, such that $a \times a^{-1} = 1$. This allows the operation of division to be defined as multiplication by the inverse.

7. The associative [$a + (b + c) = (a + b) + c$, $a \times (b \times c) = (a \times b) \times c$], commutative [$a + b = b + a$, $a \times b = b \times a$], and distributive [$a \times (b + c) = a \times b + a \times c$] laws apply.

These properties cannot be satisfied for all possible field sizes, which means that only certain sizes of finite field can be constructed. The properties can, however, be satisfied if the field size is any prime number or any integer power of a prime. Our main interest will be in finite fields whose size is an integer power of 2.

Examples of finite fields with 3 and 4 elements are shown in Tables 4.1–4.4. Note that the arithmetic in GF(3) is carried out modulo 3, whereas in GF(4) neither addition nor multiplication is carried out modulo 4. The reasons, and the method of construction of the fields, will be explained in the next two sections.

Table 4.1   Addition in GF(3)

+	0	1	2
0	0	1	2
1	1	2	0
1	2	0	1

Table 4.2   Multiplication in GF(3)

×	0	1	2
0	0	0	0
1	0	1	2
2	0	2	1

Table 4.3   Addition in GF(4)

+	0	1	2	3
0	0	1	2	3
1	1	0	3	2
2	2	3	0	1
3	3	2	1	0

Table 4.4   Multiplication in GF(4)

×	0	1	2	3
0	0	0	0	0
1	0	1	2	3
2	0	2	3	1
3	0	3	1	2

4.3   Prime size finite field GF(*p*)

Just as the appropriate arithmetic for a binary field was modulo 2, for a field whose size is a prime number p, the appropriate arithmetic is modulo p. Thus if we take any two elements in the range 0 to $p - 1$, and either add or multiply them, we should take the result modulo p.

The additive inverse of any element is easy to identify as it is just the result of subtracting the element from p. Thus in GF(7), the additive inverse of 5 is 2. The multiplicative inverse is more difficult to find, however, and the following approach will help, as well as leading towards the method for constructing other field sizes.

In any prime size field, it can be proved that there is always at least one element whose powers constitute all the nonzero elements of the field. This element is said to be primitive. For example, in the field GF(7), the number 3 is primitive since

$$3^0 = 1$$
$$3^1 = 3$$
$$3^2 = 2$$
$$3^3 = 6$$
$$3^4 = 4$$
$$3^5 = 5$$

Higher powers of 3 just repeat the pattern since $3^6 = 1$. Note that we can carry out multiplication by adding the powers of 3, thus $6 \times 2 = (3^3) \times (3^2) = 3^5 = 5$. Hence we can find the multiplicative inverse of any element 3^n as $3^{-n} = 3^{6-n}$. Thus the multiplicative inverse of 6 is 6 and the multiplicative inverse of 5 is 3.

4.4   Extensions to the binary field – finite field GF(2^m)

Finite fields can also be created where the number of elements is an integer power of any prime number p. In this case it can also be proved that there will be a primitive element in the field and the arithmetic will be done modulo some polynomial over GF(p). In the main case of interest where $p = 2$, the polynomial to be used will be one of the primitive binary polynomials encountered in the previous chapter as generators for Hamming codes.

Let us suppose that we wish to create a finite field GF(q) and that we are going to take a primitive element of the field and assign the symbol α to it. We cannot at present assign a numerical value to α and have to be content with the knowledge that it exists. The powers of α, α^0 to α^{q-2}, $q - 1$ terms in all, form all the nonzero elements of the field. The element α^{q-1} will be equal to α^0, and higher powers of α will merely repeat the lower powers found in the finite field. The method of multiplication follows straightforwardly by modulo $(q-1)$ addition of the powers of α. All we need now is to know how to add the powers of α, and this is best approached through the case where $q = 2^m$ (m is an integer).

For the field GF(2^m), we know that

$$\alpha^{(2^m - 1)} = 1$$

or

$$\alpha^{(2^m - 1)} + 1 = 0$$

This will be satisfied if any of the factors of this polynomial are equal to zero. The factor that we choose should be irreducible, and should not be a factor of $\alpha^n + 1$ for any value of n less than $2^m - 1$, otherwise the powers of α will repeat before all the nonzero field elements have been generated, i.e. α will not be primitive. Any polynomial that satisfies these properties is called a primitive polynomial, and it can be shown that there will always be a primitive polynomial and thus there will always be a primitive element. Moreover the degree of the primitive polynomials for GF(2^m) is always m. Tables of primitive polynomials are widely available in the literature and a selection was shown in Table 3.1.

Take as an example the field GF(2^3). The factors of $\alpha^7 + 1$ are

$$\alpha^7 + 1 = (\alpha + 1)(\alpha^3 + \alpha + 1)(\alpha^3 + \alpha^2 + 1)$$

Both the polynomials of degree 3 are primitive and so we choose, arbitrarily, the first, constructing the powers of α subject to the condition

$$\alpha^3 + \alpha + 1 = 0$$

The nonzero elements of the field are now

$$1$$
$$\alpha$$
$$\alpha^2$$
$$\alpha^3 = \alpha + 1$$
$$\alpha^4 = \alpha^2 + \alpha$$
$$\alpha^5 = \alpha^3 + \alpha^2 = \alpha^2 + \alpha + 1$$
$$\alpha^6 = \alpha^3 + \alpha^2 + \alpha = \alpha^2 + 1$$

Thus we have the required nonzero powers of α which can be multiplied by adding the powers of α modulo 7. Each power of α can be represented by a binary polynomial in powers of α of degree 2 or less. Addition is by modulo 2 addition of the terms of the polynomial, for example:

$$\alpha^3 + \alpha^4 = \alpha + 1 + \alpha^2 + \alpha = \alpha^2 + 1 = \alpha^6$$

Note that each element is its own additive inverse because of the modulo 2 addition, so that the operations of addition and subtraction are still equivalent.

It may be felt that the job is not yet finished because we still do not know what α represents numerically. This is not, however, a valid objection because the numeric values are unimportant and we can assign them in any way we like. If, for example, we decide to assign the value 2 to α and 3 to α^2 then we have decided that in our arithmetic $2 \times 2 = 3$. This differs from our normal concept of arithmetic and so we might as well regard the assignment of numeric values as purely arbitrary, although there will be some arrangements that are convenient to implement. Worrying about our lack of definition of α is equivalent in the field of complex numbers to worrying that we do not know the value of j, the square root of -1, and it is well established that the incomprehensibility of j is no handicap to finding uses for complex numbers. To be able to manipulate finite fields, it is sufficient to have defined the rules for multiplication and addition.

The field $GF(2^m)$ is said to be an extension field of GF(2). In principle, we could extend any field $GF(p)$ in a similar way, but as the only interest for coding is in extensions to the binary field we shall not pursue the matter further.

4.5   **Zech logarithms**

The method outlined above for addition of powers of α involves representing them as polynomials, modulo 2 adding the coefficients and then translating the resulting polynomial back to a power of α. This may prove tedious to implement, and an alternative is to use Zech logarithms.

Let

$$\alpha^{Z(n)} = \alpha^n + 1 \tag{4.1}$$

then

$$\alpha^n + \alpha^m = \alpha^m [\alpha^{n-m} + 1] = \alpha^m \alpha^{Z(n-m)} = \alpha^{Z(n-m)+m} \tag{4.2}$$

Thus with a table of $Z(n)$ we can easily perform addition. For GF(8) the Zech logarithm table is as shown in Table 4.5. Note that the value of $Z(0)$ is never needed as it only occurs if we try to add two terms that are the same, producing a zero result.

Table 4.5

n	$Z(n)$
1	3
2	6
3	1
4	5
5	4
6	2

As examples using Zech logarithms

$$\alpha^4 + \alpha^5 = \alpha^{Z(1)+4} = \alpha^7 = 1$$
$$\alpha^1 + \alpha^6 = \alpha^{Z(5)+1} = \alpha^5$$

It is not necessary to decide which is the larger power of α before carrying out the subtraction, provided the result is taken modulo $(q - 1)$

$$\alpha^5 + \alpha^4 = \alpha^{Z(6)+5} = \alpha^7 = 1$$
$$\alpha^1 + \alpha^6 = \alpha^{Z(2)+6} = \alpha^5$$

4.6   Implementation of finite field representation

The methods described in the above two sections for carrying out finite field arithmetic lead naturally to two different ways in which the numeric representation of finite field elements may be implemented. The choice of a numeric representation will therefore be governed by the arithmetic method judged to be most convenient.

The first approach is based upon the polynomial representation of the elements. The binary coefficients of polynomials are used to form a binary sequence representing the elements. For the GF(8) example of Section 4.4 this would give

$$0 = 000$$
$$1 = 001$$
$$\alpha = 010$$
$$\alpha^2 = 100$$
$$\alpha^3 = \alpha + 1 = 011$$
$$\alpha^4 = \alpha^2 + \alpha = 110$$
$$\alpha^5 = \alpha^2 + \alpha + 1 = 111$$
$$\alpha^6 = \alpha^2 + 1 = 101$$

Thus a 3-bit binary sequence is used to show the polynomial representation of the eight field elements. Addition is bit-by-bit modulo 2 addition of the sequences. Multiplication involves looking up powers in a table (log table), adding the powers modulo $(q - 1)$ and looking up the result in a table which is the inverse of the first (antilog table).

The second approach is to represent the powers of α more or less directly. There is a complication, however, in deciding whether the value 0 should represent the zero element or the element α^0. We could resolve this problem by letting the value $q - 1$ represent the zero element, leading to the following representation for GF(8)

$$0 = 111$$
$$1 = 000$$
$$\alpha = 001$$
$$\alpha^2 = 010$$
$$\alpha^3 = 011$$
$$\alpha^4 = 100$$
$$\alpha^5 = 101$$
$$\alpha^6 = 110$$

Addition is done using Zech logarithms. To multiply two nonzero numbers, take the modulo $(q - 1)$ sum of the representations.

An alternative, which avoids the possible confusion between the value zero and the zero element, is to let the powers of α be represented by the one's complement of the direct representation above. For GF(8), the representation is now

$$0 = 000 \ (= 0)$$
$$1 = 111 \ (= 7)$$
$$\alpha = 110 \ (= 6)$$
$$\alpha^2 = 101 \ (= 5)$$
$$\alpha^3 = 100 \ (= 4)$$
$$\alpha^4 = 011 \ (= 3)$$
$$\alpha^5 = 010 \ (= 2)$$
$$\alpha^6 = 001 \ (= 1)$$

With this representation, the multiplication algorithm becomes a straightforward addition of the representations, with $q - 1$ being subtracted if the result exceeds $q - 1$. Alternatively, increment by 1 if there is a carry out from the most significant bit. Addition is also straightforward provided the Zech logarithm table is held in one's complement form. For example, the table for GF(8) would be as shown in Table 4.6.

Table 4.6

n	$Z(n)$
6	4
5	1
4	6
3	2
2	3
1	5

Examples of multiplication in this field representation are

$$\alpha^4 \times \alpha^5 = 3 + 2 = 5 = \alpha^2$$
$$\alpha^2 \times \alpha^3 = 5 + 4 = 9 = 2 = \alpha^5$$

To add α^4 and α^5 we evaluate $3 + Z(2 - 3) = 3 + Z(6) = 7$, which is α^0. To add α^6 and α, evaluate $1 + Z(5) = 2$, which is α^5.

4.7   Properties of polynomials and finite field elements

There are several interesting and useful relations between a field GF(p) and its extension fields GF(p^m). We will be mainly interested in the binary field and its extensions, but it may be worth bearing in mind that the principles can be extended. Many of the results will be stated and demonstrated rather than proved.

Roots of a polynomial

Just as polynomials with real coefficients do not always have real factors but always factorize if complex numbers are allowed, an irreducible polynomial over a finite field can always be factorized in some extension field. For example, in the field of complex numbers, $X^2 = 1$ factorizes into $(X + j)(X - j)$ and the two roots, corresponding to a polynomial of degree 2, are $+j$ and $-j$. Similarly the binary polynomial $X^3 + X + 1$ is found to factorize in GF(8) as $(X + \alpha)$ $(X + \alpha^2)(X + \alpha^4)$. The values α, α^2 and α^4 are said to be the *roots* of $X^3 + X + 1$ because they represent the values of X for which the polynomial is zero.

If $f(X)$ is an irreducible q-ary polynomial, then it will have roots in some extension field GF(q^m), i.e. the polynomial can be expressed as the product of several terms $(X + \beta_i)$ where the terms β_i are elements of GF(q^m). Moreover, if we find one of the roots, β, then it can be shown that the others are β^q, β^{q^2}, β^{q^3}, etc. By analogy with the factorization of real polynomials, we may use the term *conjugates* to denote the values of the roots of an irreducible polynomial. For an irreducible binary polynomial with root β, the conjugate roots are β^2, β^4, β^8, etc.

The existence of conjugate roots of a polynomial is equivalent to another property demonstrated by the roots, namely that

$$f(X^q) = [f(X)]^q \tag{4.3}$$

If β is a root of $f(X)$, so therefore must be β^q. The polynomial $f(X)$ is called the minimum polynomial of β (or of any of its other roots). If β is a primitive element, then $f(X)$ is a primitive polynomial. We have already seen that the generation of a finite field is done in terms of a primitive element that is treated as a root of a primitive polynomial.

As an example, consider the finite field GF(8) generated by the primitive polynomial $X^3 + X + 1$. Substituting $X = \alpha$, $X = \alpha^2$ or $X = \alpha^4$ into the polynomial gives a zero result, and it is therefore the minimum polynomial of α, α^2 and α^4. Similarly substituting α^3, α^6 and α^{12} $(= \alpha^5)$ into $X^3 + X^2 + 1$ verifies that they are roots. The minimum polynomial of α^0 is $X + 1$.

If m is the smallest integer value for which $\beta^m = 1$, the element β is said to be of order m and it must be a root of $X^m + 1$. If it is also a root of some irreducible polynomial $f(X)$, then $f(X)$ is a factor of $X^m + 1$. In our example above, the lowest value of m for which $(\alpha^3)^m = 1$ is 7. The polynomial $X^3 + X^2 + 1$ is therefore a factor of $X^7 + 1$.

Finite field elements as roots of a polynomial

The roots of $X^{2^c-1} + 1$ are the nonzero elements of GF(2^c). Consider as an example the finite field GF(8). We have already seen that the factors of $X^7 + 1$ are $X^3 + X + 1$, $X^3 + X^2 + 1$ and $X + 1$. We have also seen that α is a root of

$X^3 + X + 1$, hence α^2 and α^4 are also roots, and that α^3 is a root of $X^3 + X^2 + 1$, hence α^6 and α^5 are also roots. The root of $X + 1$ is 1.

Roots of an irreducible polynomial

If we consider an irreducible binary polynomial of order c, it will have c roots β, β^2, β^4, . . ., $\beta^{2^{c-1}}$, and $\beta^{2^c} = \beta$. Hence

$$\beta^{2^c-1} = 1$$

Thus β is a root of X^{2^c-1}. Since the roots of $X^{2^c-1} + 1$ are the nonzero elements of $GF(2^c)$, it can be seen that an irreducible binary polynomial of degree c always has roots in $GF(2^c)$. Conversely, the factors of X^{2^c-1} include all the irreducible polynomials of degree c. Thus $X^3 + X^2 + 1$ and $X^3 + X + 1$ are the only irreducible polynomials of degree 3.

Note that $X^m + 1$ divides into $X^n + 1$ if and only if m divides into n. This, in conjunction with the previous results, means that all irreducible polynomials of degree c are primitive if $2^c - 1$ is prime. Thus since 7 is prime, all irreducible polynomials of degree 3 are primitive. On the other hand, the irreducible polynomials of degree 4 are not all primitive because 15 is not a prime number.

Factorization of a polynomial

If we wish to factorize a binary polynomial $f(X)$, we need to establish the finite field in which the factors may be found. To do this, we first find the binary factors of the polynomial (if any) and the order of the binary polynomial representing those factors. Now find the LCM, c', of the orders; the factors of the polynomial will be found in $GF(2^{c'})$.

Proof

$$2^{ab} - 1 = (2^a)^b - 1$$
$$2^{ab} - 1 = (2^a - 1)[(2^a)^{b-1} + (2^a)^{b-2} + (2^a)^{b-3} + \cdots + 1]$$

Thus $2^{c'} - 1$ is a multiple of $2^c - 1$ if c' is a multiple of c. By choosing c' to be a multiple of the order c of some binary factor, the roots of that binary factor in $GF(2^c)$ can also be found in $GF(2^{c'})$. If c' is a multiple of the orders of all the binary factors, then all the roots can be represented in $GF(2^{c'})$.

As an example, the polynomial $X^5 + X^4 + 1$ factorizes into $(X^3 + X + 1)(X^2 + X + 1)$. It therefore has factors in $GF(2^6)$.

4.8   Specifying codes by roots

It is possible to specify a polynomial code by saying that the codewords are binary polynomials with specific roots in $GF(2^m)$. For example, if the specified root is α from $GF(8)$, we know that the minimum polynomial is $X^3 + X + 1$, and all codewords must be divisible by the minimum polynomial. In this case the minimum polynomial acts as the generator for the code. In general, the generator polynomial will be the least common multiple of the minimum polynomials for the specified roots. The degree of the polynomial, which is equal to the number of parity check symbols for the code, is the same as the number of separate roots, so that the total number of code roots gives the number of parity check symbols.

If a code polynomial $v(X)$ has a root β, then

$$v(\beta) = 0$$

If v_n is the coefficient of X^n, then

$$v_{n-1}\,\beta^{n-1} + \cdots + v_2\beta^2 + v_1\beta^1 + v_0\beta^0 = 0$$

or in vector form

$$\mathbf{v}\begin{bmatrix} \beta^{n-1} \\ \cdot \\ \cdot \\ \cdot \\ \beta^3 \\ \beta^2 \\ \beta^1 \\ \beta^0 \end{bmatrix} = 0 \tag{4.4}$$

Similarly if there are j roots β_1 to β_j then

$$\mathbf{v}\begin{bmatrix} \beta_1^{n-1} & \beta_2^{n-1} & \cdots & \beta_j^{n-1} \\ \cdot & \cdot & \cdots & \cdot \\ \cdot & \cdot & \cdots & \cdot \\ \cdot & \cdot & \cdots & \cdot \\ \beta_1^3 & \beta_2^3 & \cdots & \beta_j^3 \\ \beta_1^2 & \beta_2^2 & \cdots & \beta_j^2 \\ \beta_1^1 & \beta_2^1 & \cdots & \beta_j^1 \\ \beta_1^0 & \beta_2^0 & \cdots & \beta_j^0 \end{bmatrix} = 0 \tag{4.5}$$

but

$$\mathbf{v}\,\mathbf{H}^{\mathrm{T}} = 0$$

which means that the large matrix above, when transposed, will give the parity check matrix of the code. The roots are polynomials in α and so may be regarded as vectors which themselves need to be transposed. Therefore

$$
\mathbf{H} = \begin{bmatrix} \beta_1^{n-1^T} & \cdots & \beta_1^{1^T} & \beta_1^{0^T} \\ \beta_2^{n-1^T} & \cdots & \beta_2^{1^T} & \beta_2^{0^T} \\ \cdot & \cdots & \cdot & \cdot \\ \cdot & \cdots & \cdot & \cdot \\ \cdot & \cdots & \cdot & \cdot \\ \beta_j^{n-1^T} & \cdots & \beta_j^{1^T} & \beta_j^{0^T} \end{bmatrix} \tag{4.6}
$$

Only one of the roots β, β^2 β^4, β^8, etc., needs to be included in the parity check matrix since the inclusion of any one implies all the others

4.9   Hamming codes

Hamming codes have generator polynomials that are primitive. Hence any primitive element can be a root of the code. If we take the element α as the root, then

$$
\mathbf{H} = [\alpha^{n-1^T} \ldots \alpha^{1^T} \alpha^{0^T}] \tag{4.7}
$$

The powers of α are just all the nonzero elements of the field, which leads to the conclusion that the columns of the parity check matrix contain all the possible combinations of 1 and 0. For example, taking the code based on GF(8), for which $\alpha^3 + \alpha + 1 = 0$, gives

$$
\mathbf{H} = \begin{bmatrix} 1 & 1 & 1 & 0 & 1 & 0 & 0 \\ 0 & 1 & 1 & 1 & 0 & 1 & 0 \\ 1 & 1 & 0 & 1 & 0 & 0 & 1 \end{bmatrix}
$$

This is in fact the parity check matrix for the cyclic Hamming code of Chapter 3.

4.10   BCH codes

A t-error correcting BCH code has $2t$ consecutive roots in $GF(q^m)$ and has length $q^m - 1$. A single-error correcting binary BCH code would have length $2^m - 1$ and would have two consecutive roots in $GF(2^m)$. If we choose these roots as α and α^2, then the second root is redundant because it is implied by the first. The code is therefore just a Hamming code as before.

A double-error correcting binary BCH code might have roots of α, α^2, α^3 and α^4. Of these, only α and α^3 are independent, the others being implied by α, and so the parity check matrix is

$$\mathbf{H} = \begin{bmatrix} \alpha^{n-1^{\mathrm{T}}} & \cdots & \alpha^{2^{\mathrm{T}}} & \alpha^{1^{\mathrm{T}}} & \alpha^{0^{\mathrm{T}}} \\ \alpha^{3(n-1)^{\mathrm{T}}} & \cdots & \alpha^{3\times 2^{\mathrm{T}}} & \alpha^{3\times 1^{\mathrm{T}}} & \alpha^{3\times 0^{\mathrm{T}}} \end{bmatrix} \tag{4.8}$$

BCH codes allow an algebraic method of decoding. Consider the case where $n = 15$ and there are errors at positions i and j. The syndrome is

$$\mathbf{s} = \mathbf{e}\,\mathbf{H}^{\mathrm{T}}$$

The syndrome has two components s_1 and s_3.

$$\begin{aligned} s_1 &= \alpha^i + \alpha^j \\ s_3 &= \alpha^{3i} + \alpha^{3j} \end{aligned} \tag{4.9}$$

Substituting the first into the second gives

$$s_1^2 \alpha^i + s_1 \alpha^{2i} + s_1^3 + s_3 = 0$$

Any value of α^i which is a root of this equation will locate an error and, since the assignment of the parameters i and j is arbitrary, both error locations can be found from the same equation. Roots can be found by trying all possible values, which is better than having to try all possible combinations of positions, or by other techniques.

Example

A double-error correcting BCH code of length 15 has roots α, α^3 in GF(16). As a result, the parity check matrix is

$$\mathbf{H} = \begin{bmatrix} \alpha^{14^{\mathrm{T}}} & \alpha^{13^{\mathrm{T}}} & \cdots & \alpha^{2^{\mathrm{T}}} & \alpha^{1^{\mathrm{T}}} & \alpha^{0^{\mathrm{T}}} \\ \alpha^{12^{\mathrm{T}}} & \alpha^{9^{\mathrm{T}}} & \cdots & \alpha^{6^{\mathrm{T}}} & \alpha^{3^{\mathrm{T}}} & \alpha^{0^{\mathrm{T}}} \end{bmatrix} \tag{4.10}$$

The column values can be filled in by constructing the field GF(16) using the primitive polynomial $X^4 + X + 1$. The field elements can be expressed as polynomials in α as follows:

$$\begin{aligned} \alpha^0 &= 0001 \\ \alpha^1 &= 0010 \\ \alpha^2 &= 0100 \\ \alpha^3 &= 1000 \\ \alpha^4 &= 0011 \\ \alpha^5 &= 0110 \\ \alpha^6 &= 1100 \\ \alpha^7 &= 1011 \\ \alpha^8 &= 0101 \end{aligned}$$

$$\alpha^9 = 1010$$
$$\alpha^{10} = 0111$$
$$\alpha^{11} = 1110$$
$$\alpha^{12} = 1111$$
$$\alpha^{13} = 1101$$
$$\alpha^{14} = 1001$$

The parity check matrix would therefore be

$$\mathbf{H} = \begin{bmatrix} 1&1&1&1&0&1&0&1&1&0&0&1&0&0&0 \\ 0&1&1&1&1&0&1&0&1&1&0&0&1&0&0 \\ 0&0&1&1&1&1&0&1&0&1&1&0&0&1&0 \\ 1&1&1&0&1&0&1&1&0&0&1&0&0&0&1 \\ 1&1&1&1&0&1&1&1&1&0&1&1&1&1&0 \\ 1&0&1&0&0&1&0&1&0&0&1&0&1&0&0 \\ 1&1&0&0&0&1&1&0&0&0&1&1&0&0&0 \\ 1&0&0&0&1&1&0&0&0&1&1&0&0&0&1 \end{bmatrix}$$

If the received sequence is 101010110010101, the syndrome is 10010110. Thus

$$s_1 = \alpha^{14}$$
$$s_3 = \alpha^5$$

Substituting in equation (4.9) gives

$$\alpha^{13+i} + \alpha^{14+2i} + \alpha^{12} + \alpha^5 = 0$$

The value $i = 2$ gives

$$\alpha^0 + \alpha^3 + \alpha^{12} + \alpha^5 = 0$$

The value $i = 13$ gives

$$\alpha^{11} + \alpha^{10} + \alpha^{12} + \alpha^5 = 0$$

The errors are therefore at positions 2 and 13, giving a transmitted sequence 111010110010001, and the syndrome of this sequence is zero, showing that it is a codeword.

We could check this result in another way, regarding the code as cyclic and generated by a polynomial. The roots α and α^3 have minimum polynomials $X^4 + X + 1$ and $X^4 + X^3 + X^2 + X + 1$ respectively. The generator polynomial is the product of these two, giving

$$g(X) = X^8 + X^7 + X^6 + X^4 + 1$$

The code is therefore a (15,7) code and the generator is found to divide into the decoded sequence with zero remainder.

Further treatment of the algebraic decoding of BCH codes will be found in later sections of this chapter.

It is possible, using similar techniques, to create the parity check matrix of a triple-error correcting code of length 15 (see Exercise 6). In this case, however, it is found that two rows of the matrix are not linearly independent of the others and that, when these are removed, the code is (15,5). The number of parity checks required may therefore be less than expected when the code is created. This point is explored from a different aspect in Section 4.13.

4.11   Fourier transform in a finite field

The analogy between elements of a finite field and complex numbers can be carried a stage further by showing that in certain circumstances we can define a discrete Fourier transform over a finite field. Moreover, it is found that the transform so defined has considerable practical value, providing us with efficient encoding and decoding techniques and an alternative view of cyclic codes that is of particular interest to those working in the field of digital signal processing. We shall start from the familiar form of the discrete Fourier transform, and then develop the finite field version.

The definition of the discrete Fourier transform (DFT) of an n-point sequence in the field of complex numbers is usually expressed in terms of the relation between the frequency domain samples X_k and the time domain samples x_i.

$$X_k = \sum_{i=0}^{n-1} x_i e^{-j\ 2\pi\ ik/n} \tag{4.11}$$

The term $e^{-j\ 2\pi\ ik/n}$ can be taken as a set of powers of $e^{-j\ 2\pi/n}$, which is the nth root of 1.

In the finite field $GF(2^m)$ there will be a transform of $v(X)$ into $V(z)$, equivalent to the Fourier transform, only if there is an nth root of 1 within the field, i.e. a term β such that $\beta^n = 1$. This will be satisfied if

$$\frac{2^m - 1}{n} = c$$

where c is some integer. It is not necessary for the polynomial being transformed to be defined over the same field as the transform; a polynomial with coefficients from $GF(2^l)$ can be transformed over a field $GF(2^m)$ provided m is a multiple of l. Thus, for example, a binary polynomial of length 7 could be transformed over $GF(2^3)$ or over $GF(2^6)$, or a polynomial of length 7 over $GF(2^3)$ could be transformed over $GF(2^6)$.

In the general case the coefficient V_k of the Fourier transform of a polynomial $v(\alpha)$ can be defined as

$$V_k = \sum_{i=0}^{n-1} v_i(\alpha^c)\alpha^{cik} \tag{4.12}$$

where the term $v_i(\alpha^c)$ indicates that a coefficient β in GF(2^l) is replaced by β^c in GF(2^m). Note, however, that the value of c is defined by the ratio of $2^m - 1$ to the *length* of the transformed sequence, *not* the value of $2^l - 1$.

The component v_i of the inverse transform is

$$v_i = \sum_{k=0}^{n-1} V_k\alpha^{-cik} \tag{4.13}$$

Depending on the values produced by the inverse transform, it may then be possible to reduce the coefficients to values in a smaller field.

There will be two particular cases of interest to us. One will be the case where a binary vector of length $2^m - 1$ is transformed over GF(2^m), the other is where a vector over GF(2^m) of length $2^m - 1$ is transformed over its own field. In both cases $c = 1$ and

$$V_k = \sum_{i=0}^{n-1} v_i(\alpha)\alpha^{ik} \tag{4.14}$$

with the inverse transform being

$$v_i = \sum_{k=0}^{n-1} V_k\alpha^{-ik} \tag{4.15}$$

Example

The transform of the sequence 0101100 over GF(8) is

$$
\begin{aligned}
V_0 &= 0 + 0 + 1 + 1 + 0 + 1 + 0 = 1 \\
V_1 &= \alpha^2 + \alpha^3 + \alpha^5 = 0 \\
V_2 &= \alpha^4 + \alpha^6 + \alpha^3 = 0 \\
V_3 &= \alpha^6 + \alpha^2 + \alpha = \alpha^3 \\
V_4 &= \alpha + \alpha^5 + \alpha^6 = 0 \\
V_5 &= \alpha^3 + \alpha + \alpha^4 = \alpha^5 \\
V_6 &= \alpha^5 + \alpha^4 + \alpha^2 = \alpha^6
\end{aligned}
$$

Thus the transformed sequence is $\alpha^6\alpha^50\alpha^3001$.

We shall see examples of vectors transformed over their own finite field when Reed Solomon codes are discussed in a later section.

4.12   Roots and spectral components

We have seen previously that codes can be defined by roots in $GF(2^m)$. Roots in the time domain are related to zero components in the transform over $GF(2^m)$. A polynomial $v(X)$ has a root α^k if and only if the component V_k of the transform is zero. Conversely, the polynomial $v(X)$ has a zero component v_i if and only if α^{-i} is a root of the transform polynomial $V(z)$. These properties follow from the definitions of the forward and inverse transforms.

As an example, the binary sequence 0101100 is a codeword of the (7,4) Hamming code for which the generator is $X^3 + X + 1$. We know also that the roots are α, α^2 and α^4. Thus we would expect the frequency components V_1, V_2 and V_4 to be zero. From the previous section, we see that this is true.

4.13   BCH codes in the frequency domain

A primitive t-error correcting q-ary BCH code of block length $n = q^m - 1$ is the set of all words whose spectrum in $GF(q^m)$ is zero in $2t$ consecutive components. In many cases the code is binary ($q = 2$) and the zeros taken as being from position 1 to position $2t$. Such codes would properly be called primitive binary BCH codes, but if the term BCH codes is used without qualification this may well be what is meant.

As an example, a triple-error correcting binary code of length 15 would have zeros at positions 1–6, implying roots α, α^2, . . ., α^6 in the time domain, of which α, α^3 and α^5 are independent. The existence of conjugate roots and the relation of spectral zeros to roots means that we would actually have zeros at other positions as well; position 1 implies zeros at positions 2^c (modulo n) for integer values of c, i.e. positions 2, 4 and 8. A zero at position 3 implies zeros at positions 6, 12 and 9, and the zero at position 5 implies a zero at position 10. There are therefore 10 zeros implying 10 parity check bits. The code thus has $n = 15$ and $k = 5$. (See also the end of Section 4.10 and Exercise 6.)

If we take a second special case, we can define a q-ary code of length $q - 1$ and define its spectral zeros in $GF(q)$. For example, if $q = 16$ we have a length 15 code with 16-level symbols. For a triple-error correcting code we again define six consecutive zeros, but now the existence of a zero at position 1 implies time domain roots α^{q^c} for integer values of c. Taking the powers modulo q, it is seen that there are no conjugates and therefore no extra spectral zeros. The code therefore has $2t$ spectral components which are constrained to the value zero, corresponding to $2t$ parity checks in the time domain. It thus meets the Singleton bound with equality (see section 2.13). Multilevel BCH codes over $GF(q)$ with length $q - 1$ are called Reed Solomon (RS) codes.

Reed Solomon codes can be encoded in a convenient, although nonsystematic, way using the frequency domain. The appropriate $n - k$ symbols are set to zero, the information is written into the remaining k symbols and an inverse transform produces a RS codeword. This method also provides a convenient approach to frequency domain decoding. Examples will be given in a later section.

4.14   BCH decoding and the BCH bound

We have previously seen that binary BCH codes can be decoded by a polynomial with roots that indicate the positions of the errors. We shall also see in the next section a process of decoding using a polynomial whose zero coefficients indicate the locations of errors in the time domain and whose roots in the frequency domain can be used to correct the errors. For the moment we will use such a polynomial to prove a property of BCH codes, namely that $2t$ consecutive zero-valued spectral components are sufficient to guarantee t-error correction.

Suppose we have a code polynomial $c(X)$ with fewer than d nonzero components, and its spectrum $C(z)$ has $d - 1$ consecutive zeros. We define a polynomial $\lambda(X)$ such that it is zero where $c(X)$ is nonzero and let the positions of the zeros be denoted i_j. The polynomial $\lambda(X)$ is usually called the *error locator polynomial* because, as we shall see, there is no codeword, apart from the all-zero sequence, which satisfies the defined conditions.

The zero components in $\lambda(X)$ mean that each α^{-i_j} will be a root of the transform $\Lambda(z)$ of $\lambda(X)$, or

$$\Lambda(z) = \prod_{j=1}^{v} (1 + z\,\alpha^{i_j})$$

Note from the above definition of $\Lambda(z)$ that Λ_0 is equal to 1.

Now in the time domain, $\lambda_i c_i = 0$ for all i, therefore in the frequency domain, replacing multiplication with a convolution

$$\sum_{j=0}^{n-1} \Lambda_j C_{k-j} = 0$$

The degree v of $\Lambda(z)$ is at most $d - 1$ and $\Lambda_0 = 1$, which leaves us with

$$C_k = \sum_{j=1}^{d-1} \Lambda_j C_{k-j} \tag{4.16}$$

This is the equation for the output of a linear feedback shift register with feedback polynomial $\Lambda(z)$, as shown in Figure 4.1.

If we know any $d - 1$ consecutive values of C_j we can use the shift registers with feedback to generate all the rest. We know, however that there are $d - 1$ consecutive zeros and using them to initialize the feedback shift register will

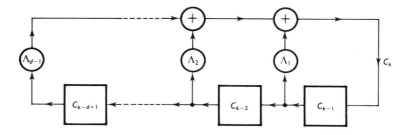

Figure 4.1 Shift register generation of transform of error locator polynomial

generate a string of zeros. Thus C_j must be zero for all j and all terms in $c(X)$ are zero. This proves that if there are $2t$ consecutive zeros in the spectrum, the nonzero codewords must have weight at least $2t + 1$ and the code can therefore correct at least t errors.

Although we are left with the possibility that the code may be able to correct more than t errors, the BCH decoding method will use the $2t$ consecutive zeros in a way that will correct up to t errors, and any extra capabilities of the code will go into error detection.

4.15   Decoding in the frequency domain

We have previously seen that BCH codes can be decoded by algebraic techniques involving the formation and solution of an equation. That equation was solved in the time domain and its roots indicated the positions of the errors. For multilevel codes, such as RS codes, we need also to find the values of the errors. It is found that a frequency domain approach yields the most efficient method of decoding RS codes, provided the information is directly available in the frequency domain. The method can also be applied to other BCH codes, although the practical implementation is more likely to be a variant of the method previously explained. In this section, therefore, the frequency domain approach will be explained and subsequent sections will concentrate on its application to RS codes.

Assume that we transmit a code sequence $c(X)$ and that it is received with the addition of an error sequence $e(X)$. We take the transform of the received sequence, giving

$$R(z) = C(z) + E(z)$$

where $R(z)$, $C(z)$ and $E(z)$ are the transforms of the received sequence, the codeword and the error sequence respectively. We know that $C(z)$ is zero in $2t$ consecutive spectral locations, so we can use these locations to give us a window on $E(z)$, i.e. $2t$ components of $E(z)$ can easily be obtained and can be considered to form a syndrome $S(z)$. We assume that there are $v \leqslant t$ errors and define an error locator polynomial $\lambda(X)$ such that it is zero in the positions where $e(X)$ is nonzero. The product of the received sequence and the error locator sequence in the time domain will therefore be zero, which means that in the frequency domain the convolution will be zero.

$$\sum_{j=0}^{t} \Lambda_j E_{k-j} = 0 \tag{4.17}$$

Here we have used the fact that $\lambda(X)$ has at most t zeros, hence $\Lambda(z)$ has at most t roots and is therefore a polynomial of degree no greater than t. If we know the error spectrum from positions m to $m + 2t - 1$, we can form t equations by letting k take values from $m + t$ to $m + 2t - 1$. Assuming the spectral zeros of the code are from positions zero to $2t - 1$, the equations are as follows:

$$\Lambda_0 E_t + \Lambda_1 E_{t-1} + \cdots + \Lambda_t E_0 = 0$$

$$\Lambda_0 E_{t+1} + \Lambda_1 E_t + \cdots + \Lambda_t E_1 = 0$$

$$\Lambda_0 E_{2t-1} + \Lambda_1 E_{2t-2} + \cdots + \Lambda_t E_{t-1} = 0$$

This set of t equations in $t + 1$ unknowns is called the *key equation*, which we can solve for the different values of Λ_j, provided we impose an arbitrary value on one of the roots, corresponding to the fact that the value of the error locator polynomial is arbitrary in the nonzero positions in the time domain. In practice the condition we impose is $\Lambda_0 = 1$. The procedure for solving the key equation may be straightforward if t is small, but in the general case special methods have to be devised that are computationally efficient and take into account the fact that the number of errors may be less than t. One such method, Euclid's algorithm, will be explained in a later section. For the moment it is sufficient to believe that the task can be accomplished.

Once we know the values of the Λ_j, we can generate all the values of E_k by using Λ as the feedback polynomial for a linear shift register, primed with t known values of E_k

$$E_k = \sum_{j=1}^{v} \Lambda_j E_{k-j} \tag{4.18}$$

This procedure is known as recursive extension.

When the spectrum of the errors has been found, an inverse transform on the corrected frequency domain sequence will produce the time domain codeword. As we shall see in the next section, this final step is unnecessary for RS codes provided they are encoded in the frequency domain.

4.16   Encoding and decoding example

As an example of frequency domain encoding and decoding, we will look at a RS code. This example is chosen for two reasons. Firstly, we can encode from the frequency domain by an inverse transform, which means that when we obtain the errors in the frequency domain the decoding task is finished and no final inverse transform is required. Secondly, the frequency domain technique will produce the error values as well as the locations; the standard time domain techniques for RS codes produce the error locations and a second stage is needed for the values. The processes involved in encoding and decoding are illustrated in Figure 4.2.

We will choose a (7,3) double-error correcting RS code over $GF(2^3)$. Let the information be α^3, α, α^6 and let the zeros in the frequency domain occupy the positions 0–3. We therefore put the information into positions 4, 5 and 6 in the frequency domain with zeros in the other positions, producing the transform of the codeword as

$$C(z) := \alpha^3 z^6 + \alpha z^5 + \alpha^6 z^4$$

An inverse transform (see equation 4.15) generates the codeword as follows:

$$c_0 = \alpha^3 + \alpha + \alpha^6 = \alpha^2$$
$$c_1 = \alpha^3 \alpha^1 + \alpha \alpha^2 + \alpha^6 \alpha^3 = 1$$

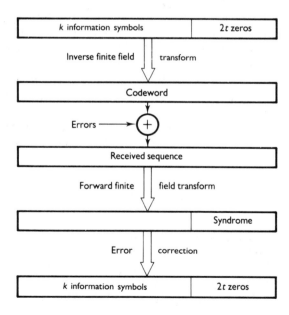

Figure 4.2 Frequency domain encoding and decoding of Reed Solomon codes

$$c_2 = \alpha^3\alpha^2 + \alpha\alpha^4 + \alpha^6\alpha^6 = \alpha^5$$
$$c_3 = \alpha^3\alpha^3 + \alpha\alpha^6 + \alpha^6\alpha^2 = \alpha^4$$
$$c_4 = \alpha^3\alpha^4 + \alpha\alpha + \alpha^6\alpha^5 = \alpha^3$$
$$c_5 = \alpha^3\alpha^5 + \alpha\alpha^3 + \alpha^6\alpha = \alpha^6$$
$$c_6 = \alpha^3\alpha^6 + \alpha\alpha^5 + \alpha^6\alpha^4 = \alpha$$

Hence the code polynomial is

$$c(X) = \alpha X^6 + \alpha^6 X^5 + \alpha^3 X^4 + \alpha^4 X^3 + \alpha^5 X^2 + X + \alpha^2$$

We now create a two-symbol error, say $\alpha X^4 + \alpha^4 X$. The received polynomial is

$$r(X) = \alpha X^6 + \alpha^6 X^5 + X^4 + \alpha^4 X^3 + \alpha^5 X^2 + \alpha^5 X + \alpha^2$$

Now the task of decoding may begin. The transform of the received sequence is obtained (using equation 4.14) as follows

$$R_0 = \alpha + \alpha^6 + 1 + \alpha^4 + \alpha^5 + \alpha^5 + \alpha^2 = \alpha^2$$
$$R_1 = \alpha\alpha^6 + \alpha^6\alpha^5 + \alpha^4 + \alpha^4\alpha^3 + \alpha^5\alpha^2 + \alpha^5\alpha^1 + \alpha^2 = 0$$
$$R_2 = \alpha\alpha^5 + \alpha^6\alpha^3 + \alpha + \alpha^4\alpha^6 + \alpha^5\alpha^4 + \alpha^5\alpha^2 + \alpha^2 = 1$$
$$R_3 = \alpha\alpha^4 + \alpha^6\alpha + \alpha^5 + \alpha^4\alpha^2 + \alpha^5\alpha^6 + \alpha^5\alpha^3 + \alpha^2 = \alpha^2$$
$$R_4 = \alpha\alpha^3 + \alpha^6\alpha^6 + \alpha^2 + \alpha^4\alpha^5 + \alpha^5\alpha + \alpha^5\alpha^4 + \alpha^2 = \alpha^2$$
$$R_5 = \alpha\alpha^2 + \alpha^6\alpha^4 + \alpha^6 + \alpha^4\alpha + \alpha^5\alpha^3 + \alpha^5\alpha^5 + \alpha^2 = \alpha^5$$
$$R_6 = \alpha\alpha + \alpha^6\alpha^2 + \alpha^3 + \alpha^4\alpha^4 + \alpha^5\alpha^5 + \alpha^5\alpha^6 + \alpha^2 = \alpha^4$$

Hence the transformed polynomial is

$$R(z) = \alpha^4 z^6 + \alpha^5 z^5 + \alpha^2 z^4 + \alpha^2 z^3 + z^2 + \alpha^2$$

We now form the key equation with $t = 2$ and $\Lambda_0 = 1$, knowing that the four lowest coefficients of $R(z)$ represent a part of $E(z)$.

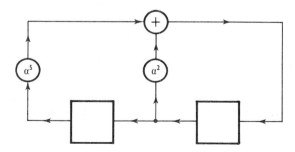

Figure 4.3 Shift register for recursive extension

$$1 + \alpha^2\Lambda_2 = 0$$

$$\alpha^2 + \Lambda_1 = 0$$

In this case the equations are easy to solve, giving $\Lambda_1 = \alpha^2$ and $\Lambda_2 = \alpha^5$. The shift register configuration is therefore as shown in Figure 4.3.

We now load the value α^2 into the leftmost stage of the shift register, and zero into the other stage. Cycling the shift register will give the outputs α^2, 0, 1, α^2, 1, α^6, α^6. Thus

$$E(z) = \alpha^6 z^6 + \alpha^6 z^5 + z^4 + \alpha^2 z^3 + z^2 + \alpha^2$$

and adding this to the spectrum of the received signal gives

$$C(z) = \alpha^3 z^6 + \alpha z^5 + \alpha^6 z^4$$

Thus we have shown that double error correction can be achieved for this case.

4.17 Further examples of Reed Solomon decoding

The previous section worked through an example in which the number of errors was exactly equal to the error correcting ability of the code. There are two other types of case where the outcome is not obvious and which we need to study. They are the cases where the number of errors is less than the error correcting capability and where there are more errors than the code can correct.

Looking first at the case where we have fewer than the maximum number of correctable errors, it is obvious that if there are no errors, then the transform of the codeword will exhibit zeros in the expected places and no decoding is required. If there are some errors, but less than t, the transform of the error locator polynomial will have fewer than t unknown roots and the t simultaneous equations will not be linearly independent. This will be illustrated by returning to the example of the previous section but this time introducing only one error.

Let us assume that we receive a sequence

$$r(X) = \alpha X^6 + \alpha^6 X^5 + X^4 + \alpha^4 X^3 + \alpha^5 X^2 + X + \alpha^2$$

which is the same as the previous example except that position 1 does not contain an error, the sole error being in position 4. The transform is

$$R(z) = \alpha^6 z^6 + \alpha^3 z^5 + \alpha^4 z^4 + \alpha^6 z^3 + \alpha^2 z^2 + \alpha^5 z + \alpha$$

from which the key equations are found to be

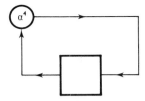

Figure 4.4 Recursive extension with single error

$$\alpha^2 + \alpha^5\Lambda_1 + \alpha\Lambda_2 = 0$$
$$\alpha^6 + \alpha^2\Lambda_1 + \alpha^5\Lambda_2 = 0$$

The second equation is seen to be the same as the first, multiplied by α^4, which tells us that there is only one error and we must set Λ_2 equal to zero. The solution to the key equation is thus

$$\Lambda_1 = \alpha^2\alpha^{-5} = \alpha^4$$

and loading the value α into the shift register of Figure 4.4 gives the sequence α, α^5, α^2, α^6, α^3, 1, α^4. The transform of the decoded codeword is thus

$$C(z) = \alpha^3z^6 + \alpha z^5 + \alpha^6z^4$$

which is correct.

The fact that in the above example each term in the syndrome is a constant factor times the previous term is characteristic of single-symbol errors, and the position of the error in the time domain can be readily determined from the factor. In this case because $S_j = \alpha^4 S_{j-1}$, the error is in position 4, whence $\Lambda(z) = \alpha^4z + 1$ and $\Lambda_1 = \alpha^4$. It is usually worth including a check for single errors in a decoder and a special decoding routine, because in many practical examples single errors will make up a significant proportion of the sequence errors.

Now let us suppose that three errors are introduced into the transmitted codeword and that the received sequence is

$$r(X) = \alpha^3X^6 + \alpha^6X^5 + X^4 + \alpha^4X^3 + \alpha^5X^2 + \alpha^5X + \alpha^2$$

where, in comparison with the example of Section 4.16, an extra error value 1 has been applied to position 6. The transform is

$$R(z) = \alpha^2z^6 + \alpha^3z^5 + \alpha^5z^4 + \alpha z^3 + \alpha^4z^2 + \alpha^6z + \alpha^6$$

from which the key equations are found to be

$$\alpha^4 + \alpha^6\Lambda_1 + \alpha^6\Lambda_2 = 0$$

$$\alpha + \alpha^4\Lambda_1 + \alpha^6\Lambda_2 = 0$$

Substituting for Λ_2 gives

$$\alpha^2 + \alpha^3\Lambda_1 = 0$$
$$\Lambda_1 = \alpha^6$$
$$\Lambda_2 = \alpha$$

The registers for recursive extension are shown in Figure 4.5. After initializing with values α^6, α^6, the error sequence generated is α^6, α^6, α^4, α, α^4, α^5, 1. This gives the transform of the decoded codeword as

$$C(z) = \alpha^6 z^6 + \alpha^2 z^5 + z^4$$

From our privileged position of knowing what the original information was, we can tell that the decoding has failed; the question is whether there is any way of detecting the decoding error or whether the error is undetectable. Clearly with a code of minimum distance 5, there must be instances where a three-symbol error is indistinguishable from a two-symbol error on a different codeword. On the other hand, if the code is not a perfect code (and RS codes are not), some triple errors must be detectable. How can we tell which is which?

It is tempting to assume that because the process of error detection, location and correction all appeared to work, any decoding error must be undetectable. A study of these processes will indicate, however, that they cannot fail to give some sort of result. Our key equations will always give up to t roots, and if there are fewer than t linearly independent equations we will just reduce the assumed number of roots to match. Having obtained the roots, these will always be consistent with the known part of the error sequence and so the generation of the errors in the frequency domain will give apparently valid results. If we want to

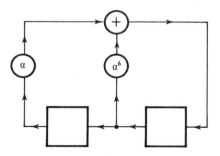

Figure 4.5 Attempted recursive extension after triple error

detect uncorrectable errors, then the method must involve something other than the processes already tried.

If we apply an inverse transform to obtain the decoded codeword, the result is

$$c(X) = \alpha^3 X^5 + \alpha^5 X^4 + \alpha X^3 + \alpha X^2 + \alpha^2 X$$

This has more than two differences from the received sequence (in fact it differs in every place) and so we can see that the decoding process has somehow gone wrong and the errors were therefore detectable. We do not, however, wish to perform the inverse transform in our decoder because that would destroy the advantage of encoding in the frequency domain. We therefore prefer to find some evidence in the frequency domain that uncorrectable errors have occurred.

The detection of uncorrectable errors can in fact be achieved in the frequency domain after recursive extension. If the roots of the error locator polynomial do indeed correspond to a pattern of t or fewer errors in the time domain, then the sequence generated by the shift registers will be cyclic with the same length as the code. At the end of the correction, the contents of the shift registers should be the same as the initialization. This was the case for the double- and single-error patterns above. It is not, however, the case for the triple-error pattern where at the end the registers hold values 0, α, compared with the initialization of α^6, α^6. We can therefore tell at the end of recursive extension whether the process has been successful.

The fact that we have encoded and decoded via the frequency domain does have one effect that is worth noting in the case where an undetectable decoding error occurs. In such a case, it can be assumed that the decoder will introduce an extra t errors, but these extra errors are in the time domain. The information is in the frequency domain, and there the effect of the decoding error is more difficult to quantify. The best assumption is that after any decoding error, each symbol in the frequency domain will have a random error applied, and that therefore the probability of being correct is $(q - 1)/q$ for each symbol. As a result, the approximate expressions for output error rates must be modified from those given in Section 1.7.

4.18   Decoding of binary BCH codes

As a final example of error correction via the frequency domain, let us examine the example of the (15,7) binary BCH code from Section 4.10. There we received a sequence 101010110010101 which was found to have two errors, in positions 2 and 13. We now examine the decoding by means of a transform over GF(16), the field being generated by the polynomial $X^4 + X + 1$.

The transform of the received sequence is

$$R(z) = \alpha^5 z^{12} + z^{10} + \alpha^{10} z^9 + \alpha^7 z^8 + \alpha^{10} z^6 + z^5 + \alpha^{11} z^4 + \alpha^5 z^3 + \alpha^{13} z^2 + \alpha^{14} z$$

The zeros should be between positions 4 and 1, so the key equation becomes

$$\alpha^5 + \alpha^{13} \Lambda_1 + \alpha^{14} \Lambda_2 = 0$$
$$\alpha^{11} + \alpha^5 \Lambda_1 + \alpha^{13} \Lambda_2 = 0$$

Substituting for Λ_2 gives

$$\Lambda_1 = \alpha^{14}$$

hence

$$\Lambda_2 = 1$$

Decoding can now be by finding the roots of $z^2 + \alpha^{14} z + 1$, which are α^2 and α^{13}. Hence the errors are at positions -2 and -13, or 13 and 2 respectively. As the code is binary, that completes the decoding. Alternatively, we could use recursive extension to generate the sequence α^{14}, α^{13}, α^5, α^{11}, 1, α^{10}, α^7, α^7, α^{10}, 1, α^{11}, α^5, α^{13}, α^{14}, 0. Adding these values to positions 1–14 and position 0 of the transform of the received sequence gives

$$C(z) = \alpha^{14} z^{14} + \alpha^{13} z^{13} + \alpha^{11} z^{11} + \alpha^7 z^7$$

The inverse transform restores the originally transmitted codeword.

4.19   Polynomial form of the key equation

In previous sections we have been involved in solving simultaneous equations in order to carry out error correction. This we can do manually by substitution or other means. For automatic implementation we need to find an approach that can be efficiently and routinely implemented. To do this we first of all convert the key equation from its expression as a summation into a polynomial format.

We wish to find a solution to the key equation, which can be expressed as

$$\sum_{j=0}^{t} \Lambda_j E_{k-j} = 0$$

for values of k from t to $2t - 1$. This expression represents a convolution which can, alternatively, be given a polynomial form. We have seen on a number of occasions previously that the convolution of two sequences corresponds to the product of the sequence polynomials. In this case it is equivalent to all the terms of degree between t and $2t - 1$ in $\Lambda(z)E(z)$. Hence we can say

$$\Lambda(z)E(z) = f(z)z^{2t} + \Omega(z) \tag{4.19}$$

The terms on the left-hand side of degree t to $2t - 1$ are zero. The terms of degree $2t$ or more are represented by $f(z)z^{2t}$. $\Omega(z)$ represents the terms of degree less than t, and is known as the error evaluator polynomial because it is used for such a purpose in the time domain decoding of multilevel BCH codes such as RS codes.

Two methods are commonly used for solving the key equation in this form: Euclid's algorithm and the Berlekamp–Massey algorithm. The latter is more efficient, but is more difficult to understand than Euclid's method and is related to it. We shall study the Euclid algorithm in detail and merely outline the steps involved in the other.

4.20   Euclid's algorithm

Euclid's algorithm is most commonly encountered in finding lowest common multiples of numbers. In the process of so doing it identifies common factors so that these can be taken into account in computing the lowest common multiple. Many authors preface a discussion of Euclid's method with an illustration of its use for such a purpose. Unfortunately, the connection between using it in this way and solving the key equation is not easy to spot and the numeric application may not be of much help in understanding the application to polynomials. For that reason, I prefer to confine the discussion to the solution of equations involving polynomials. Euclid's method enables us to find minimum degree solutions for polynomials $f(z)$ and $g(z)$ such that

$$a(z)f(z) + b(z)g(z) = r(z)$$

where $r(z)$ is known to have degree less than some fixed value. In our case, $r(z)$ will have degree $<t$, $a(z) = z^{2t}$ and $b(z)$ is the syndrome polynomial $S(z)$. The polynomial $g(z)$ will give us $\Lambda(z)$ which is what we need to know. The method involves repeated division of polynomials until a remainder is found of degree $<t$.

The first step is to divide $a(z)$ by $b(z)$ to find the quotient $q_1(z)$ and remainder $r_1(z)$.

$$a(z) = q_1(z)b(z) + r_1(z) \tag{4.20}$$

If the degree of $r_1(z)$ is less than t, then we have reached our solution with $f(z) = 1$, $g(z) = q_1(z)$ and $r(z) = r_1(z)$. Otherwise set $g_1(z) = q_1(z)$ and proceed to the next stage.

The second step is to divide $b(z)$ by $r_1(z)$ giving

$$b(z) = q_2(z)r_1(z) + r_2(z) \tag{4.21}$$

Note that the degree of $r_2(z)$ must be less than that of $r_1(z)$ so that this process is reducing the degree of the remainder. If we eliminate $r_1(z)$ from equations (4.20) and (4.21) we obtain

$$q_2(z)a(z) = [q_2(z)g_1(z) + 1]\,b(z) + r_2(z) \qquad (4.22)$$

Set $g_2(z) = q_2(z)g_1(z) + 1$. If the degree of $r_2(z)$ is less than t, then $g(z) = g_2(z)$, otherwise continue to the next step.

The third step continues in similar vein, dividing $r_1(z)$ by $r_2(z)$

$$r_1(z) = q_3(z)r_2(z) + r_3(z) \qquad (4.23)$$

Again the degree of the remainder is decreasing. Using equations (4.21) and (4.22) to eliminate $r_1(z)$ and $r_2(z)$ gives

$$[1 + q_2(z)q_3(z)]a(z) = [g_1(z) + q_3(z)g_2(z)]b(z) + r_3(z) \qquad (4.24)$$

If the degree of $r_3(z)$ is less than t then $g(z) = g_3(z) = q_3(z)g_2(z) + g_1(z)$.

The method continues in this way until a remainder of degree less than t is found, at each stage setting

$$g_n(z) = q_n(z)g_{n-1}(z) + g_{n-2}(z) \quad [g_0(z) = 1,\ g_{-1}(z) = 0] \qquad (4.25)$$

Summary of Euclid's algorithm

Set $g_{-1}(z) = 0$, $g_0(z) = 1$.

Set n = 1. Divide z^{2t} by $S(z)$ to find quotient $q_1(z)$ and remainder $r_1(z)$. Calculate $g_1(z)$ from equation (4.25).

While degree of remainder is greater than or equal to t, continue by incrementing n, divide previous divisor by previous remainder and calculate $g_n(z)$ by equation (4.25).

When desired degree of remainder is obtained, set $\Lambda(z) = g_n(z)$.

Example

We shall now solve the key equation from Section 4.16 using Euclid's algorithm. The syndrome $S(z)$ is

$$S(z) = \alpha^2 z^3 + z^2 + \alpha^2$$

Divide z^4 by $S(z)$ to give

$$z^4 = (\alpha^5 z + \alpha^3)(\alpha^2 z^3 + z^2 + \alpha^2) + \alpha^3 z^2 + z + \alpha^5$$

Set $g_1(z) = \alpha^5 z + \alpha^3$.

Divide $S(z)$ by $\alpha^3 z^2 + z + \alpha^5$ to give

$$\alpha^2 z^3 + z^2 + \alpha^2 = (\alpha^6 z + \alpha^6)(\alpha^3 z^2 + z + \alpha^5) + \alpha^3 z + \alpha$$

Set $g_2(z) = (\alpha^6 z + \alpha^6)(\alpha^5 z + \alpha^3) + 1$. As the remainder is of degree <2, this is the end of Euclid's algorithm.

Multiplying the terms in $g_2(z)$, we now have

$$\Lambda(z) = \alpha^4 z^2 + \alpha z + \alpha^6$$

This does not quite correspond to our usual form for recursive extension, as we have previously set $\Lambda_0 = 1$. We can achieve this by dividing by α^6 to give

$$\Lambda(z) = \alpha^5 z^2 + \alpha^2 z + 1$$

The terms of this polynomial give the same arrangement for recursive extension as in Section 4.16.

Applying Euclid's algorithm to the single-error example of Section 4.17 would terminate with a polynomial of degree 1. This is left as an exercise for the reader.

4.21 The Berlekamp–Massey algorithm

Another way to find the arrangement of shift registers with feedback for recursive extension is to use the Berlekamp–Massey algorithm. This algorithm is difficult to understand, although simple to implement; consequently it will be described here but an explanation of why it works will not be attempted. Essentially it creates the minimum complexity arrangement of shift registers with feedback to carry out recursive extension. In the following description, the parameter l represents the degree of the error locator polynomial and n represents the degree of the syndrome polynomial being examined. The algorithm is as follows:

```
begin
l := 0;
n := 0;
k := −1;
Λ(z) := 1;
D(z) := zΛ(z);
while (n < 2t) do
```

```
        begin
          δ := ∑_{i=0}^{l} Λ_iS_{n-i};
          if (δ <> 0) then
            begin
            Λ*(z) := Λ(z) + δD(z)
            if (l < n − k) then
              begin
              l* := n − k;
              k:= n − l;
              D(z) := Λ(z)/δ;
              l := l*
              end;
            Λ(z) := Λ*(z)
            end;
          D(z) := zD(z);
          n := n + 1
          end;
        end.
```

Example

The steps in solving the double-error correction example of Sections 4.16 and 4.20 are as follows:

$$\delta := \alpha^2$$
$$\Lambda^*(z) := \alpha^2 z + 1$$
$$l^* := 1$$
$$k := 0$$
$$D(z) := \alpha^5$$
$$l := 1$$
$$\Lambda(z) := \alpha^2 z + 1$$
$$D(z) := \alpha^5 z$$
$$n := 1$$
$$\delta := \alpha^4$$
$$\Lambda^*(z) := 1$$
$$\Lambda(z) := 1$$
$$D(z) := \alpha^5 z^2$$
$$n := 2$$
$$\delta := 1$$
$$\Lambda^*(z) := \alpha^5 z + 1$$
$$l^* := 2$$
$$k := 1$$
$$D(z) := 1$$

$$l := 2$$
$$\Lambda(z) := \alpha^5 z^2 + 1$$
$$D(z) := z$$
$$n := 3$$
$$\delta := \alpha^2$$
$$\Lambda^*(z) := \alpha^5 z^2 + \alpha^2 z + 1$$
$$\Lambda(z) := \alpha^5 z^2 + \alpha^2 z + 1$$
$$D(z) := z^2$$
$$n := 4$$

The algorithm therefore terminates with $\Lambda(z)$ holding the correct coefficients of the feedback polynomial. Applied to the single-error example of Section 4.17 it will also terminate correctly with a polynomial of degree 1.

4.22   Extended Reed Solomon codes

It is possible to create a q-ary RS code of length $q + 1$, and such a code is known as an extended code. The code will still correct $t = (n - k)/2$ symbols and can be thought of either as adding two parity symbols to a code which corrects $t - 1$ errors (expansion) or as adding two extra information symbols to a t-error correcting code. The extended code is not cyclic, but can be encoded and decoded using frequency domain techniques. Proofs of the properties of extended RS codes can be found in Blahut (1983).

The process of encoding is as follows. Put $k - 2$ ($= q - 1 - 2t$) information symbols and $2t$ consecutive zeros into a vector of length $q - 1$. Put the two remaining information symbols into the two outside zero positions, one at the low-order end and one at the high-order end, as in Figure 4.6. We now have the spectrum of a $t - 1$ error correcting RS code. The last two information symbols are known as the edge frequencies.

The vector of length $q - 1$ is now given an inverse Fourier transform over GF(q) to produce a RS codeword that can correct $t - 1$ errors. The high-order edge frequency is appended at the beginning (high-order end) of the codeword and the low-order edge frequency at the (low-order) end of the codeword. The codeword is now of length $q + 1$. This is shown in Figure 4.6.

To decode a received sequence using the extended code, strip the symbols from the beginning and end, and forward transform the remaining sequence of length $q - 1$. The full syndrome consists of the sum of the high-order edge frequency plus the stripped symbol received in the high order position, the subsequent $2t - 2$ symbol values and the sum of the low-order edge frequency plus the stripped symbol received in the low-order position, as shown in Figure 4.7. Decoding, however, starts off with an attempt at $t - 1$ error correction, using

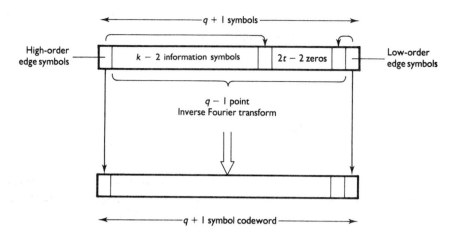

Figure 4.6 Encoding of extended Reed Solomon code

only the central $2t - 2$ symbols of the syndrome. A standard RS decoder is used in conjunction with some additional logic as follows:

1. Remove the edge symbols and attempt $t - 1$ error correction on the remaining symbols. If decoding succeeds, then accept the result if at least one of the edge symbols corresponds with the appropriate edge frequency or if $t - 2$ or fewer symbols required correction. Otherwise proceed to the next stage.

2. If the stage 1 decoding is unsuccessful or the result is not accepted, the received edge symbols are taken as being correct. The full syndrome is used to attempt t-error correction on the remaining symbols.

Example

We consider the case of a (9,5) RS code over GF(8), based on the example of Section 4.16, but in this case we have a five-symbol information sequence 1, α^3, α, α^6, α^2. We treat the first and last of these as edge symbols, placing them in positions 3 and 0 respectively in the frequency domain. Thus we start from the spectrum of a single-error correcting RS code

$$C(z) = \alpha^3 z^6 + \alpha z^5 + \alpha^6 z^4 + z^3 + \alpha^2$$

The inverse transform gives the codeword of a (7,5) RS code:

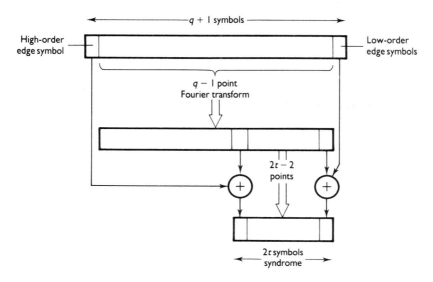

Figure 4.7 Syndrome formation for extended Reed Solomon code

$$c(X) = \alpha^6 X^6 + \alpha^2 X^5 + \alpha^3 X^4 + \alpha^6 X^3 + X^2 + \alpha^3 X + 1$$

The two extra information symbols are now added to the ends of the codeword to produce the (9,5) RS codeword

$$c'(X) = X^8 + \alpha^6 X^7 + \alpha^2 X^6 + \alpha^3 X^5 + \alpha^6 X^4 + X^3 + \alpha^3 X^2 + X + \alpha^2$$

Now assume that an error occurs at positions 8 and 5, producing a received sequence

$$r'(X) = \alpha^3 X^8 + \alpha^6 X^7 + \alpha^2 X^6 + \alpha^5 X^5 + \alpha^6 X^4 + X^3 + \alpha^3 X^2 + X + \alpha^2$$

The additional symbols are stripped from the sequence to give

$$r(X) = \alpha^6 X^6 + \alpha^2 X^5 + \alpha^5 X^4 + \alpha^6 X^3 + X^2 + \alpha^3 X + 1$$

which transforms to

$$R(z) = \alpha^2 z^6 + \alpha^3 z^4 + \alpha^3 z^2 + \alpha^6 z$$

The terms in z^2 and z are extracted to form a single-error correcting syndrome

$$S(z) = \alpha^3 z + \alpha^6$$

The solution of the key equation is $\Lambda_1 = \alpha^4$. The spectrum of the error sequence is generated by recursive extension starting from the rightmost syndrome position (position 1) with the rightmost information position (position 0) generated last. The result is found to be

$$E(z) = \alpha^5 z^6 + \alpha z^5 + \alpha^4 z^4 + z^3 + \alpha^3 z^2 + \alpha^6 z + \alpha^2$$

which, when added to $R(z)$ gives

$$C(z) = \alpha^3 z^6 + \alpha z^5 + \alpha^6 z^4 + z^3 + \alpha^2$$

Since one of the edge frequencies now corresponds with the appropriate received edge symbol, the decoding is accepted and all the information is directly available from $C(z)$.

Decoding in other circumstances, either with both errors in the edge symbols or both errors in the central part of the codeword, is left to the reader in Exercise 11.

4.23   Erasure decoding of BCH codes

One feature that is sometimes incorporated into decoders for BCH codes is the ability to recover events known as erasures. These are instances when there is knowledge that a symbol should have been present at a particular point in a coded sequence, but there is no information as to what that symbol was. Erasure decoding can be regarded as a first step in soft-decision decoding because, in comparison with what was transmitted, an extra level has been introduced into the received sequence. Unfortunately erasure decoding does not give worthwhile gains on a Gaussian channel, but it may be useful in the presence of certain types of interference. It is also an important part of certain soft-decision strategies, for which further reading will be suggested at the end of this chapter.

When an erasure occurs, the maximum likelihood decoding method is to compare the received sequence with all codewords, but ignoring the symbol values in the erased positions. The erasures are then filled using the values from the selected codeword. With e erasures there will still be a minimum distance of $d_{min} - e$ between codewords, counting only the unerased places. Thus we will obtain decoding provided $2t$ is less than this reduced minimum distance.

$$2t + e < d_{min} \tag{4.26}$$

At this point, one might well ask whether there is any point in declaring erasures on a binary symmetric channel. A t-error correcting code will be able to fill up to $2t$ erasures, but if a guess was made for the values of all the erased symbols, then on average half would be correct and the error correction would cope with the rest. It will be seen shortly that erasures do give some advantage in that erasure filling is equivalent to carrying out error correction on two possible sets of reconstituted bit values, and then choosing the better of the two. On the other hand, the demodulator need only have a slight inclination towards one or other value to make choosing the more likely bit value a better strategy than erasure.

For any binary code there is a straightforward, nonalgebraic decoding method. Replace all the erased bits by zero and decode. If no more than half of the erasures should have been ones and equation (4.26) was satisfied, then the number of errors will still be less than half of d_{min} and the decoding will be correct. If, on the other hand, more than half the erasures should have been ones, then we may get a decoding error that will introduce extra errors into the sequence. In this case, replacing all the erased bits with ones will be successful. The procedure is therefore to decode twice, replacing all the erased bits firstly with zeros and then with ones. If the decoded sequences differ, choose the one that is closer to the received sequence.

Reed Solomon codes may be decoded in the presence of erasures by an algebraic technique to be explained below. The minimum distance of these codes is $n - k + 1$, which means that in the absence of errors, equation (4.26) shows that $n - k$ erasures can be filled. We thus have the interesting result that a RS codeword can be recovered from any k correct symbols.

To decode algebraically, we replace the erasured symbols by some arbitrary value, usually zero. We adopt the polynomial approach in the frequency domain and multiply the product of the syndrome polynomial $S(z)$ and the error locator polynomial $\Lambda(z)$ by an erasure polynomial $\Gamma(z)$, which is known because the positions of the erasures are known. For every two erasures, the degree of the error locator polynomial is reduced by one so that the degree of the product of erasure and error locator polynomials is increased by one. The number of simultaneous equations that can be formed will thus be reduced by one, which matches the reduction in the number of unknowns. This all sounds rather horrific, but is fairly straightforward if considered in the context of an example.

4.24   Example of erasure decoding of Reed Solomon codes

We choose as our example the first case from Section 4.17 in which there was one error in the received sequence, but we introduce also two erasures. The received sequence will be taken as

$$r(X) = \alpha X^6 + X^4 + \alpha^5 X^2 + X + \alpha^2$$

with known erasures at positions 5 and 3. The transform of the received sequence is

$$R(z) = \alpha^6 z^6 + \alpha^5 z^5 + \alpha^6 z^4 + z^3 + \alpha^3 z^2 + 1$$

The low-order terms of $R(z)$ form a syndrome of the received sequence.
The erasure polynomial is

$$\Gamma(z) = (\alpha^5 z + 1)(\alpha^3 z + 1)$$

the error locator polynomial is

$$\Lambda(z) = \Lambda_1 z + 1$$

and the product is

$$\Gamma(z)\Lambda(z) = \alpha\Lambda_1 z^3 + (\alpha + \alpha^2\Lambda_1)z^2 + (\alpha^2 + \Lambda_1)z + 1$$

As this polynomial is of degree 3, we can only carry out a single place convolution with a known section of the error spectrum to produce a key equation. We are therefore only interested in the terms of degree 3 when we multiply by the syndrome

$$S(z) = z^3 + \alpha^3 z^2 + 1$$

giving as our key equation

$$\alpha\Lambda_1 + \alpha^5 + \alpha^3\Lambda_1 + 1 = 0$$
$$\Lambda_1 = \alpha^4$$

We can now substitute this value back into the expression for $\Gamma(z)\Lambda(z)$, which will be the polynomial used to generate the errors in the frequency domain by recursive extension.

$$\Gamma(z)\Lambda(z) = \alpha^5 z^3 + \alpha^5 z^2 + \alpha z + 1$$

This gives rise to the circuit shown in Figure 4.8 for recursive extension.
Initializing the registers with the values 1, 0, α^3 from the syndrome generates the further terms of the error spectrum as 1, 0, α^6, α^4, which when added to $R(z)$ gives

$$C(z) = \alpha^3 z^6 + \alpha z^5 + \alpha^6 z^4$$

The decoding has therefore been successful.

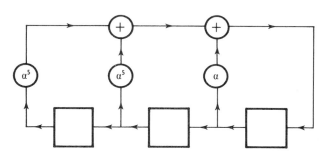

Figure 4.8 Recursive extension with one error and two erasures

Euclid's algorithm may be used to solve for the feedback polynomial in the presence of erasures by initializing $g_0(z)$ as $\Gamma(z)$, using $S(z)\Gamma(z) \bmod z^{2t}$ as the initial divisor and terminating when the degree of the remainder is less than $t + e/2$ (t is the number of errors that can be corrected without erasures, e is the number of erasures, assumed to be even). To operate the Berlekamp–Massey algorithm, set l and n to e and initialize $\Lambda(z)$ to $\Gamma(z)$.

4.25   Further reading

The material of this chapter has been the most difficult to be found in this book. Although I have tried to make it as straightforward as possible and to give simple examples of all the topics treated, the reader who is seriously interested in finite field methods and codes will want to refer also to other sources, if only to get a clear picture of the conventional, time domain approach. Most books on error control coding will have some treatment of the subject, but I will comment on the value of a few of the leading contenders.

Perhaps the prime source for the frequency domain approach is Blahut (1983). He has been perhaps the leading exponent of this approach and his book contains just about all the material from the various papers that he previously published on the subject. The reader will also find there full treatment of finite field arithmetic, proofs of the various properties of polynomials and their factors plus further treatment of advanced methods such as the Berlekamp–Massey algorithm.

Possibly the best feature of Blahut's book, however, is the treatment of fast algorithms for finite field Fourier transforms, a subject that I have avoided entirely. It is well known that the obvious way of calculating discrete Fourier transforms contains many duplicated operations. Anyone who is not familiar with this fact would do well to look at Brigham (1988) where the Cooley–Tukey radix-two algorithm for fast Fourier transforms is explained in great detail. The approach is to start with a number of points which is an integral power of 2 and decompose into a number of two-point transforms. This is not directly of much use to us because the number of points in sequence for a finite field transform is usually one less than an integer power of 2, e.g. 255 rather than 256. The Cooley–Tukey approach can, however, be applied to other radices or to mixed radices and so can reduce the computation when the length of the transform factorizes. There are other fast algorithms that may be useful too, such as the Winograd and Good–Thomas methods, all of which are covered by Blahut.

Clark and Cain (1981) also adopt a frequency domain approach to BCH and RS codes, and they explain the time domain methods well too. As always their treatment is worthy of study. In this chapter, I have broached the subject of soft-decision decoding of block codes, and for this too I can do no better than to refer the reader to the appropriate chapter of Clark and Cain's book. The nonalgebraic erasure decoding method for BCH and other binary codes, explained in Section 4.23, is actually closely related to the Chase algorithm for soft-decision decoding, which is the most commonly encountered method and is well covered by Clark and Cain.

Michelson and Levesque (1985) have good coverage of both time and frequency domain approaches, the latter in the context of RS codes. They also have a useful appendix with a full list of irreducible polynomials of degree up to 16 and a reduced list up to degree 34. Lin and Costello (1983) have a good, if lengthy, treatment of finite fields and take in other nonessential but interesting matters such as groups, rings and vector spaces. Their approach to BCH and RS codes is time domain only. Although the reader should by now know how to construct generator polynomials for BCH codes, the list of such generators in an appendix is a useful reference source.

4.26   Exercises

1   Use the primitive polynomial $X^3 + X^2 + 1$ to create a polynomial representation of the field elements of GF(8). Evaluate the products $(111) \times (100)$, $(101) \times (010)$, $(011) \times (110)$ and the divisions $(100)/(101)$, $(111)/(110)$ and $(010)/(011)$.

2   For the field GF(8) created in Exercise 1, construct the Zech logarithm table. Hence perform the sums $\alpha + \alpha^2$, $\alpha^5 + 1$, $\alpha^6 + \alpha^3$, $\alpha^4 + \alpha^5$.

3   Use the primitive polynomial $X^4 + X^3 + 1$ to create the field GF(16) in a polynomial form. Construct the Zech logarithm table.

4   If $Z(n)$ represents the Zech logarithm, prove that

$$Z[Z(n)] = n$$

and

$$Z(q - 1 - n) = Z(n) - n.$$

5   Find the minimum polynomials for each of the nonzero elements of GF(8) as defined
        in Exercise 1.

6   Starting from the parity check matrix of a double-error correcting BCH code of
        length 15 (equation 4.10), construct the parity check matrix for the triple-error
        correcting code. Show that two of the extra rows of the parity check matrix are
        redundant and that therefore the parity check matrix corresponds to a (15,5) code.

7   Given that

$$X^{15} + 1 = (X + 1)(X^4 + X + 1)(X^4 + X^3 + 1)(X^4 + X^3 + X^2 + X + 1)$$
$$(X^2 + X + 1)$$

        find the generator polynomial of a triple-error correcting BCH code of length 15.

8   For the BCH code defined by equation (4.10), decode the sequence
        100010110010001.

9   Find the forward and inverse transforms of the binary sequence 101100100000000
        over GF(16).

10   Using the (7,3) RS code example of this chapter, carry out the decoding if the errors
        are

$$e(X) = \alpha^5 X^4 + \alpha^2 X^2$$

        using Euclid's algorithm for solution of the key equation.

11   Encode the 8-ary information sequence α^2, 0, α^6, 1, α into a (9,5) extended RS code.
        Carry out the decoding if errors are introduced as follows:

        1 in position 8 and α in position 0

        α^2 in position 7 and α^3 in position 2

12   In the example (7,3) RS code of Section 4.16, erase the transmitted symbols at
        positions 6, 5, 3 and 0. Carry out the decoding.

5
Convolutional codes

5.1   Introduction

In Chapter 1 it was explained that codes for error control generally fell into two categories, namely block codes and convolutional codes. The subsequent three chapters were devoted to block codes for random error correction, and the time has now come to look at convolutional codes. The space devoted to convolutional codes will be rather less than that used for block codes, but this fact should not be taken as an indication of their relative importance. Indeed in some ways the reasons why it is difficult to say a lot about convolutional codes are the same as the reasons why convolutional codes should be given serious consideration for error control, particularly forward error correction on Gaussian channels.

The most obvious feature of convolutional codes in comparison with block codes is that they do not exhibit the same sort of algebraic complexity. Convolutional encoders are relatively simple and the codes do not usually fall into families in the same way as block codes. In addition there is one decoding method which is in a definable sense optimal, which is in principle applicable to all convolutional codes and which permits the use of soft-decision decoding with little increase in complexity. As a result this method, known as Viterbi decoding, is the usual choice for real-time applications. It is only the restrictions on code complexity and decoding speed that stop the Viterbi method from being ideal for all convolutional code applications.

A few years ago there appeared on British television an advertisement for a well-known brand of beer whose message could be taken as applying to convolutional codes. Two beer drinkers are shown in a bar. They order different beers and one of them proceeds to treat the other to a lecture on the merits of the former's chosen tipple. The second drinker says nothing, but finishes his drink whilst the first has barely started. The punch line is 'the less said, the better the beer.' As it happens, the beer was not one that I ever drink and neither am I a particular exponent of convolutional codes, nevertheless the point is well made. This is my excuse for the relative paucity of the treatment of convolutional codes.

As background to this chapter most of the first chapter is relevant, even though the examples in Chapter 1 were based on a block code. Some of the characteristics of convolutional codes are presented as an analogy with the block code features, so the information on block codes will be needed. (This approach of block codes first, convolutional second is not necessary but it is convenient, and even authors whose personal bias is towards convolutional codes tend to follow it.) Because of the relevance of soft-decision decoding to convolutional codes, Sections 1.3 and 1.4 will be of interest. The discussion of linearity in Chapter 2 is also relevant because convolutional codes are linear, although the property that linearity implies the existence of an equivalent systematic code does not apply to convolutional codes.

5.2   General properties of convolutional codes

An example schematic diagram of a convolutional encoder is shown in Figure 5.1. Note that the information bits do not flow through directly into the code-stream, i.e. the code is not systematic. The difference between systematic and nonsystematic codes is not trivial with convolutional codes, and nonsystematic codes can give better performance when coupled with an appropriate decoding method.

The way in which the encoder works is that the input bit is modulo 2 added to stored values of previous input bits, as shown in Figure 5.1, to form the outputs which are buffered ready for transmission. The input bit is then moved into the shift registers and all the other bits shift to the left (the leftmost, i.e. oldest, stored bit being lost). The encoder starts with the registers clear, and if a 1 is input the outputs will be 11 and the encoder will contain 1 in the right-hand shift register stage. If the next input is 0 then the encoder will output 10, the right shift register will contain 0 and the left shift register 1.

There are few well-defined families of convolutional codes. The designer of the coding scheme usually chooses a decoding method and then chooses a suitable code for that method, the code having been selected by computer search techniques. Study of convolutional codes therefore tends to concentrate more on

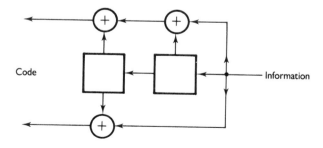

Figure 5.1 Convolutional encoder

decoding than on the codes themselves, but some appreciation of the encoding process will first be required.

5.3   Generator polynomials

The encoding operation could be described by two polynomials, one to represent the generation of the each output bit from the input bit. For the above code they are

$$g^{(1)}(X) = X^2 + X + 1$$
$$g^{(2)}(X) = X^2 + 1$$

The operator X represents a single frame delay.

The interpretation of these polynomials is that the first output bit is given by the modulo 2 sum of the bit that has been remembered for two frames (the X^2 term), the bit remembered for one frame (X) and the input bit (1). The second output is the bit remembered for two frames (X^2) modulo 2 added to the input (1).

The concept of generator polynomials can be applied also to cases where several bits are input at once. There would then be a generator to describe the way that each of the input bits and its previous values affected each of the outputs. For example, a code that had 2 bits in and 3 out would need six generators designated $g_1^{(1)}(X)$, $g_1^{(2)}(X)$, $g_1^{(3)}(X)$, $g_2^{(1)}(X)$, $g_2^{(2)}(X)$ and $g_2^{(3)}(X)$.

5.4   Terminology

Terminology is a particularly tricky and confusing part of convolutional codes. The major problem is a lack of uniformity in the terms used by different authors, with many instances where two people use different words for the same thing and, even worse, where two people use the same word for different things. As a result there cannot be said to be any consensus around the terms I have used and although I think I can find some support for each term, I cannot point to another author who uses the same terms for everything.

The terms to be used here to describe a convolutional code are as follows:

Input frame – the number of bits, k_0, taken into the encoder at once.

Output frame – the number of bits, n_0, output from the encoder at once.

Memory order – the maximum number, m, of shift register stages in the path to any output bit.

Memory constraint length – the total number, v, of shift register stages in the encoder, excluding any buffering of input and output frames.

Input constraint length – the total number, K, of bits involved in the encoding operation; equal to $v + k_0$.

Output constraint length – the number, n, of output bits for which the effect of any one input bit persists; equal to $(m + 1) n_0$.

The term that causes particular problems is *constraint length*. Used without qualification, it might well mean what I have called *input constraint length*, but it could also be one of the two other possibilities or another related but differently defined parameter. Curiously enough, the symbol used (v, K or n) is often more widely accepted than the term to describe it, and so may give a clue to the real meaning. The general message, however, is to be wary of the terms used by other authors and be sure to know what is meant.

A convolutional code may be termed a (n_0, k_0, m) code or a (n, k) convolutional code, where $k = (m + 1)k_0$. The latter stems from a philosophy that treats convolutional codes similarly to block codes and will not be followed here. Conversion from the latter to the former terminology can often be achieved by recognizing the common factor $m + 1$ between n and k. The term code rate, meaning $k_0 n_0$, is also often applied to convolutional codes.

For our example, $k_0 = 1$, $n_0 = 2$, $m = 2$, $v = 2$, $K = 3$ and $n = 6$. The code is a $(2,1,2)$ convolutional code, the code rate being $1/2$.

Convolutional codes are part of a larger family of codes called tree codes, which may be nonlinear and have infinite constraint length. If a tree code has finite constraint length, which means in practice that the encoder has no feedback, then it is a trellis code. A linear trellis code is a convolutional code.

5.5   Encoder state diagram

If an encoder has v shift register stages, then the contents of those shift registers can take 2^v states. The way in which the encoder transits between states will depend on the inputs presented in each frame. The number of possible input permutations to the encoder in a single frame is 2^{k_0}. Hence if $v > k_0$ not all states can be reached in the course of a single frame, with only certain states being connected by allowed transitions. The encoder states can be represented in diagrammatic form with arcs to show allowed transitions and the associated input and output frames, as in Figure 5.2 which shows the transitions for the encoder of Figure 5.1. The label given to each state indicates the contents of the encoder memory, and the bits in the input and output frames are listed in an arbitrary, but consistent, order. Since the input frame is represented in the end state number, it is not always necessary to include input values in the state diagram.

It is also fairly easy to work in reverse order and to derive the encoder

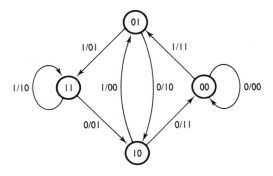

Figure 5.2 Encoder state diagram

circuit or the generator polynomials from the state diagram. The memory constraint length is easily determined from the number of states. The number of branches from each state (and the labels if inputs are shown) allows the size of the input frame to be determined. The shortest path from the zero state (memory clear) to the state where the memory is filled with ones gives the memory order. To find the generator polynomials describing the output contribution of a single bit of the input frame, we start with the encoder clear, inject one frame in which just that input bit is 1, then continue with a number of zero frames until the encoder is again clear. The first output frame will give the unity terms in the generator polynomials, the second output frame gives the X terms of the polynomials and so on.

For our example, the first output frame would be 11, indicating that the unity term is present in both polynomials. The second output frame of 10 indicates that the X term is present in $g^{(1)}(X)$ but not in $g^{(2)}(X)$. The third output frame of 11 indicates that both polynomials contain the X^2 term.

5.6   Distance structure of convolutional codes

As with block codes, there are concepts of distance that determine the error correcting power of the code. Because of linearity, one can assess the distance properties of the code relative to the all-zero path, but since the code sequence may be infinite in length, it is not at all clear how long the sequences to be compared should be. There are $m + 1$ frames involved in any encoding operation, which means that the minimum sensible path length for comparison would be $m + 1$ frames, i.e. a sequence of n bits. On the other hand, we might want to compare infinite sequences. The significance of these two possible approaches can be appreciated by consideration of the encoder state diagram of Figure 5.2.

We want to compare two paths which start from the same point and then diverge. Linearity means that we can use any path as the baseline for our comparison, and as in the block code case the all-zero sequence is convenient. We define a minimum distance as the weight of the minimum weight sequence of length $m + 1$ frames which deviates from the all-zero path. Thus we can see for the code in question that we must consider the possible paths of length 3, and we find that the minimum weight path follows the state sequence 00–01–10–01, giving $d_{min} = 3$.

Now consider what happens if we extend the length of the paths we are comparing. The lowest weight path of length 4 follows the state sequence 00–01–10–01–10 and has weight 4. The lowest weight five-frame path is 00–01–10–01–10–01, again with weight 4. If we now move on to six-frame paths, a new path comes into contention, namely 00–01–10–00–00–00–00 which has weight 5, as does 00–01–10–01–10–01–10. This new path, however, has the property that it can be extended to infinite length without any increase in weight, merely by following the loop from 00 back to 00. Thus for a path of infinite length, the least value of Hamming distance is in this case 5. We call this value the free distance of the code and define it as the weight of the minimum weight sequence which deviates from the all-zero path and returns to it a number of frames later. The symbol used for free distance is either d_{free} or d_∞. The number of frames in the nonzero segment of the path used to calculate free distance is called the free length, n_{free}, of the code. In our example case, the free length is 6.

Of the two distances defined above, the one that is important in determining the error control properties of the code depends on the decoding method used. Some methods look at just one output constraint length at a time, treating the code almost as if it were a block code, and in that case it is d_{min} that is important. True maximum likelihood methods, however, compare complete received sequences with possible code sequences and for such methods d_∞ is the appropriate distance measure. In the example code, a free distance of 5 means that maximum likelihood decoding of any error pattern affecting not more than 2 bits would result in the original code sequence being recovered. Of course errors affecting more than 2 bits may be successfully decoded if the incorrect bits are sufficiently far apart.

It is in this context that the importance of nonsystematic codes arises, because they are needed to obtain values of free distance that are higher than d_{min}. Odenwalder (1970) provides generators for rate 1/2 codes chosen for optimal output bit error rates at high signal-to-noise ratios, which is not necessarily the same as choosing the best value of free distance, although there is obviously a close link. These codes are shown in Table 5.1 with the generators shown as octal characters so that, for example, 15 represents the pattern 1101 or $X^3 + X^2 + 1$.

Table 5.1   Rate 1/2 convolutional codes

v	$g^{(1)}, g^{(2)}$	d_∞
2	7,5	5
3	17,15	6
4	35,23	7
5	75,53	8
6	171,133	10
7	371,247	10
8	753,561	12

5.7   Evaluating distance and weight structure

In the previous section, the method used for finding the minimum weight paths of different lengths relied heavily on inspection and it would have been easy to miss one. If we confine ourselves to paths that start and end at the zero state, then there is a more formal method which finds the number of paths of any weight or length. The method is explained in the context of the previous example, based on the state diagram of Figure 5.2. The start point is to rearrange the state diagram so that the state 00 appears at each end of a network of paths, thus representing both the start and end points of the paths of interest. This is shown in Figure 5.3.

As the encoder moves from state to state, three things of possible interest happen. The length of the code sequence increases and the weights of both the input and output sequences either increase or remain the same. We define operators D, corresponding to an increase of 1 in the output weight: L, corresponding to an increase of one frame in the code sequence length; and N, representing an increase of 1 in the input sequence weight. We can now label each arc of the modified state diagram with the appropriate operators, as has been done on Figure 5.3; let X_i represent the accumulated weights and lengths

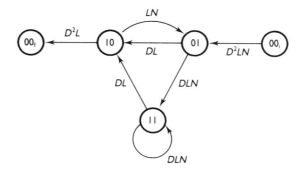

Figure 5.3 Modified encoder state diagram

associated with state i and multiply the initial values by the values against the arcs to represent final state values. Of course each state can be entered from more than one start state, but if we show the sums of the contributions from each of the possible start states, all the possible paths through the encoder will appear as separate terms in the final expression. We can thus set up a number of simultaneous equations representing the different states as follows:

$$X_{01} = D^2LNX_{00_i} + LNX_{10}$$

$$X_{10} = DLX_{01} + DLX_{11}$$

$$X_{11} = DLNX_{01} + DLNX_{11}$$

$$X_{00_f} = D^2LX_{10}$$

We want to know what happens when moving from state 00_i to 00_f (where the subscripts i and f indicate the initial and final states respectively), so we divide X_{00_f} by X_{00_i} to yield the input and output weights and the lengths of all the possible paths. From the above equations we eventually obtain

$$\frac{X_{00_f}}{X_{00_i}} = \frac{D^5L^3N}{1 - DLN(1 + L)}$$

A binomial expansion on this expression gives

$$\frac{X_{00_f}}{X_{00_i}} = D^5L^3N[1 + DLN(1 + L) + D^2L^2N^2(1 + L)^2 + \cdots]$$

$$\frac{X_{00_f}}{X_{00_i}} = D^5L^3N + D^6L^4N^2 + D^6L^5N^2 + D^7L^5N^3 + 2D^7L^6N^3 + D^7L^7N^3 + \cdots$$

This tells us that between states 00_i and 00_f there is one path of length 3, output weight 5 and input weight 1; a path of length 4, output weight 6 and input weight 2; a path of length 5, output weight 6 and input weight 2; a path of length 5, output weight 7 and input weight 3; two paths of length 6, output weight 7 and input weight 3; a path of length 7, output weight 7 and input weight 3, etc.

The expression for X_{00_f}/X_{00_i} is called the *generating function* or the *transfer function* of the encoder. It will be used to find the performance of convolutional codes with maximum likelihood decoding in Section 5.13.

5.8 Catastrophic error propagation

Consideration of encoder state diagrams raises another important possibility in the properties of the code. Suppose that another state, apart from state zero, had a zero-weight loop returning to it. It would now be possible to devise a code sequence that starts from the zero state and ends with a sequence of zeros, but in which the encoder has not returned to the zero state. Moreover, since the encoder state is the result of recent inputs, it cannot be a sequence of input zeros that is maintaining the encoder in that nonzero state. Thus comparing this sequence with the all-zero sequence, we could have two information sequences which differ in an infinite number of places, but which when encoded differ in a finite number of places. This has serious implications for the decoding process, because it means that a finite number of channel errors could be translated into an infinite number of decoding errors. This phenomenon is called catastrophic error propagation. Fortunately it is possible to spot catastrophic properties of codes from the existence of common factors in the generator polynomials for the code or in the inability to solve for the code-generating function. A computer program to find good convolutional codes can therefore easily avoid catastrophic codes.

Example

A convolutional code has generator polynomials

$$g^{(1)}(X) = X + 1$$
$$g^{(2)}(X) = X^2 + 1$$

which have a common factor $X + 1$. An input sequence 1111 . . . results in an output sequence 11 01 00 00 . . ., from which we can see that a simple error sequence of finite length could cause reception of 00 00 00 00 which results in an infinite number of decoding errors, i.e. there is catastrophic error propagation.

5.9   Maximum likelihood decoding

In principle the best way of decoding against random errors is to compare the received sequence with every possible code sequence. This process is best envisaged using a code trellis which contains the information of the state diagram, but also uses time as a horizontal axis to show the possible paths through the states. Code trellises get very complex for large constraint lengths and so we shall take just one example, shown in Figure 5.4, for the encoder of Figure 5.1.

The apparent problem with maximum likelihood decoding is that over L code frames there are 2^{Lk_0} paths through the trellis, and comparing what is received with every possible path seems unmanageable. Fortunately, Viterbi realized that not all of these paths need be considered, and that at any stage only 2^v paths need to be retained, provided the errors show no correlation between frames (memoryless channel). He devised a technique that simplifies the problem of decoding without sacrificing any of the code's properties.

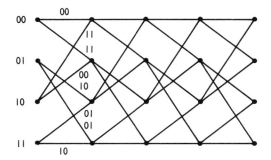

Figure 5.4 Code trellis

5.10   The Viterbi algorithm

If we look at all the paths going through a single node in the trellis, and consider only the part from the start of transmission up to the selected node, we can compute the distance between the received sequence and each of these trellis paths. When we look at these distance metrics we will probably find that one of the paths is better than all the others. Viterbi realized that if the channel errors are random, then the paths that are nonoptimal at this stage can never become optimal in the future; in other words, we need keep only one path for each node. The Viterbi method therefore keeps only 2^v paths through the trellis and at each frame it decides which paths to keep and which to discard. The procedure at each received frame is as follows:

1. For each of the 2^v stored paths, compute the distance between the received frame and the 2^{k_0} branches.

2. For each of the 2^v nodes which represent the end states of the frame, construct the 2^{k_0} paths which terminate at that node and select and store the best.

The decoding procedure can be regarded as updating a table after each frame containing the following parameters:

end states (2^v values)
start states (2^{k_0} values for each end state)
output frame associated with each transition
branch metric (distance between output frame and corresponding received frame)
initial path metric (the accumulated distance to the start state)
final path metric (sum of previous two quantities)
whether the path is to be retained

The first three columns will be the same for every frame as they represent properties of the code. There is no need to record the inputs associated with each transition as these are in effect stored as part of the final state. All start states except zero are given initial path metrics of infinity to represent the fact that the encoder starts in the clear state. There is also a need to provide storage for all the paths that are being retained. If ever there is a tie as to which path should be kept, the choice is made arbitrarily.

5.11   Example of Viterbi decoding

Consider an example based on Figure 5.4. Let the information be 1011001, for which the code sequence can be seen from Figure 5.1, or from the generator polynomials, to be 11 10 00 01 01 11 11 10 11. This includes two extra zero input frames to clear out the decoder. Introduce two errors to give a received sequence 11 11 00 01 00 11 11 10 11. For our example, the table held after the first frame will be as shown in Table 5.2. The final path metric (f path in the table) corresponding to a particular end state is now copied to the initial path metric (i path in the table) of the states with the corresponding start state. For example, the lowest final path metric for end state 00 is 2. This becomes the initial path metric for start state 00 in the next frame, as shown in Table 5.3.

Table 5.2   First frame − 11 received

End state	Start state	o/p	Branch	i path	f path	Keep
00	00	00	2	0	2	Y
00	10	11	0	∞	∞	N
01	00	11	0	0	0	Y
01	10	00	2	∞	∞	N
10	01	10	1	∞	∞	Y
10	11	01	1	∞	∞	N
11	01	01	1	∞	∞	Y
11	11	10	1	∞	∞	N

Table 5.3   Second frame − 11 received

End state	Start state	o/p	Branch	i path	f path	Keep
00	00	00	2	2	4	Y
00	10	11	0	∞	∞	N
01	00	11	0	2	2	Y
01	10	00	2	∞	∞	N
10	01	10	1	0	1	Y
10	11	01	1	∞	∞	N
11	01	01	1	0	1	Y
11	11	10	1	∞	∞	N

The tables held for the subsequent frames are shown in Tables 5.4–5.10.

Table 5.4   Third frame – 00 received

End state	Start state	o/p	Branch	i path	f path	Keep
00	00	00	0	4	4	N
00	10	11	2	1	3	Y
01	00	11	2	4	6	N
01	10	00	0	1	1	Y
10	01	10	1	2	3	N
10	11	01	1	1	2	Y
11	01	01	1	2	3	N
11	11	10	1	1	2	Y

Table 5.5   Fourth frame – 01 received

End state	Start state	o/p	Branch	i path	f path	Keep
00	00	00	1	3	4	N
00	10	11	1	2	3	Y
01	00	11	1	3	4	N
01	10	00	1	2	3	Y
10	01	10	2	1	3	N
10	11	01	0	2	2	Y
11	01	01	0	1	1	Y
11	11	10	2	2	4	N

Table 5.6   Fifth frame – 00 received

End state	Start state	o/p	Branch	i path	f path	Keep
00	00	00	0	3	3	Y
00	10	11	2	2	4	N
01	00	11	2	3	5	N
01	10	00	0	2	2	Y
10	01	10	1	3	4	N
10	11	01	1	1	2	Y
11	01	01	1	3	4	N
11	11	10	1	1	2	Y

Table 5.7   Sixth frame – 11 received

End state	Start state	o/p	Branch	i path	f path	Keep
00	00	00	2	3	5	N
00	10	11	0	2	2	Y
01	00	11	0	3	3	Y
01	10	00	2	2	4	N
10	01	10	1	2	3	Y
10	11	01	1	2	3	N
11	01	01	1	2	3	Y
11	11	10	1	2	3	N

Table 5.8   Seventh frame – 11 received

End state	Start state	o/p	Branch	i path	f path	Keep
00	00	00	2	2	4	N
00	10	11	0	3	3	Y
01	00	11	0	2	2	Y
01	10	00	2	3	5	N
10	01	10	1	3	4	Y
10	11	01	1	3	4	N
11	01	01	1	3	4	Y
11	11	10	1	3	4	N

Table 5.9   Eighth frame – 10 received

End state	Start state	o/p	Branch	i path	f path	Keep
00	00	00	1	3	4	Y
00	10	11	1	4	5	N
01	00	11	1	3	4	Y
01	10	00	1	4	5	N
10	01	10	0	2	2	Y
10	11	01	2	4	6	N
11	01	01	2	2	4	Y
11	11	10	0	4	4	N

Table 5.10   Ninth frame – 11 received

End state	Start state	o/p	Branch	i path	f path	Keep
00	00	00	2	4	6	N
00	10	11	0	2	2	Y
01	00	11	0	4	4	Y
01	10	00	2	2	4	N
10	01	10	1	4	5	Y
10	11	01	1	4	5	N
11	01	01	1	4	5	Y
11	11	10	1	4	5	N

At this stage we have come to the end of the received sequence, and we have one path that is clearly better than the others. Indeed if there had been any doubt at this stage, we could have selected the path that ended at the state zero because we know that the encoder is cleared out at the end.

Following the selected path backwards shows that the code sequence is 11 10 00 01 01 11 11 10 11, which corresponds to what was transmitted. The actual implementation of the decoder might not be concerned with the transmitted sequence, but could just keep a record of the encoder states; the inputs associated with each transition can be inferred from the least-significant bit of the end state and enables us to reconstruct the information sequence as 1011001 plus the final two zeros used to clear the encoder.

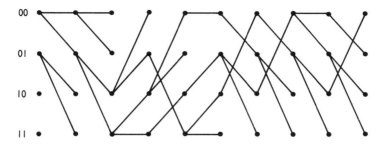

Figure 5.5 Survivor paths in Viterbi decoding

A number of points arise from this example. Firstly, although the correct code sequence was showing the best metric after seven frames, the final two frames in which the encoder was cleared did clarify the position and improve the discrimination between paths. Secondly, at some stages we had to make arbitrary decisions as to which path should be retained, but none of the doubtful decisions featured in the final solution. Thirdly, if we plot out the surviving paths through the trellis at each stage, as in Figure 5.5, we see that after three frames all the survivors correspond in the first frame. At this stage, therefore, we could have decoded the first frame. On the other hand, the second frame is not resolved until the final path selection at the end. In general it is found that we do not have to wait until the end of a message before any decoding can start, although the number of frames that we have to wait is variable and depends on the errors. If we set a maximum to the number of frames to be held as a path history, experience shows that we will have few problems provided this decoding window is at least four times the memory order.

5.12   Applicability of convolutional codes

Many of the features of the above example affect the suitability of convolutional codes for certain applications, at least in conjunction with Viterbi decoding. These factors are the need to treat the information as a continuous stream, computational limitations on the power of the codes used and the nature of the decoding error events. These are perhaps, although not necessarily, negative factors against which must be weighed the ease with which soft decisions can be incorporated into algorithm.

If we feed information into a convolutional encoder, at the end of the information stream the encoder's memory will not be clear, as it will still contain information about the final frames of the information. A total of m frames of extra zeros must therefore be added to the information sequence to clear out the encoder and round off the code sequence. Thus there will be a tail of mn_0 bits on the code [although with a systematic code one need not transmit the mk_0 zeros, only the $m(n_0 - k_0)$ parity bits]. This tail can represent a significant overhead on short transmissions using encoders with a high memory order. Since higher memory order means more powerful codes, convolutional codes are most suitable when the information can be regarded as a long continuous flow. This is not necessarily as restrictive as it might seem, however. Time division systems with each transmitter's information being placed in widely separated slots might be thought to necessitate a clearing of the encoder at the end of each slot. If, however, each slot can be viewed as a compressed section of a continuous data flow, then the code sequence can be regarded as continuous from the end of one slot to the beginning of the next one assigned to the same source.

At every frame received, the decoder has to update 2^v states and for each of these states there are 2^{k_0} paths to be evaluated. Thus the amount of computation in the decoder is roughly proportional to $2^{v+k_0} = 2^K$. This sets an upper limit to constraint lengths of the codes which can be decoded in this way. The limit depends on technology and required bit rate, but figures of $K = 8$–10 are commonly quoted as typical present-day maxima. Larger constraint lengths, which mean more powerful codes, can only be decoded at reasonable rates by other techniques such as sequential decoding to be described in Section 5.15.

If the decoder makes a mistake it will output a long stream of errors. The length of this error burst will depend on the precise error pattern and the path and weight distributions of the code, and for this reason simulation is often required to evaluate the performance of convolutional codes. Typically, however, the number of frames spanned by the error pattern may be around four times the memory order of the encoder. Fortunately, the codes do eventually resynchronize to the correct sequence, provided the code does not exhibit catastrophic error propagation. It should not be thought, however, that this long error burst is necessarily a disadvantage. In some applications the worse the error, the easier it is to detect. As always, the implications must be considered in the context of the nature of the data and the extent to which decoding errors can be tolerated.

One of the attractions of convolutional codes in conjunction with Viterbi decoding is that this coding can easily accept soft decisions. There is no reason why the distance computations should not use a soft-decision metric, although the amount of computation is increased because we need more than 1 bit to represent the metrics. It is found, however, that 3-bit (eight level) quantization of the channel is sufficient to provide the benefits of soft-decision decoding. For the small increase in decoder complexity, plus of course the possibly large increase in demodulator complexity, a further 2 dB or so of coding gain can be provided on a Gaussian channel, providing in many cases significantly more gain than can easily be achieved by other means.

5.13 Performance of convolutional codes

In Section 5.7 we saw how to obtain the weight distribution of a convolutional code. The performance of a convolutional code with maximum likelihood decoding can be obtained straightforwardly from the transfer function $T(D,N)$, which is equivalent to X_{00_f}/X_{00_i} with the parameter L eliminated. The output bit error rate can be shown to be upper bounded by

$$BER \leq \frac{1}{k_0} \frac{\partial T(D,N)}{\partial N}\bigg|_{N=1,\ D=Z} \tag{5.1}$$

where Z is a function of channel transition probabilities.

If $T_{d,n}$ is the coefficient of $D^d N^n$ in $T(D,N)$, equation (5.1) is equivalent to

$$BER \leq \frac{1}{k_0} \sum_{d=d_\infty}^{\infty} A_d Z^d \tag{5.2}$$

where

$$A_d = \sum_{n=1}^{\infty} n T_{d,n} \tag{5.3}$$

On a binary input Q-ary discrete memoryless channel, i.e. a random error channel with binary transmissions and Q levels of detection, the parameter Z is defined as

$$Z = \sum_{j=0}^{Q-1} \sqrt{p(j|0)p(j|1)} \tag{5.4}$$

where $p(j|0)$ and $p(j|1)$ represent the probabilities that level j will be received when the transmitted symbol has values 0 and 1 respectively. For a binary symmetric channel, i.e. hard decision, the expression for Z becomes

$$Z = 2\sqrt{p(1-p)} \tag{5.5}$$

where p is the channel bit error rate.

For a binary input AWGN channel, i.e. unquantized soft decision, the parameter Z is given by

$$Z = e^{-RE_b/N_0} \tag{5.6}$$

where R is the code rate.

The rate 1/2 code whose transfer function was found in Section 5.7 has

$$T(D,N) = D^5 N + 2D^6 N^2 + 4D^7 N^3 + \cdots$$

We therefore see that $A_5 = 1$, $A_6 = 4$, $A_7 = 12$. The output bit error rate is therefore

$$BER \leqslant Z^5 + 4Z^6 + 12Z^7 + \cdots$$

As Z is usually small, the expression for bit error rate is normally dominated by the first few terms, despite the fact that the coefficients are increasing.

The most commonly encountered convolutional code is rate 1/2 and has input constraint length $K = 7$ and generators

$$g^{(1)}(X) = X^6 + X^5 + X^4 + X^3 + 1$$

$$g^{(2)}(X) = X^6 + X^4 + X^3 + X + 1$$

The upper bound on output bit error rate for this code is

$$BER \leqslant 36Z^{10} + 211Z^{12} + 1404Z^{14} + 11633Z^{16} + \cdots$$

Generators and error rates for other good convolutional codes can be obtained from Michelson and Levesque (1985).

5.14   Punctured convolutional codes

Although it is possible to define good generator sets for convolutional codes of any rate and to use Viterbi decoding, the computation may become rather complex at high rates. Take, for example a rate 3/4 code for which $v = 3$ and $K = 6$. There are 64 path computations in the decoding of every 4-bit output frame, each involving a 4-bit comparison. Now suppose instead we use a rate 1/2 code and delete two output bits every three frames. For this code, we keep $v = 3$ for comparability, but $K = 4$ giving 16 path computations per frame with three frames required to give the equivalent of the 4-bit output frame of the original. Thus we have 48 comparisons, each of only 1 or 2 bits. Similar considerations show that the computational gains are even greater at higher rates, and are even worthwhile for rate 2/3.

Of course, computational considerations would be worthless if the codes produced by the above process, known as puncturing, did not produce codes of comparable performance. Fortunately, however, there are many punctured codes with a performance which, in terms of coding gain, comes within 0.1 or 0.2 dB of the optimum code. There is therefore little point in using codes other than punctured codes for higher rates. Table 5.11, based on data from Cain et al. (1979), shows rate 1/2 codes that can be punctured to produce good rate 2/3 or 3/4 codes. For the rate 2/3 codes, the first two generators (octal) are used to produce the first 2-bit output frame and in the next frame only the third generator (which

Table 5.11   Rate 1/2 codes punctured to rates 2/3 and 3/4

ν	Generators $R = 1/2$	d_∞	Generators $R = 2/3$	d_∞	Generators $R = 3/4$	d_∞
2	7, 5	5	7, 5, 7	3	7, 5, 5, 7	3
3	15, 17	6	15, 17, 15	4	15, 17, 15, 17	4
4	31, 33	7	31, 33, 31	5	31, 33, 31, 31	3
4	37, 25	6	37, 25, 37	4	37, 25, 37, 37	4
5	57, 65	8	57, 65, 57	6	65, 57, 57, 65	4
6	133, 171	10	133, 171, 133	6	133, 171, 133, 171	5
6	135, 147	10	135, 147, 147	6	135, 147, 147, 147	6
7	237, 345	10	237, 345, 237	7	237, 345, 237, 345	6

is the same as one of the other two) is used. For rate 3/4 codes there is then a third frame in which the fourth generator is used.

Apart from the computational consideration, punctured convolutional codes are important because of the possibility of providing several codes of different rates with only one decoder. It would be possible, for example, to operate with a rate 3/4 code in reasonably good reception conditions but allow the transmitter and receiver to agree criteria for a switch to rate 2/3 or 1/2 if noise levels increased and higher values of d_∞ are required. Such a scheme is known as *adaptive coding*.

5.15   **Sequential decoding**

The Viterbi algorithm is satisfactory only for codes of relatively short constraint lengths because of the number of paths that must be updated and stored. If we examined the actions of a Viterbi decoder we usually find that a small number of paths are established as being the most likely with the other stored paths being much less likely. Sequential decoding aims to simplify the decoding task by concentrating the search on the most likely paths. In this way it can use codes with much longer constraint lengths. There are several slightly different implementations of sequential decoding but two of them – the Fano algorithm and the stack algorithm – are illustrative of the basic approaches that are possible.

The Fano algorithm works frame by frame, examining the received sequence, deciding the most likely code frame and advancing to the appropriate point in the trellis. The path metric to be minimized over l frames is

$$- \sum_{j=1}^{l} \sum_{i=1}^{n_0} \left[\log_2 \left(\frac{p(v_{ij}|u_{ij})}{p(v_{ij})} \right) - R \right]$$

where j represents the frame number, i the bit within the frame, v_{ij} the received bit, u_{ij} the appropriate bit of the code path being followed and R the code rate. This quantity is called the *Fano metric*.

At each stage in decoding, the path metric is compared with a running threshold to decide whether the decoder should move forwards or backwards. On the first visit to any node in the trellis, the threshold is set as tightly as possible. Generally the metric should be no greater than the threshold and if the threshold is exceeded, the decoder has to decide whether to backtrack or to loosen the threshold. The latter action is taken when backtracking does not bring the metric down below the current threshold. Changes to the threshold are made in multiples of some fixed value Δ which is a design parameter. Too small a value of Δ will increase the amount of backtracking, too large and the decoder will follow incorrect paths for a considerable distance before backtracking begins.

The stack algorithm eliminates the tendency of the Fano algorithm to visit certain nodes several times, thus reducing computation but at the expense of increased storage. A number of previously examined paths and their accumulated metrics are held on a stack, the path with the lowest metric at the top. The decoder takes the path at the top, creates 2^{k_0} successor paths, computes their metrics and places them in the appropriate positions on the stacks. The stack may overflow, but the paths lost will have high metrics and are unlikely to figure in the maximum likelihood solution. The reordering of paths is also a problem, but Jelinek (1969) proposed an approach that has been widely adopted.

Both the Fano and the stack methods operate within a fixed decoding window, as do Viterbi decoders, and output the first frame from a full decoding window. There are other distinct characteristics of sequential decoding which may affect its suitability for particular applications. The speed of the decoding will depend on the method used, but there is also variability in decoding speed, which can cause problems for real-time operation. This variability may be smoothed out by provision of a buffer for the incoming frames, but in certain circumstances it may be necessary to force the decoder along a particular path or to abandon the decoding of a section of the code. This is not necessarily a bad thing; correct design can ensure that problems of this type occur mainly when the error rates are so high that decoding errors are in any case highly likely, and at least it is known that a decoding problem has occurred. Nevertheless, sequential decoding is more at home with non-real-time and off-line applications.

The principal advantage of sequential decoding is that the reduced computation allows for the use of greater constraint lengths, values around 40 being commonly quoted. This means that more powerful codes with higher values of free distance and higher coding gains can be employed. On the other hand, soft-decision decoding, although simple to incorporate in principle, does greatly slow down the decoder in its progress through the trellis. As a result it is less common to find soft decision with sequential decoding than is the case with Viterbi decoding, and the greater constraint length may do little more than compensate for the loss of soft decision.

5.16   Syndrome decoding

There are several decoding methods for convolutional codes in which the decoding window consists of $m + 1$ frames, the code is systematic and error correction is up to a maximum of $(d_{min} - 1)/2$ bits in any run of $m + 1$ frames. These methods all treat the code rather like a block code, calculating a syndrome to identify the error. They all sacrifice some of the power of convolutional codes, including soft-decision decoding, in the interests of speed and simplicity. The names given to these methods include syndrome decoding, table look-up decoding, feedback decoding, majority logic decoding and threshold decoding, some of which may be synonymous.

The syndrome of a systematic convolutional code can be defined in a way that is exactly equivalent to the definition for a block code. The received information bits are encoded and the recalculated parity bits compared (modulo 2 added) with the received parity bits.

Consider, for example, a (4,3,2) systematic code, with the following generators:

$$g_1^{(1)}(X) = 1 \quad g_2^{(1)}(X) = 0 \quad g_3^{(1)}(X) = 0$$
$$g_1^{(2)}(X) = 0 \quad g_2^{(2)}(X) = 1 \quad g_3^{(2)}(X) = 0$$
$$g_1^{(3)}(X) = 0 \quad g_2^{(3)}(X) = 0 \quad g_3^{(3)}(X) = 1$$
$$g_1^{(4)}(X) = X^2 + X + 1 \quad g_2^{(4)}(X) = X + 1 \quad g_3^{(4)}(X) = X^2 + 1$$

This code has a minimum distance of 3, which means that it can correct one bit error every $m + 1$ (3) frames. If we consider a sequence that is all-zero except for a single 1, the recalculated parity bit plus the received parity bit will be nonzero for up to three frames as the error passes through the decoder. Thus, writing bit 1 of the frame and the oldest syndrome bit on the left of the sequence, the results will depend on the position of the error as shown in Table 5.12. Thus if the error is in bit 2, the syndrome will be zero as the error enters the decoder and one for the next two frames. The presence of an error in the oldest frame is easily detected by the fact that the oldest bit of the syndrome is one and the other two bits determine the position. Suppose the sequence entering the decoder is 1100 0100 1010 0011, then the syndrome sequence is 0101. There was therefore an error entering the decoder on the second frame, and the subsequent syndrome bits can be looked up in the table to identify the error as being bit 3 of that frame. The correct code sequence was therefore 1100 0110 1010 0011 and the information sequence 110 011 101 001.

Table 5.12

Error pattern	Syndrome
1 0 0 0	1 1 1
0 1 0 0	1 1 0
0 0 1 0	1 0 1
0 0 0 1	1 0 0

If the above code had been multiple-error correcting, then it is possible to find and correct errors in the oldest frame and still leave correctable errors in the later frames. If, after correcting the errors in the oldest frame, the syndrome is modified to take account of the correction, then the decoder is said to employ feedback. The principle is the same as that which may be found in a multiple-error correcting Meggit decoder (Sections 3.14 and 3.15) for cyclic block codes. Feedback can be a dangerous thing because a decoding error may propagate throughout the subsequent decoding. If this is purely a result of the decoding algorithm then it is called *ordinary error propagation*, as opposed to catastrophic error propagation which results from the properties of the code itself.

One form of particular interest is when the syndrome bits can be split into sets with each of the sets consisting of a number of votes as to whether a particular received bit is correct. If the number of votes against (i.e. nonzero syndrome bits) exceeds some threshold then the bit is altered. This is called threshold decoding, or majority logic decoding if the threshold is 50 percent of the votes.

The advantage of syndrome decoding is speed and the fact that the decoder complexity grows only linearly with constraint length, so that larger constraint lengths can be used than for other methods. The disadvantage is that the codes are not very powerful compared with equivalent nonsystematic codes used to full advantage, and soft-decision decoding is not generally applicable. Threshold decodable codes in particular are rarely very powerful, but could be the only choice at extremely high bit rates.

5.17   Further reading

Virtually all books on coding will have some treatment of convolutional codes, but that of Lin and Costello (1983) seems to me to be the most comprehensible and comprehensive. It deals with other methods of representing the action of a convolutional encoder and quotes an inspection rule, taken from Mason and Zimmerman (1960), to write down the generating function from the modified state diagram. It has separate chapters on maximum likelihood decoding, sequential decoding and majority logic decoding. Lin and Costello do not, however, deal very well with the derivation and meaning of the generating function. For this, Michelson and Levesque (1985) are to be recommended, particularly in bringing out the analogy with the *z*-transform.

Every designer of a Viterbi decoder has to go through the process of making complex decisions on the implementation of the algorithm and how best to keep track of all the things that the decoder must remember. Clark and Cain (1981), as always, treat such practical aspects well, as do Michelson and Levesque (1985), although there is still scope for more extensive treatment in some, as yet unwritten, book. Clark and Cain are at the forefront of code puncturing techniques and should be consulted on this topic also.

5.18   Exercises

1   An encoder has the following generator polynomials:

$$g_1^{(1)}(X) = X + 1$$
$$g_1^{(2)}(X) = X$$
$$g_1^{(3)}(X) = X$$
$$g_1^{(4)}(X) = X + 1$$
$$g_2^{(1)}(X) = X^2$$
$$g_2^{(2)}(X) = X + 1$$
$$g_2^{(3)}(X) = 0$$
$$g_2^{(4)}(X) = X^2 + X + 1$$
$$g_3^{(1)}(X) = 0$$
$$g_3^{(2)}(X) = X$$
$$g_3^{(3)}(X) = X^2 + 1$$
$$g_3^{(4)}(X) = X^2 + 1$$

Draw the encoder schematic diagram. Encode the information sequence 101 011 100 010. Quantify the following terms:

(a) input frame;
(b) output frame;
(c) input constraint length;
(d) output constraint length;
(e) memory order;
(f) memory constraint length.

2   An encoder has generator polynomials

$$g^{(1)}(X) = X^3 + X^2 + 1$$
$$g^{(2)}(X) = X^3 + X^2 + X + 1$$

Draw the state transition diagram. Find the values of d_{min} and d_∞.

3   Find the generating function for the code of Exercise 2. Hence check your value of d_∞. What are the lengths and input weights of all paths with the three lowest values of output weight?

4   A code has generators

$$g^{(1)}(X) = X^2 + 1$$
$$g^{(2)}(X) = X^2 + X$$

From the state diagram, or by considering the encoding of the sequence 1111 . . ., deduce that the code exhibits catastrophic error propagation.

5   From the encoder state diagram below, find the generator polynomials of the code.

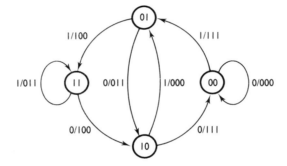

6   For the convolutional encoder of Figure 5.1, decode the sequence 11 01 11 00 10 00 01 11 11.

7   Find the hard-decision coding gains at a bit error rate of 10^{-5} for the rate $1/2\ K = 3$ code whose weight structure is analysed in Section 5.7, assuming binary PSK modulation. How much does the gain change if unquantized soft decision is used?

8   Repeat Exercise 7 for the rate $1/2\ K = 7$ code whose bit error rate is given in Section 5.13, but assuming that the soft-decisions have 8-level quantisization.

9∗   Prove that for a rate R convolutional code operating on a binary PSK channel (bit error rate given in equation 1.15), the coding gain at low bit error rates is of the order of $Rd_\infty/2$ for hard-decision decoding and Rd_∞ for soft-decision decoding.

10   A decoder for the systematic code of Section 5.16 receives a sequence 0111 0001 1000 0100 1101 1111 0011. Find the decoder output.

6
Coding for bursty channels

6.1   Introduction

Although the first five chapters have discussed a wide range of coding techniques, they have all had one thing in common, namely that they were aimed towards errors that show no correlation from one symbol to another. As a result, the decoding techniques aim to minimize a symbol-by-symbol measure of discrepancies between received and code sequences. If, on the other hand, errors tend to occur in bursts, then different decoding metrics will be appropriate and thus different codes may be required to optimize performance with respect to those metrics. This chapter addresses the question of what techniques are available and appropriate for bursty channels.

Although random error mechanisms exist on most channels, few can be said to behave purely as AWGN channels. The deep space channel is perhaps the closest to the AWGN model, but once any terrestrial lines, radio or satellite links are included in the system, other mechanisms ensure that to a greater or lesser extent the error control problems faced will differ in some respects from the AWGN case. These mechanisms include various types of interference, multipath, shadowing and variable attenuation caused by precipitation. It is not the intention here to discuss the causes and characteristics of these factors, but in general they may have significant impact both on code design and on the benefits that can be achieved by coding.

In principle, bursty errors should be easier to combat than random errors for a given symbol error rate, because the location of a single random error gives no information as to the likely location of other errors, whereas in a bursty channel one knows that there will be several adjacent symbols which have a relatively high error probability. In theory the best way to combat bursty errors is therefore to use the particular characteristics of the channel to identify the most likely error patterns. In practice, however, the channel characteristics may not be sufficiently well known and the error control scheme may need to be designed to be robust against a range of possibilities rather than optimized for actual channel conditions. In particular, some sort of mix of bursts and random errors is often encountered, in which case the channel is said to be *compound* or *diffuse*.

The considerations affecting the choice of error control method on a bursty channel also show in the assessment of the benefits of coding. If the channel conditions are not well known, it is difficult to obtain an assessment of coding gain. On the other hand, where an assessment is possible, either by theoretical analysis or by measurement, then the coding gains obtained are commonly much better than is possible than on AWGN channels, being measured perhaps in tens of decibels rather than 3 or 4 dB. Indeed some uncoded channels may exhibit a minimum bit error rate that cannot be improved upon regardless of signal strength. If coding can get down below that level, the coding gain is in theory infinite! On the other hand, some cautious scepticism is a good idea when interpreting theoretical coding gains. In particular it is wise to check whether the assumed channel conditions and E_b/N_0 would allow a real demodulator to operate close to the theoretical error rates.

An understanding of Chapters 1–3 and 5 will be necessary for a full appreciation of this chapter, although the reader interested only in block codes could omit Chapter 5 and those concerned mainly with convolutional codes could skip some of Chapter 2 and all of Chapter 3. The proper control of errors on real channels is, however, such a difficult and important problem that it seems unwise to overlook any of the methods available.

6.2   Description of bursty errors

The conventional way of describing an error burst is by burst length, which is the number of bits spanned by the burst, i.e. the length from the first to the last bit of the burst including both end bits. Defined in this way, a burst of length 10 is illustrated in Figure 6.1. Note that not all bits within a burst are necessarily corrupt, and that therefore this way of defining burst length allows several ways of expressing any particular error pattern. For example, the error pattern of Figure 6.1 could be considered to be a burst of length 2 and one of length 7, or one of length 2 one of length 3 and one of length 1, or even 6 bursts of length 1.

The error control schemes for bursty channels are generally categorized in terms of the number and length of the bursts they can correct within a given span on the channel, or whether they can cope with mixtures of bursts and random errors. As we have seen, there may be several ways of describing a burst error pattern, but if we think in terms of the capabilities of the code we can then decide whether any particular error pattern falls within those that are correctable.

Figure 6.1 Error burst of length 10

6.3   Block codes for single-burst error correction

There are a number of block codes that will correct single bursts within a block. Cyclic codes are generally used because of the particular properties of burst error detection that they all possess. This does not, however, mean that all cyclic codes are good for burst error correction, and for this they must be specially chosen.

As we saw in Chapter 3, a (n,k) cyclic code can be formulated in a systematic way with the $n - k$ parity check symbols in the low-order position. The cyclic property means, however, that any consecutive $n - k$ symbols can be shifted into the parity positions and we will still have a codeword. Any error that affects only the parity symbols cannot produce a codeword result because the parity symbols are firmly fixed by the information. It therefore follows that any error that spans $n - k$ symbols or less of a cyclic codeword cannot produce a codeword result, and is therefore detectable. The cyclic nature of the code means that errors affecting the first few and last few symbols can be considered as a single 'end-around' burst. Figure 6.2 shows an error pattern that by normal considerations would be a burst of length 14, but viewed as an end-around burst its length is only 6.

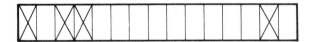

Figure 6.2 End-around burst of length 6

If the code is suitable for burst correction, then the maximum length of a correctable single burst within one codeword is $(n - k)/2$. This result, known as the *Reiger bound*, may be seen by analogy with the random error case in which the error correction capability is half that of error detection, or by considering the principle of decoding when the maximum likelihood error pattern is considered to be the shortest possible burst.

The usual decoding method is called error trapping, and is very similar to Meggit decoding. Remembering that the syndrome of an error in the parity symbols is equal to the error pattern itself, we see that if the syndrome is shifted around a Meggit decoder we will eventually reach a point where it shows directly in the syndrome. If the error pattern occupies at most $(n - k)/2$ consecutive symbols, then we can detect this condition by the existence of $(n - k)/2$ consecutive zeros in the syndrome. The number of shifts to achieve this condition will show where the burst is located.

Example

A (15,9) cyclic code generated by

$$g(X) = X^6 + X^5 + X^4 + X^3 + 1$$

can correct bursts of length up to 3. An error pattern

$$e(X) = X^9 + X^8 + X^7$$

has the syndrome as formed by a circuit as in Figure 3.3

$$s^{(6)}(X) = X^5 + X + 1$$

This pattern of 100011 when shifted gives 111111, 000111, 001110, 011100 and 111000. We now have three zeros in the low-order bits of the syndrome and the error pattern trapped in the high-order bits. The fact that it took five extra shifts to achieve this shows that the error pattern starts from bit 9, i.e. it affects bits 9, 8 and 7. We have thus correctly identified the pattern and location of the error.

6.4   Fire codes

Fire codes are single-burst error correcting cyclic codes with a syndrome that can be split into two components for faster decoding. The form of the generator polynomial for a Fire code correcting single bursts of length up to l is

$$g(X) = (X^{2l-1} + 1)h(X)$$

where $h(X)$ is an irreducible binary polynomial of degree $m \geq l$ which is not a factor of $X^{2l-1} + 1$, i.e. the period p of $h(X)$ is not a factor of $2l - 1$. The length of the code is the lowest common multiple of p and $2l - 1$.

As an example, let $h(X) = X^4 + X + 1$. This is a primitive polynomial of degree 4 which is therefore not a factor of $X^7 + 1$. The polynomial

$$g(X) = (X^7 + 1)(X^4 + X + 1)$$

therefore generates a (105,94) Fire code which can correct single bursts of length 4.

We could construct a decoder in which the received sequence passes through the shift registers before feedback is applied, i.e. of the type shown in Figure 3.1 but based on $g(X)$ for the Fire code. In that case if a burst error occurred which affected bits $n + l - i - 1$ to $n - i$ (both values taken modulo n), then after a further i shifts in the registers the errors would appear in bits $l - 1$ to 0 of the syndrome. At most $n - 1$ shifts would be required to achieve this condition in which the error would be trapped and could be located.

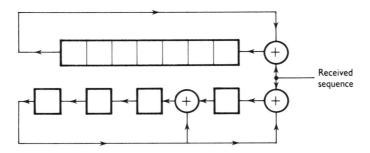

Figure 6.3 Split syndrome formation for (105,94) Fire code

There is an alternative, faster decoder structure in which the generator polynomial is broken down into its factors $X^{2l-1} + 1$ and $h(X)$. Such an arrangement is shown for our example code in Figure 6.3. Any error pattern that is not a codeword will leave a nonzero remainder in one or both of the syndrome registers. Clearly any error pattern of length $2l - 1$ or less cannot leave a zero remainder when divided by $X^{2l-1} + 1$ and no error pattern of length 4 or less could leave a zero remainder when divided by $h(X)$. Thus the correctable error patterns will leave a nonzero remainder in both registers.

If, with a correctable error pattern, we cycle the registers which divide by $X^{2l-1} + 1$, after λ_1 shifts the error pattern will appear in the l low-order bits of the register leaving the $l - 1$ high-order bits zero. Because the period of these registers is $2l - 1$, the same pattern would reappear every $2l - 1$ further shifts and one of these occasions would correspond with the number of shifts (i) required to trap the error in a standard error-trapping decoder as discussed above. Hence

$$i = A_1(2l - 1) + \lambda_1 \tag{6.1}$$

where A_l is an unknown integer.

The next stage is to cycle the registers which divide by $h(X)$. After λ_2 shifts the error pattern appears in the registers and can be recognized because it is the same as that in the other registers. The period of $h(X)$ is p and by the same logic as before

$$i = A_2p + \lambda_2 \tag{6.2}$$

where A_2 is an unknown integer.

Eliminating i from equations (6.1) and (6.2) gives

$$A_1(2l - 1) - A_2p = \lambda_2 - \lambda_1 \tag{6.3}$$

and they can also be combined to give

$$i(\lambda_2 - \lambda_1) = A_1(2l - 1)\lambda_2 - A_2 p \lambda_1 \qquad (6.4)$$

We can certainly find a pair of integers A_1 and A_2 which satisfy equation (6.3) and then substitute into (6.4). A better way, however, is to find the pair of integers I_1 and I_2 which satisfy

$$I_1(2l - 1) - I_2 p = 1 \qquad (6.5)$$

and then take $(\lambda_2 - \lambda_1)I_1$ and $(\lambda_2 - \lambda_1)I_2$ as the solutions of equation (6.3) to give the following expression for equation (6.4):

$$i = I_1(2l - 1)\lambda_2 - I_2 p \lambda_1 \qquad (6.6)$$

The value for i is taken modulo n. The advantage of this approach is that I_1 and I_2 can be calculated in advance and their values stored to use in equation (6.6) once λ_1 and λ_2 are known. For example, in our case where $2l - 1$ is 7 and p is 15, the values of I_1 and I_2 are 13 and 6 respectively.

If we wish to be able to correct bursts up to length l and simultaneously to detect bursts up to length $d(d > l)$, we can construct a Fire code generator

$$g(X) = (X^c + 1)h(X)$$

where $c = l + d - 1$ and $h(X)$ is not a factor of $X^c + 1$.

6.5 Convolutional codes for burst error correction

If convolutional codes are used to correct burst errors, there must be an error-free guard space between bursts. If all bursts of length b are to be corrected by a code of rate R, then the ratio of guard to burst length is

$$\frac{g}{b} \geqslant \frac{1 + R}{1 - R}$$

This result is called the *Gallager bound*.

The best-known convolutional codes for burst error correction are the Iwadare–Massey codes, which can correct bursts up to length λn_0 for any integer λ and require a guard space of $n_0(m + 1) - 1$. They are $(n_0, n_0 - 1)$ codes with memory order $m = (2n_0 - 1)\lambda + 2n_0 - 3$. A second type exists for which the memory order is $(2n_0 - 1)\lambda + (n_0^2 - n_0 - 2)/2$. Neither type is optimum with respect to the Gallager bound. A form of feedback decoding is used.

It can be shown that if the decoder allows a small fraction of bursts to pass, then the constraint on guard space may be relaxed to an approximate value

$$\frac{g}{b} \geqslant \frac{R}{1 - R}$$

A family of majority-logic decodable convolutional codes, known as Gallager codes, comes close to meeting this lower bound.

6.6   Phased-burst error correcting codes

There are some codes where the correction capabilities depend on the location of the burst; such codes are said to correct phased bursts because they work best if the bursts are confined within certain natural boundaries in the code. In the case of block codes, there are two families that correct phased bursts, namely Burton codes and RS codes. Berlekamp–Preparata codes are a family of phased-burst error correcting convolutional codes.

Burton codes are closely allied to Fire codes, having a generator of the form

$$g(X) = (X^m + 1)h(X)$$

where $h(X)$ is an irreducible binary polynomial of degree m and period p. The length of the code is the lowest common multiple of p and m. The code can be regarded as grouped into a number (σ) of sub-blocks of length m and is a (σm, $\sigma m - 2m$) code. It can correct any error which affects only one sub-block. The parameters and error correcting properties of the code are, however, the same as those of an equivalent single-error correcting RS code, and so Burton codes can be regarded as being superseded.

The most important phased-burst error correcting block codes are the RS codes, which are a special case of multilevel BCH codes. They thus have symbols that consist of several bits and the error correcting performance is measured in terms of the number of symbol errors that can be corrected, not the number of bit errors.

For a t-error correcting RS code with symbols consisting of l bits

$$n = 2^l - 1$$
$$n - k = 2t$$

Note that n and k are measured in l-bit symbols and that t is the number of symbols that can be corrected. For example, a (31,15) RS code is 155 bits long, of which 75 are information, and up to eight symbol errors can be corrected regardless of the number of bits that are wrong in each symbol. As the symbol boundaries occur at fixed points in the code, the RS codes are multiple-phased burst-error correcting codes.

Reed Solomon codes can be very powerful for their rate, particularly if errors are bursty. They are random symbol-error correcting codes and can be used to good advantage on diffuse channels, but against random binary errors they may be a little inefficient as the number of symbol errors approaches the number of bit errors. Eight bit errors might corrupt eight symbols, thus exhausting the power of the code. On the other hand, if eight bit errors occurred as a burst of length 8, then only two or three symbols would be affected, leaving something in hand for further bursts or random errors.

The encoding and decoding of RS codes was dealt with in Chapter 5. Decoders for RS codes commonly allow for filling of erasures, i.e. symbols for which the value is completely unknown. If the number of erasures is e, then

$$d_{\min} > s + t + e \quad (s \geqslant t)$$

provides the upper bound on the combinations of error correction, error detection and erasure filling that can be achieved.

Berlekamp–Preparata codes are rate $(n_0 - 1)/n_0$ systematic, convolutional codes that are optimum with respect to the Gallager bound for phased bursts, i.e. bursts affecting only a single frame of n_0 bits. For codes of this rate, the ratio of guard space to burst length is

$$\frac{g}{b} = 2n_0 - 1$$

The correctable burst length is a single frame and the guard space is just m frames, where m is the memory order. Hence the memory order is also equal to $2n_0 - 1$.

If Berlekamp–Preparata codes are interleaved to degree λ (see Section 6.8), then they can correct bursts affecting λ frames with a guard space of $m\lambda$ frames. As λ becomes large, the phased nature of the bursts becomes less important and the interleaved code approaches the performance of an ordinary burst-error correcting code which is optimum with respect to the Gallager bound.

6.7   Techniques for compound channels

When a channel contains a mixture of burst errors and random errors, several techniques may be considered for error control. These techniques are amongst the most commonly encountered coding schemes because compound channels are widely encountered in practice.

It is possible to adapt burst-error correcting block codes to handle random errors as well. The idea is that a cyclic code is used with generator polynomial

$g(X) = \text{LCM}[a(X),\ b(X)]$, where $a(X)$ is the generator of a burst-error correcting code (e.g. a Fire code) and $b(X)$ is the generator of a random-error correcting code. Syndrome-computing registers are constructed separately for each factor of $g(X)$ and used to decode separately. If the results agree, or if one code gives a correctable error and the other an uncorrectable pattern, then the error can be corrected. If neither part can correct the error, then an uncorrectable error is indicated.

When using convolutional codes, it is sometimes possible to determine whether a burst or random error pattern has been received and switch to the appropriate circuit. Alternatively, specific codes exist that correct particular combinations of burst and random errors. For example, there are systematic rate 1/2 diffuse codes which correct bursts up to length 2λ and for which the generator of the redundant bit is

$$g^{(2)}(X) = X^{3\lambda+1} + X^{2\lambda} + X^{\lambda} + 1$$

These codes have $m = 3\lambda + 1$ and

$$\frac{g}{b} = \frac{6\lambda + 2}{2\lambda}$$

Thus for large λ they are close to the Gallager bound for rate 1/2 codes.

Many important compound channels have the characteristic that they are basically Gaussian, but are occasionally corrupted by bursts of noise or interference. In that case, it may well be possible to detect the occurrence of the burst noise and erase the symbols affected. Symbol erasure is a near-optimum strategy in these circumstances, as opposed to the pure Gaussian channel where it is of very little value. It was pointed out in Section 4.22 that there is a simple nonalgebraic decoding strategy in the presence of erasures that can be used for any binary block code. Algebraic methods also exist for BCH codes and are commonly applied in decoding RS codes, as explained in Section 4.23.

It has already been seen in Section 5.13 that convolutional codes can be decoded with deliberately introduced erasures when a code is punctured. The same principle applies to Viterbi-decoded convolutional codes when erasures are created by burst noise; the erased symbols do not contribute to the branch metrics and the decoding copes well with the erasures, provided the number of symbols affected is small compared with the constraint length.

Other techniques suitable for diffuse channels are interleaving and product codes. These will be treated in subsequent sections.

6.8   Interleaving

Interleaving is a common technique for bursty or diffuse channels that aims to randomize bursts so that they can be corrected by a random-error correcting

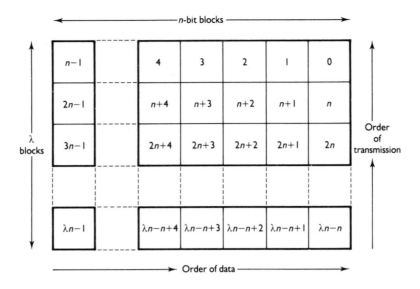

Figure 6.4 Block interleaving

code. The three main methods of interleaving are block, convolutional and pseudorandom interleaving. The latter is mainly used to counteract jamming when someone with a knowledge of the system attempts to produce error bursts that will defeat it. Convolutional interleaving is better at avoiding periodic interference than block interleaving but it is more complex. We shall therefore look at block interleaving first and then go on to convolutional interleaving.

Block interleaving is illustrated in Figure 6.4. A number (λ) of codewords are written into an array with each row of the array consisting of one codeword. The array is then read out column by column for transmission. If a burst of up to λ symbols occurs on the channel, then no more than one symbol in any codeword will be wrong. Thus the burst is spread out over a number of codewords. The parameter λ is called the degree of interleaving.

Block interleaving can be obtained on convolutional codes by providing λ encoders in parallel or by using just one encoder employing λ shift register stages for every 1 in a single encoder. Each bit therefore comes into the encoding operation at every λ stages. For example, the code produced by the convolutional encoder of Figure 5.1 could be interleaved to degree 3 using the encoder of Figure 6.5. Note, however, that all the bits of each output frame would appear consecutively in the final transmitted stream so that it is frames, rather than bits, that are interleaved to degree 3.

If a syndrome decoding method is used, the same trick of using multiple shift register stages can be used in forming syndromes of the de-interleaved received sequence.

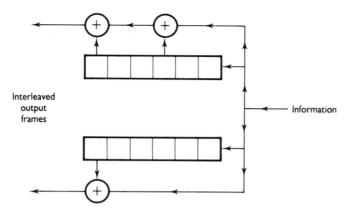

Figure 6.5 Rate 1/2 convolutional encoder with interleaving to degree 3

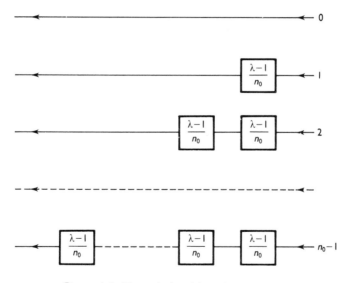

Figure 6.6 Convolutional interleaving

Convolutional interleaving can be considered to be an additional process to be carried out on a block-interleaved convolutional code in order to interleave the bits of each output frame and, at the same time, protect against bursts that are periodic with the same period as the interleaving. A stepped sequence of delays is applied to the n_0 bits of each output frame prior to multiplexing, as illustrated in Figure 6.6. Channel $i(0 \leq i \leq n_0 - 1)$ has $i(\lambda - 1)/n_0$ delay stages, where λ is the

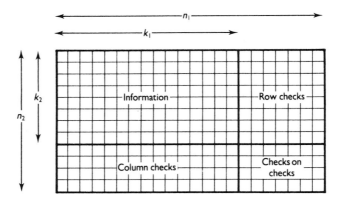

Figure 6.7 Product code

degree of interleaving. It is assumed that λ is chosen such that $\lambda - 1$ is a multiple of n_0. As each delay line advances only once every n_0 bits, the total delay on channel i is $i(\lambda - 1)$. If, for example, we have $n_0 = 3$ and $\lambda = 4$, a portion of the stream from $v_{-\infty}$ to v_{∞} would be $v_0, v_{-2}, v_{-4}, v_3, v_1, v_{-1}, v_6, v_4, v_2, v_9$, etc. At the receiving end the channels are again demultiplexed, subjected to $(n_0 - i - 1)(\lambda - 1)/n_0$ delay stages to equalize all the delays, and then further demultiplexed into λ parallel decoders.

6.9   Product codes

Product codes are similar to interleaved block codes in that the codewords are written into an array, but in this case an extra code is applied down the columns. This is illustrated in Figure 6.7. The segment of the array marked 'checks on checks' will be the same regardless of whether the row code or column code is applied first.

Product codes are a way of producing complex codes from simple components. For example, if both the row and column codes are simple parity checks (single-error detecting), the overall code can correct single errors. Any single error will fail one row and one column parity check, and these failures can then be used to locate the error. In general, if the minimum distance of the row code is d_1, correcting t_1 errors, and of the column code is d_2, correcting t_2 errors then for the product code it is d_1d_2, correcting $2t_1t_2 + t_1 + t_2$ errors. Achieving this performance, however, is not necessarily straightforward as the strategy for row and column decoding may not be easy to define.

Take, for example, the product of two single-error correcting codes that should correct four random errors. If those errors are arranged so that there are two errors in each of two rows and two columns, then a simple strategy of alternately correcting rows and columns will only make things worse. The row correction will add an extra error into each of the affected rows and the column correction will then do the same into each of the affected columns. The product code will thus be wrongly decoded.

There is, in fact, an approach to decoding that will always find a codeword if one exists within $(d_1 d_2 - 1)/2$ of the received sequence. Assuming that the order of transmission is along the rows, the decoding method relies on having an error correcting decoder for the rows and an error-and-erasure correcting decoder for the columns.

1. Decode the rows. For any row that cannot be decoded, erase it. For any row i in which corrections are made, record ω_i the number of corrections.

2. If an odd number of row erasures has taken place, erase one more row, choosing the one for which ω_i is largest.

3. Calculate the error correction capability of the product code as $[d_1(d_2 - e) - 1]/2$ where e is the number of rows erased.

4. Decode one column. If decoding succeeds, count $d_1 - \omega_i$ for every position in which the value is corrected and ω_i for every (unerased) position in which no correction occurs. If this count is less than or equal to the error correction capability of the code, then the column is correctly decoded. Otherwise, or if the original decoding failed, erase two more rows (with largest ω_i), recalculate the error correction capability, and repeat.

5. After each successful column decoding, move on to the next column. Rows previously erased remain erased.

There will often be a tie for which columns should be selected for erasure. Such ties may be broken arbitrarily.

Consider what happens when we have a product of single-error correcting codes and a 4-bit error pattern affecting two rows and two columns as above. Let the row and column codes be the (7,4) cyclic Hamming code described in Chapter 3 and let rows 5 and 2 contain errors in bits 5 and 3, as shown in Figure 6.8. The row decoder now introduces errors into bit 2 of each of those rows and records that the rows have had single-error correction (Figure 6.9).

The column decoder first decodes column 6 with no error correction being needed. It counts the two row corrections that have taken place, compares these with the error correction capability of the code (4), and accepts the column decoding. When column 5 is decoded, however, it introduces another error into bit 3 of the column. Since row 3 has had no errors corrected, accepting the column decoding implies that there were three errors in that row in addition to the errors corrected in rows 5 and 2, making a total of 5 – which exceeds the error correcting capability of the code (Figure 6.10). The column decoding is thus not accepted, rows 5 and 2 are erased (Figure 6.11), the error correction power of the

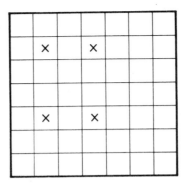

Figure 6.8 Quadruple-error correcting product code with four errors

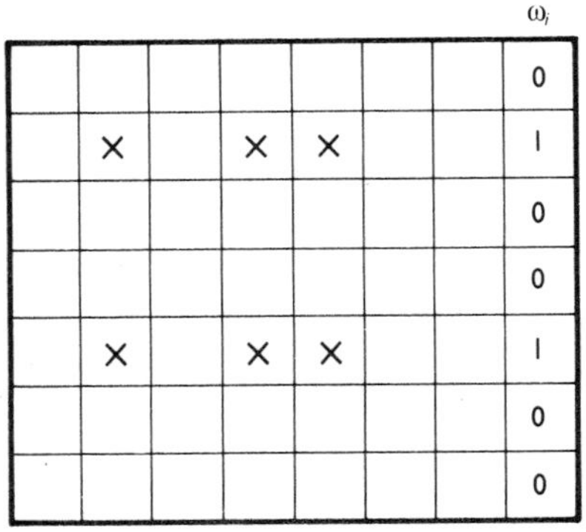

							ω_i
							0
	×		×	×			1
							0
							0
	×		×	×			1
							0
							0

Figure 6.9 Product code after row decoding

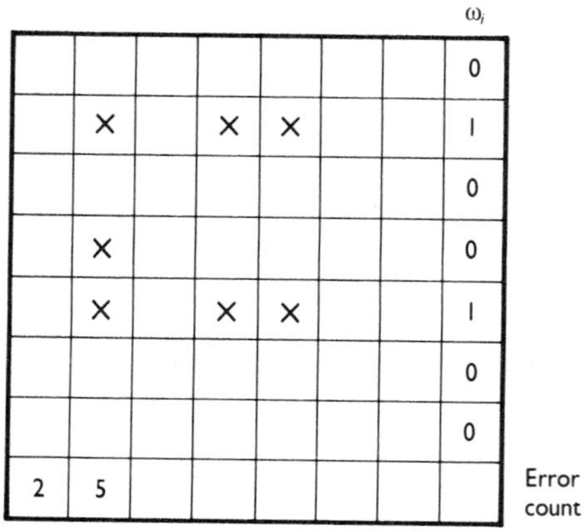

							ω_i
							0
	×		×	×			1
							0
	×						0
	×		×	×			1
							0
							0
2	5						Error count

Figure 6.10 Product code after decoding of two rows

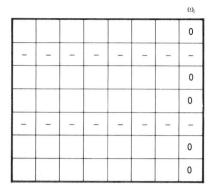

Figure 6.11 Product code after row erasure

code is now recalculated as $[3(3 - 2) - 1]/2 = 1$, and the column decoder will now successfully fill the erasures.

Because of the interleaving, a product code will correct burst as well as random errors. Bursts of up to $n_1 t_2$ in length may be corrected if the order of transmission is along the rows. Moreover the code can correct bursts of this length or random errors at the same time. That does not mean that one array can contain a full complement of both burst and random errors, but that there can never be confusion between a burst error and a different random error pattern if both fall within the error correcting power of the code. The two patterns must have different syndromes and so can in principle be corrected by a single decoder. If the above decoding method were used with transmission down the columns, then it is apparent that the effect of interleaving will be to ensure that burst errors as well as random errors are corrected. In fact this will also be the case if transmission is along the rows; miscorrected rows containing the burst will eventually be erased as the column decodings fail.

If n_1 and n_2 are relatively prime, and the row and column codes are both cyclic, then the whole product code can be turned into a cyclic code provided an appropriate transmission order is chosen. This creates other strategies for decoding the array in one operation. The appropriate order is such that bit j in the transmitted stream is found in column $j \bmod n_1$ and in row $j \bmod n_2$, as shown in Figure 6.12. The generator polynomial of the cyclic product code is the highest common factor of $X^{n_1 n_2} + 1$ and $g_1(X^{b n_2}) g_2(X^{a n_1})$ where $g_1(X)$ and $g_2(X)$ are the generators of the row and column codes respectively, and the integers a and b are chosen such that

$$an_1 + bn_2 = 1$$

The random-error and burst-error correcting properties of the code are not

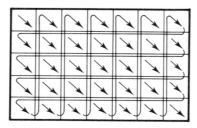

Figure 6.12 Cyclic ordering for product code

diminished by ordering the transmission in this way, so an appropriate decoder for the cyclic product code should provide maximum decoding capability.

6.10   Further reading

The description of burst length used here is the conventional one found in most texts, but another measure was proposed in Wainberg and Wolf (1972) and was taken up in Farrell and Daniel (1984). Bursts are defined as starting, but not necessarily finishing, with an error so that a burst of a particular length includes all shorter lengths. It is claimed that it is relatively easy to obtain a burst distance, similar to Hamming distance, through which minimum burst distance decoding could be obtained.

The various burst-error correcting codes mentioned briefly in this chapter, i.e. Iwadare–Massey, Gallager, Berlekamp–Preparata and Burton codes, are described in more detail by Lin and Costello (1983). Lin and Costello also cover all the other topics in this chapter, but split between block and convolutional codes. Their treatments of product codes and convolutional interleaving are particularly recommended.

The most succinct description of Fire codes and the proofs of their properties are to be found in Blahut (1983). The general technique for decoding random errors with product codes can also be found, with proofs and more detail, in this source.

Abramson (1968) describes a cascade decoding method for cyclic product codes. It would appear that the functioning of this method depends on a different definition which he gives for the generator polynomial. The effect is to alter the order of the transmitted symbols in a way that is still cyclic but allows the decoding to take place in two stages.

Clark and Cain (1981) have a section on coding for burst noise channels in which they concentrate on erasure techniques and the performance of codes in the presence of erasures. As always, their work is recommended reading.

6.11   **Exercises**

1   What is the maximum burst length that is guaranteed to be detected by a cyclic Hamming code of length 15? Could the code be decoded to enable reliable correction of bursts up to length 2?

2   Starting from the polynomial $X^3 + X + 1$, construct the generator of a Fire code of length 35 that can detect and correct all bursts of length 3 or less. Find the constants I_1 and I_2. Decode the sequence

$$X^{34} + X^{32} + X^{31} + X^{30} + X^{29} + X^{25} + X^{23} + X^{22} + X^{18} + X^{16} + X^{15} + X^3 + X + 1$$

3* Verify that the polynomial $X^{15} + X^{10} + X^9 + X^6 + X + 1$ generates a Fire code. Find the length of the code and the correctable burst length. Amend the generator so that the code can also detect and correct all random 2-bit errors.

4   Compare the burst correcting abilities of a (15,11) RS code with those of a (15,11) BCH code interleaved to degree 4. For a random channel bit error rate of 10^{-2}, compare the output bit error rates of the two codes. For simplicity, assume that any decoding error from the RS code gives five symbol errors, each of which has two bit errors, and that a decoding error in a BCH block results in three bit errors.

5   A half-rate convolutional code is to be convolutionally interleaved to degree 5. How many parallel encoders are required and how many delay stages in each line of the convolutional interleaver? If the bits going into the interleaver are numbered 0, 1, 2, 3, etc., what is the sequence coming out of the interleaver?

6   A product code uses a (7,4) Hamming code for the rows and a (15,11) Hamming code for the columns. Find the minimum distance of the code and describe one codeword that has a weight equal to this minimum distance. Compare the burst-error correction capabilities if the code is transmitted across the rows or down the columns.

7* In the example of product code decoding, illustrated in Figures 6.8–6.11, it is found during the final column decodings that the product code is still capable of correcting one more error. Does this mean that a five-error pattern could have been decoded?

7
Concatenated codes

7.1　　　　Introduction

When any error correcting code is decoded, there will be occasional decoding errors. These errors will inevitably be bursty in nature regardless of the code used. For block codes the decoding error will be confined to the block in which it occurred. Viterbi-decoded convolutional codes will exhibit decoding errors that last for a few constraint lengths. Concatenation is a method of putting a second code on top of the first to correct the majority of the decoding errors which occur after the first decoding. The second, or outer, code must be burst-error correcting and for practical purposes can be assumed always to be a Reed Solomon (RS) code.

Concatenation can be thought of as a way of converting channel errors into bursts so that they can be tackled by a burst-error correcting code. It should be remembered that for the same bit error rate, bursty errors are in principle easier to combat than random errors. It will also be seen that in many cases the burst errors can be constrained to be phased bursts corresponding with the natural boundaries of the RS outer code. In this way concatenation can make the most efficient use of RS codes.

This chapter does not require a detailed knowledge of any previous chapters, but rather a good general understanding. Topics that underly the discussion are code performance (Chapter 1), block code characteristics (Chapter 2), convolutional code characteristics (Chapter 5), RS codes and interleaving (Chapter 6).

7.2　　General principle of concatenation

Concatenation or nesting of codes is achieved by a two-stage encoding and decoding process, as shown in Figure 7.1. The first code to be applied to the data is called the outer code. It will be a RS code and the symbols N and K will be used to represent the length and dimension. It must be remembered that RS

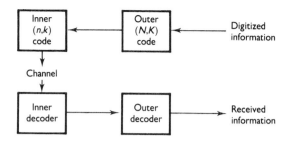

Figure 7.1 Code concatenation

codes are multilevel codes, so that each symbol consists of several bits. The choice of number of bits per symbol will depend on characteristics of the second code to be applied.

The second code to be applied is called the inner code. It may be either a block code or a convolutional code. The combination of inner code and channel produces a *superchannel* which has, it is to be hoped, a lower bit error rate than the uncoded channel and the errors are confined to bursts of known duration. For a block inner code the decoder will produce output in blocks of k bits and any or all of these could be wrong if a decoding error occurs. For a convolutional inner code, a decoding error produces a sequence containing many errors lasting for at least the input constraint length, and perhaps three or four times that long depending on the structure of the code and the effect of channel errors during the recovery time.

The symbol size of the outer code is chosen such that inner decoding errors affect relatively few symbols, often only one. Thus if the inner code is a short block code, its dimension k is usually used as the symbol size of the outer code. Inner decoding errors therefore result in only one symbol error in the outer code. If the inner code is convolutional, the choice of symbol size is more difficult and is generally set equal to some multiple of the input frame of the inner code. Decoding errors will affect several consecutive symbols and so the outer code needs to be able to correct multiple symbol errors. This is often achieved by interleaving a number of outer code blocks together, symbol by symbol.

In the case where a short block inner code is used, each symbol consists of k bits and there are K information symbols in the outer code block. The output of the outer encoder consists of N symbols, each of k bits. These symbols are then treated as k-bit information blocks for the inner code, and are encoded into n-bit blocks. Thus the inner encoder output consists of N blocks, each of n bits. The overall code is therefore a (Nn, Kk) code.

Producing reasonable concatenated schemes is actually a difficult problem, especially because of the need to balance the relative error correcting power of the two codes. For a fixed overall code rate, it might be possible to reduce the rate and increase the power of one code, compensating with an increased rate and reduced error correcting power of the other. Somewhere will be an optimum balance, but this is not easy to find. The inner code must be able to achieve reasonable error control on the channel and may need to be burst correcting or interleaved if the channel characteristics are predominantly bursty. If the inner code is not powerful enough, or not well suited to the channel, it is wasted and serves only to increase the error rates that the outer code has to handle. In such circumstances the outer code might do better on its own. Similarly, the outer code must be able to cope with the symbol error rates on the superchannel.

7.3   Concatenation using inner block code

In principle, any short block code could be used as the inner code. Choosing the dimension of the inner code to be equal to the symbol size of the outer code ensures that the superchannel errors are in phase with the symbol boundaries of the outer code for maximum efficiency. It does, however, restrict the values of k we would wish to use because of the increasing complexity of RS decoding for large symbols. On the other hand, short codes often give the realistic possibility of soft-decision decoding to provide a worthwhile extra gain.

There are certain specific families of block codes that have commonly been proposed and evaluated for use as inner codes. These are principally the maximal length (simplex) codes, orthogonal codes and bi-orthogonal (Reed Muller) codes which can be decoded by correlative methods and which give optimum or near-optimum performance. The drawback to all these codes, however, is that they are very low rate, so some higher rate possibilities should be considered too. These will generally be soft-decision decoded, using a method such as the Chase algorithm (discussed below) to give a performance that is close to maximum likelihood.

7.4   Maximal length codes

Maximal length codes are codes that have length $n = 2^k - 1$ for dimension k. They are the *dual codes* of Hamming codes, which means that the generator matrix of a Hamming code can be used as the parity check matrix of a maximal length code, and vice versa. They can be generated as cyclic codes by taking

$$g(X) = \frac{X^n + 1}{p(X)}$$

where $p(X)$ is a primitive polynomial of degree k.

The codewords consist of the all-zero sequence and the n positions of the generator sequence. Thus there are $n + 1$ codewords, giving the relation between n and k shown above.

The minimum distance of a maximal length code is 2^{k-1} and all the nonzero codewords are at this distance from the all-zero codeword. Linearity, however, means that the distance structure of the code looks the same from any codeword, so we reach the conclusion that every codeword is at the same distance from every other.

For a fixed outer code with symbol size k, the appropriate maximal length code as an inner code will allow operation at the lowest possible value of E_b/N_0.

7.5   Orthogonal codes

Orthogonal signalling is a commonly used technique that may be regarded either as a modulation or as a low-rate code. Viewed as a code, it is closely related to the maximal length code. An orthogonal signal set may be used as the inner code of a concatenated scheme.

Two signals $S_n(t)$ and $S_m(t)$ are orthogonal over some period T if

$$\int_0^T S_n S_m \, dt = \begin{cases} 0 & m \neq n \\ K & m = n \end{cases}$$

where K is some positive constant.

Orthogonal signal sets are commonly provided, at the expense of bandwidth, by the use of multilevel frequency-shift keying (MFSK). Another way is to use an orthogonal code.

An orthogonal code results from adding an overall parity check to a maximal length code to produce a $(2^k, k)$ code. It provides an orthogonal set of 2^k signals, one for each of the possible input values. The code is, however, less efficient than the maximal length code because the additional parity check is always zero and contributes nothing to the minimum distance of the code.

7.6   Reed Muller codes

Adding in the all-ones codeword to the generator matrix of an orthogonal code doubles the number of possible codewords and produces a *bi-orthogonal* code. The number of information bits has increased by 1 compared with the same length orthogonal code, but the minimum distance is unchanged. Hence $n = 2^{k-1}$ and $d_{min} = 2^{k-2}$. Bi-orthogonal codes are also known as first-order Reed Muller codes.

The generator matrix of the first-order Reed Muller codes has k rows and 2^{k-1} columns. Bearing in mind its derivation from maximal length codes, we can derive it in three stages. Firstly, produce a $(k - 1) \times (n - 1)$ matrix whose columns consist of all the combinations of $k - 1$ bits except all zeros. This is using the parity check matrix of a Hamming code as the generator of a maximal length code. Now add an all-zero column to represent the overall parity check of the orthogonal codes, producing a $(k - 1) \times n$ matrix. Finally add another row which is all ones, leaving a $k \times n$ matrix.

Rows of the generator matrices of higher order Reed Muller codes can be produced by taking products of all pairs of the first $k - 1$ rows for second order, then all triplets for third order, etc. Higher-rate codes are thus produced but the minimum distance is reduced by a factor of two for every increment in order.

All Reed Muller codes can be decoded by majority logic, although several steps are needed for the higher-order codes. Our interest here, however, is in the bi-orthogonal codes because, being so closely related to maximal length codes, they give very similar performance, and there are some implementation advantages. For small k, soft decision decoding can be carried out using correlative techniques in which there are a number of matched filters looking for single codewords. Because half the codewords of the Reed Muller codes are the complements of the other half, we can use half the number of matched filters and take the sign of the correlation to decide which of two codewords has been received.

7.7   Block codes with soft-decision decoding

The codes of the above three sections have all been low-rate codes, and their use in concatenated coding schemes reduces the rate still further. Other block codes are therefore often used to produce overall code rates of around 0.5 or greater. Soft-decision decoding is preferred for best overall gain provided it is practicable.

There are several methods for soft-decision decoding of block codes that become practicable when the codes are short and give a performance close to true maximum likelihood decoding. The Chase algorithm is probably the most widely used of these and is certainly applicable to concatenated schemes. We shall therefore study the method first before considering the codes to which it might be applied.

The intention of the Chase algorithm is to generate a list of codewords that will almost always contain the maximum likelihood codeword. The basic procedure consists of three steps. Firstly, hard decisions are made on the bits of the received sequence. Secondly, a number of error sequences are generated and added to the hard-decision received sequence. Finally each of the sequences produced in step 2 is decoded and compared with the (soft decision) received sequence and the one that is closest is selected.

The important part of the algorithm is the method of generating the test patterns. If the hard-decision decoded result is not the best answer, then one of its nearest codewords usually will be, and the aim is that the error sequences should, after decoding, produce a good set of these near codewords. Chase proposed three different methods that generate different numbers of error sequences, the largest number giving the best performance. However, the 'second best' of his methods gives virtually identical performance to the best with greatly reduced complexity and is therefore the most widely encountered. The i least reliable bits are identified, where i is the largest integer that does not exceed $d_{min}/2$. The error patterns consist of all the 2^i possible values in these positions and zero in the rest.

Typical short block codes used in concatenated schemes have d_{min} equal to 4. The Chase algorithm therefore requires only four decoding operations to achieve a performance that is, in typical operating conditions, within a few tenths of a decibel of that obtained by maximum likelihood decoding.

Another alternative that is sometimes encountered is the use of a simple parity check code ($d_{min} = 2$). To achieve maximum likelihood decoding, accept the hard-decision received sequence if the parity is satisfied, otherwise complement the least reliable bit.

7.8 Concatenation using inner convolutional code

When the inner code is a convolutional code, the choice of symbol size for the outer code is less straightforward than with an inner block code. One logical choice for the symbol size would be the size k_0 of the convolutional code's input frame, because decoding errors will persist for a certain number of frames and the errors will be in phase with the RS symbol boundaries. Unfortunately the value of k_0 is usually too small to use as the symbol size; a symbol size of three is the absolute minimum for a sensible outer code, whereas three is a large value for the input frame of a convolutional code. We therefore choose some multiple of k_0, usually at least $(m + 1)k_0$, because a decoding error will normally affect at least that number of bits and the number of symbol errors will be reduced by having a large symbol. Unfortunately, the errors may not correspond exactly with the symbol boundaries and we need to cater for one more symbol error than would be the case for phased errors.

Whatever the choice of symbol size, it will usually be necessary to interleave several outer codewords together, symbol by symbol, in order to spread the inner decoding errors over several codewords. Decoding errors from a convolutional code typically last for a few constraint lengths and will therefore affect several symbols of the outer code. Interleaving will result in fewer occasions when the outer code is defeated, because of the greater length over which inner decoding errors are averaged. Obviously the need is greater the smaller the symbol size of the outer code, but in any case spreading the errors widely will reduce the severity of fluctuations in symbol error rates and reduce the incidence of outer decoding errors.

As an example, a rate 3/4 code might produce bursts of errors lasting 15 frames when decoding fails. We could concatenate with an outer (7,5) RS code with 3-bit symbols to produce an overall code rate of 0.54. The outer code is single-error correcting, so we would want to interleave to degree 15 at least, but probably no more since we could not guarantee to correct more decoding errors even with a greater interleaving degree. As a result we could cater for one inner decoding error per 225 bits of information. If, on the other hand, we choose a 9-bit RS symbol, we can have an outer (511,365) code with the same rate. Inner decoder bursts might now affect six symbols, so we interleave to degree 6 at least. The outer code is able to correct 73 symbol errors, so 73 inner decoding errors per six blocks (19710 information bits) can be corrected. Thus for an increase in length by a factor of 87.6, the number of errors corrected has increased by a factor of 73. The apparent reduction in error correcting efficiency is entirely due to the loss of phasing of the inner decoding errors with the RS symbols, and should be more than compensated by the benefits of extended noise averaging.

7.9   Performance of concatenated codes

In Section 1.10 it was stated that code performance could be represented by an error exponent and that if the exponent is positive, error probabilities can be reduced to an arbitrarily small value by increasing the length of the code. Unfortunately, all known codes produced by single-stage encoding can maintain their error exponent only by reducing the rate to zero as the length increases towards infinity. Concatenated codes do not suffer this disadvantage. For the information rate obtained, however, their error exponent is less than Shannon's lower bound on achievable value. Thus concatenated codes are a good way of creating long codes and are capable of high coding gains, but still fall short of realizing Shannon's predictions.

The performance of a concatenated coding scheme can be evaluated from separate knowledge of the performance of the inner and outer codes. We have previously seen that simple approximate expressions can be obtained for the probability of decoding error using hard decision on a block code. This would then give us the symbol error rate p_s, which can be used in the equations of Section 1.7 to obtain output bit error rate from the RS code. The assessment is complicated, however, by the fact that we rarely use block codes with hard decision as the inner code. Thus we may have to resort to simulation of the inner code to give us our symbol error rate on the superchannel.

Typical coding gains against the AWGN channel would be around 7 dB at bit error rates of 10^{-5} using an inner convolutional code, 6 dB with an inner bi-orthogonal code, 5 dB with a $d_{min} = 4$ inner block code and 4 dB with a simple parity check code as the inner code. At bit error rates of 10^{-8} the gains are typically 2 dB higher. All these figures assume hard decision decoding of the outer code.

In principle, erasure decoding of the outer code should increase the coding gain by over 1 dB. The difficulty is in setting the level of inner decoding confidence for which erasures should be declared. As a result, gains of this sort are not seen. There is a method, however, by which an erasure-filling decoder for RS codes can give soft-decision decoding when the symbols have confidence information attached. This method, known as *generalized minimum distance decoding*, is formulated on the assumption that the symbol values lie at an equal distance from each other. This is the case when an orthogonal modulation is used, or when the inner code is a maximum length code or an orthogonal code.

The method carries out a series of hard decision with erasure decodings. First, the entire sequence is decoded, next the two least-reliable symbols are erased and the sequence is decoded. This continues until at most $d - 1$ symbols have been erased or the best codeword is found. The best codeword can be identified by comparing with the original sequence as follows. If symbol i has confidence α_i then count α_i if the decoded and original symbols correspond, $-\alpha_i$ if they do not. Sum over all the n symbols and if the sum comes to more than $n - d_{min}$, then the best codeword has been found. At most $(d_{min} + 1)/2$ iterations will be needed.

7.10   **Further reading**

In a book of this sort, aimed at students of the subject rather than seasoned practitioners, the treatment of an essentially practical subject such as concatenation is necessarily brief. This should not obscure the importance of the topic; concatenated coding is bound to be of increasing interest in communication systems, especially when high gains are needed. It is at present probably less well established in the literature than the more mature topics, but the later texts quoted here will act as sources of further reference papers.

Concatenated codes were first proposed by Forney (1966a) and this is still a valuable source, particularly for the consideration of relative power of inner and outer codes and the capabilities of concatenated codes relative to the Shannon results.

Clark and Cain (1981) look in some detail at concatenation and quote, with references, many performance figures. Similar, but briefer, coverage is to be found in Michelson and Levesque (1985). Lin and Costello (1983) are strong on concatenation using inner convolutional codes and they also mention certain generalizations of concatenation that have been proposed, e.g. Justesen codes. Blahut (1983) gives a full example of concatenation with an inner block code, in this case also a RS code, and also has a full treatment of Justesen codes. Orthogonal modulations, which may be regarded as inner codes, are explained by Sklar (1988).

The method for soft-decision decoding of block codes was described by Chase (1972) and is also treated by Clark and Cain (1981). Forney (1966b) introduced the idea of generalized minimum distance decoding, which is also described by Blahut (1983).

7.11   Exercises

1   Messages of length 1100 bits are to be sent over a bursty channel. The bursts last for up to 10 bits. Suggest a concatenated scheme using a double-error correcting outer code and a (15,11) BCH inner code.

2   The scheme devised in Exercise 1 is to be used on a Gaussian channel with bit error rate of 10^{-2}. Estimate the output bit error rate and the coding gain at this rate assuming BPSK modulation.

3   A rate 1/2, $K = 6$, convolutional code produces decoding errors that last for up to 30 frames. Suggest an outer code with minimum distance 11 and an appropriate interleaving degree.

4   Find the codewords of the cyclic code whose generator polynomial is $g(X) = X^4 + X^3 + X^2 + 1$. By inspection, verify that the code has the properties described for a maximal length code, i.e. all nonzero codewords are cyclic shifts of a single sequence.

       The demodulator gives soft decisions with 3-bit quantization. The sequence 0067342 is received, where value 0 represents high confidence in received 0 and value 7 represents high confidence in received 1. Values 0–3 represent hard-decision 0 and values 4–7 represent hard-decision 1. Find the closest codeword to the received sequence. Verify that the Chase algorithm, as described in Section 7.7, would generate the maximum likelihood codeword.

       If the probability of decoding error from this code is 1 percent, suggest an outer code that will give a block decoding error rate below 10^{-4}. Find the overall code rate. Would interleaving the outer code produce a lower overall decoding error rate?

8
Coding for bandwidth-limited channels

8.1   Introduction

In almost all of the previous sections of this book it has been tacitly assumed that transmission is over a binary channel, as opposed to a multilevel channel in which each signal can take on several values. The major exception was in considering concatenation, where the use of multilevel orthogonal modulations (or orthogonal codes) can reduce the channel error rates, which are then further reduced by an outer code. Unfortunately, orthogonal signalling requires increasing bandwidth as the number of levels increases if the data rate is to be maintained, and thus cannot be used in bandwidth-limited conditions. Certain other forms of multilevel modulation, however, work the opposite way, reducing the required bandwidth at the expense of increased error rates. In such conditions, error control may be particularly required.

There are many difficulties in applying error control coding to multilevel channels. The first problem is that the errors tend to affect several bits at once. Another difficulty is that not all errors are equally likely, whereas on a binary channel there are only two (equally likely) error events, namely a transmitted 0 being received as 1 or transmitted 1 received as 0. As a result, the following conclusions may be reached:

1. Decoding should take into account the distance in signal space between the sequences, i.e. the energy required to alter one code sequence to another. This distance is termed *squared Euclidean distance* and the problem of decoding by Euclidean distance is identical to that of soft-decision decoding. Thus the codes should be soft-decision decodable.

2. The code should be specially chosen to maximize squared Euclidean distance between sequences. This means that it must be chosen in conjunction with the modulation. The necessity of linking coding and modulation is a particular feature of multilevel channels.

159

The need for soft-decision decoding leads naturally to the use of convolutional codes with Viterbi decoding, although the codes must be specially designed. Although work has been done on block codes for multilevel applications, convolutional codes are better established. In particular, convolutional codes are often used in conjunction with an expanded signal set to achieve lower error rates than an uncoded channel, with no increase in bandwidth or reduction in data rate. In these cases we often refer to *Ungerboeck coding*, named after the pioneer of such schemes. This chapter will essentially be devoted to Ungerboeck codes.

As prerequisites to this chapter, the reader should be familiar with the material of Chapters 1 and 5.

8.2   *M*-ary phase shift keying (MPSK)

One way to carry several bits in a single signal without bandwidth penalties is to use multiple phase signalling in which the transmitted signal can take M different phase values ($M = 4, 8, 16, 32$, etc.). Such a modulation is known as M-ary phase shift keying (MPSK), and the bandwidth depends on the signalling rate, not on the number of levels. The value of E_b/N_0 required to maintain the error rate does, however, increase substantially as the number of levels increases.

Figure 8.1 shows that for a given signal amplitude, the shortest distance from a signal point to the edge of a demodulator decision boundary is proportional to $\sin(\pi/M)$. In the case where the predominant errors are corruptions from the transmitted point to one of its nearest neighbours (i.e. at low

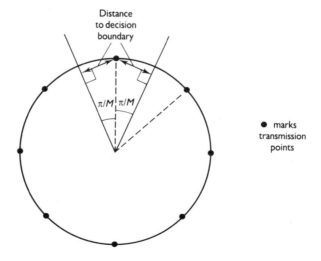

Figure 8.1 Demodulator decision boundaries for MPSK

error rates), the signal energy needs to be increased by a factor of $1/\sin^2(\pi/M)$ to maintain the same symbol error rate. If E_b/N_0 is maintained, the actual increase in symbol energy will be $\log_2(M)$. For the same symbol error rate, MPSK therefore shows a loss of $1/[\log_2(M)\sin^2(\pi/M)]$ compared with binary PSK. For large M, this amounts to a loss of 6 dB each time M is doubled.

8.3 Quadrature amplitude modulation

Another way to expand the signal constellation without bandwidth penalties is to adopt quadrature amplitude modulation (QAM). Two signals in phase quadrature are combined such that the resultant can take a large number of discrete amplitude and phase combinations, as shown in Figure 8.2 for a 16-level constellation. The number of points in the constellation may be doubled with approximately the same mean symbol energy by insertion of a number of intermediate points as shown in Figure 8.3. The distance between the points is

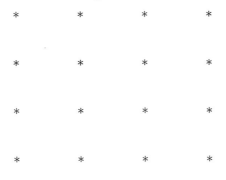

Figure 8.2 A 16-point QAM constellation

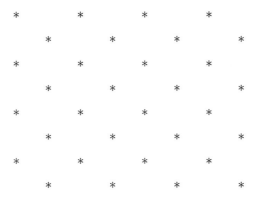

Figure 8.3 A 32-point QAM constellation

now reduced by a factor of $\sqrt{2}$, so that symbol energy must be doubled for the same symbol error rate. To maintain E_b/N_0 the symbol energy must be increased by a factor of $[1 + \log_2(M)]/\log_2(M)$. In the limit of large M, each doubling of M requires a 3 dB increase in E_b/N_0 for the same symbol error rate, i.e. a 3 dB coding loss.

From the above, it can be seen that the losses of expanding the signal set using QAM are less severe than those resulting from the use of MPSK. On the other hand, MPSK has a constant power delivery, which may pose fewer problems in many applications. Both MPSK and QAM constellations are therefore encountered, the former having relatively low values of M.

8.4   Ungerboeck codes

The original work on coding for multilevel channels was done by Ungerboeck and there are a number of convolutional codes bearing his name which he devised for particular constellations. His work addresses the specific problem of improving bit error rates over existing channels without increasing the mean signal power or the bandwidth; the constellation is expanded and a code of suitable rate is added so that the transmitted information rate is maintained.

If we start from a constellation that has 2^l levels, we can expand to 2^{l+1} levels, thereby increasing the number of bits per symbol from l to $l + 1$. A convolutional code with $k_0 = l$, $n_0 = l + 1$ would therefore allow us to send data over the expanded channel at the same rate as over the original unencoded channel. In practice, we do not always encode every data bit; some are passed unencoded to the modulator. For example, we might start from a 32-point (5-bit) transmission, encode 2 bits of every 5 in a rate 2/3 encoder and pass on the 3 encoded and 3 unencoded bits of each frame to the modulator for a 64-point constellation.

Ungerboeck's method is based on set partitioning of the transmitted points; this process is carried out in several stages, each stage doubling the number of sets and reducing the number of points within each set. The encoded bits are used to select the set and the unencoded bits to select the point within the set. Thus the number of stages of partitioning required is equal to the number of bits in the output frame of the convolutional encoder.

Examples of convolutional encoders for use with two-stage and three-stage partitioning are rate 1/2 and 2/3 encoders with generators

$$g^{(1)}(D) = D$$
$$g^{(2)}(D) = D^2 + 1$$

and

$$g_1^{(1)}(D) = D$$
$$g_1^{(2)}(D) = D + 1$$
$$g_1^{(3)}(D) = D^2 + D + 1$$
$$g_2^{(1)}(D) = 0$$
$$g_2^{(2)}(D) = D$$
$$g_2^{(3)}(D) = D + 1$$

respectively.

8.5   Set partitioning

Ungerboeck's set partitioning method will be explained using a 64-point constellation based on a rectangular grid. The procedure to be adopted for partitioning of a circular constellation (MPSK) will be exactly analogous.

The points on the constellation could be taken as representing a signal that can vary in both phase and amplitude in 64 predetermined combinations. Such a constellation is shown in Figure 8.4, partitioned into two sets labelled A and B. If we separate out the two sets, as in Figures 8.5 and 8.6 we can see that each forms a 32-point constellation. The closest points within a set now lie along diagonals, and to maintain symmetry about the axes we need to rotate them by 45°. Note that the minimum squared Euclidean distance between points in either set has been doubled compared with the 64-point constellation. Nevertheless, each set represents a 32-point constellation as would be used without coding, so it is the minimum squared Euclidean distance within one of these two sets that provides the basis for any comparisons of encoded and unencoded performance.

A	B	A	B	A	B	A	B
B	A	B	A	B	A	B	A
A	B	A	B	A	B	A	B
B	A	B	A	B	A	B	A
A	B	A	B	A	B	A	B
B	A	B	A	B	A	B	A
A	B	A	B	A	B	A	B
B	A	B	A	B	A	B	A

Figure 8.4 A 64-point constellation partitioned into two sets

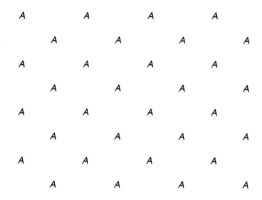

Figure 8.5 Set A of a partitioned 64-point constellation

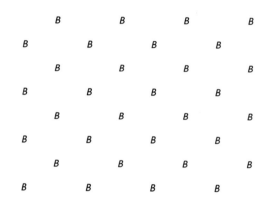

Figure 8.6 Set B of a partitioned 64-point constellation

The next step is to take the rotated subsets and alternately assign the points in set A to subsets A_0 and A_1. Similarly the B points are split into B_0 and B_1. The result is shown in Figure 8.7.

After a further rotation we can partition yet again. A_0 is partitioned into subsets A_{00} and A_{11} and A_1 into A_{01} and A_{10}. The points in set B are partitioned likewise. The result is shown in Figure 8.8.

The subscripts used for the last partition are different from those used by Ungerboeck. The reason for doing it in this way is that, if d_0 is the minimum squared Euclidean distance between points within sets A or B, the minimum squared distance between two subsets of A or B can be found as $2d_0^2$ multiplied by the Hamming distance between the subscripts. For example, between points in A_{01} and A_{10} it is $4d_0^2$. This property can be used in analysing the performance of

$$
\begin{array}{cccccccc}
A_0 & B_0 & A_0 & B_0 & A_0 & B_0 & A_0 & B_0 \\
B_1 & A_1 & B_1 & A_1 & B_1 & A_1 & B_1 & A_1 \\
A_0 & B_0 & A_0 & B_0 & A_0 & B_0 & A_0 & B_0 \\
B_1 & A_1 & B_1 & A_1 & B_1 & A_1 & B_1 & A_1 \\
A_0 & B_0 & A_0 & B_0 & A_0 & B_0 & A_0 & B_0 \\
B_1 & A_1 & B_1 & A_1 & B_1 & A_1 & B_1 & A_1 \\
A_0 & B_0 & A_0 & B_0 & A_0 & B_0 & A_0 & B_0 \\
B_1 & A_1 & B_1 & A_1 & B_1 & A_1 & B_1 & A_1
\end{array}
$$

Figure 8.7 A 64-point constellation partitioned twice

$$
\begin{array}{cccccccc}
A_{00} & B_{00} & A_{11} & B_{11} & A_{00} & B_{00} & A_{11} & B_{11} \\
B_{10} & A_{10} & B_{01} & A_{01} & B_{10} & A_{10} & B_{01} & A_{01} \\
A_{11} & B_{11} & A_{00} & B_{00} & A_{11} & B_{11} & A_{00} & B_{00} \\
B_{01} & A_{01} & B_{10} & A_{10} & B_{01} & A_{01} & B_{10} & A_{10} \\
A_{00} & B_{00} & A_{11} & B_{11} & A_{00} & B_{00} & A_{11} & B_{11} \\
B_{10} & A_{10} & B_{01} & A_{01} & B_{10} & A_{10} & B_{01} & A_{01} \\
A_{11} & B_{11} & A_{00} & B_{00} & A_{11} & B_{11} & A_{00} & B_{00} \\
B_{01} & A_{01} & B_{10} & A_{10} & B_{01} & A_{01} & B_{10} & A_{10}
\end{array}
$$

Figure 8.8 A 64-point constellation partitioned three times

the codes. Any further partitioning destroys this property, but more stages of partitioning are rarely required.

8.6   Integration of coding with partitioning

When the convolutional codes described earlier are used in conjunction with the partitioned constellation, the first bit from the encoder output determines the set (A or B) and other outputs determine the subscript. Unencoded bits can be used in some arbitrary manner to select a point within the subset. If the rate 1/2 encoder is used, then two stages of partitioning would suffice, leaving 16 points within each subset. Four unencoded data bits would then be used to select one of those points. If the rate 2/3 encoder is used, three stages of partitioning are needed, leaving eight points per subset and requiring three unencoded data bits to select the point.

8.7   Performance of Ungerboeck codes

The initial doubling of the number of points in the constellation halved the minimum squared Euclidean distance, an effect offset by the first partitioning. Thereafter each stage of partitioning produces a doubling of minimum squared Euclidean distance within a subset. If the code gave us absolute certainty of knowledge of the subset, two-stage partitioning would then produce a coding gain of 3 dB and 6 dB for three-stage partitioning. Achievable coding gains will be less than these figures; how close we come to achieving them will depend on the power of the code. When Ungerboeck coding is applied to MPSK, it should be remembered that the losses incurred in expanding the signalling constellation are greater than for QAM and that the potential gains of coding are therefore greater.

The asymptotic coding gain of an Ungerboeck coding scheme may be found by comparing the minimum squared Euclidean distance between coded paths with the squared Euclidean distance between nearest neighbours on the smaller constellation that would be used for uncoded transmissions. The ratio between these distances, expressed in decibels, gives the asymptotic coding gain. For example, the rate 1/2 code specified in Section 8.4 has the trellis shown in Figure 8.9. If that code is applied to an 8-ary PSK constellation, then there will be two-stage partitioning and one uncoded bit in every frame. Hence each path in the trellis will in reality represent two possible transmitted points, one for each value of the uncoded bit. The Ungerboeck-mapped constellation (with the rightmost bit being the one that is uncoded) and the squared Euclidean distance from 000 to each of the other points is as shown in Figure 8.10. Euclidean squared distances are shown as a multiple of the squared distance between points in a QPSK (quaternary, or 4-level, PSK) constellation.

If we assume an error on the coded bits, then the code path at the lowest squared Euclidean distance from the all-zero sequence is found to be 010 100 010 (or 011 100 010 or 010 100 011 or 011 100 011). The ratio of squared distance to the reference value is 2.293 (1 + 0.293 + 1). Hence if this were the most likely error, the asymptotic coding gain would be $10 \log_{10}(2.293) = 3.6$ dB. A single error on an uncoded bit is, however, more likely, being at a squared Euclidean distance of 2 (relative to the reference value) from the all-zero path. Hence the asymptotic

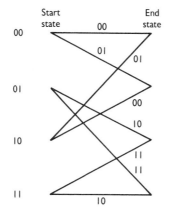

Start
state   End
00   state
00
01
01
01
00
10
10
10
11
11
11
10

Figure 8.9 Trellis for rate 1/2 code

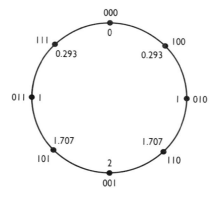

000
0
111   100
0.293   0.293
011 ● I   I ● 010
1.707   1.707
101   110
2
001

Figure 8.10 Partitioned 8-PSK constellation

coding gain is limited by the error rate on the uncoded bits and will be of the order of 3 dB.

8.8   **Further reading**

The analysis given here of MPSK and QAM has been slightly simplified and has concentrated on maintaining the symbol error rate. It might be more useful to compare constellations with the same bit error rate, but this is complicated by the need to consider the mapping of the symbol values onto the constellation. Proakis (1983) derives expressions for symbol error rates of MPSK and QAM. Sklar

(1988) quotes expressions for the bit error rates and compares the different levels of the constellations in those terms.

Ungerboeck (1977, 1982) carried out the original work in this field, devising codes for a variety of constellations. Both Haykin (1988) and Clark and Cain (1981) have summaries of Ungerboeck coding methods. Forney *et al.* (1984) give an admirable summary of the whole subject of coding for bandwidth-limited conditions, including the use of block codes. Wei (1984a, 1984b) describes methods that overcome problems of phase ambiguity.

In addition to techniques of the type discussed in this chapter, there are many modulation schemes designed to be spectrally efficient and which can be regarded as incorporating coding. For example, minimum shift keying (MSK) can be regarded as incorporating a simple convolutional code and Masamura *et al.* (1979) describe a demodulation process that makes use of this. There are other, more complex, bandwidth-efficient modulations that appear under a variety of names and use Viterbi decoding in the demodulation. Such schemes are described by Lender (1964), Kobayashi (1971), Anderson and Taylor (1978), Anderson *et al.* (1981), Aulin *et al.* (1981), Muilwijk (1981), Mazur and Taylor (1981), Aulin and Sundberg (1982) and Raveendra and Srinivasan (1987).

8.9   Exercises

1   Devise a partitioning scheme for 16-ary PSK. Show the symbol mappings that would occur using each of the convolutional codes specified in Section 8.4.

2   An uncoded communication channel uses 8-ary modulation. It is decided to go over to an Ungerboeck-coded 16-ary channel with two-stage partitioning. Compare the expected coding gains at constant symbol error rate if the constellation is MPSK against those for QAM. What would be the effects of three-stage partitioning?

3   Starting from an 8-point QAM constellation arranged as one of the subsets in Figure 8.8, carry out two-stage partitioning. Use the rate 1/2 Ungerboeck encoder for the information sequences 11 00 11 11 00 00 01 10 and 11 01 10 10 10 01 01 11, and find the squared Euclidean distance between the coded sequences. Compare this with the squared Euclidean distance between the uncoded sequences on an equivalent 4-point QAM constellation.

4   Repeat Exercise 3 using MPSK modulation.

5   Partition a 16-point rectangular QAM constellation three times. Use the rate 2/3 Ungerboeck encoder for the information sequences 100 111 001 011 and 101 110 100 011, and find the squared Euclidean distance between the coded sequences. Compare this with the squared Euclidean distance between the uncoded sequences on an 8-point QAM channel.

9
Error detection methods

9.1   Introduction

The preceding chapters have largely assumed that the purpose of coding was to allow the receiver to recover the information from the received sequence with a higher certainty than would be obtainable without coding. Many error control schemes do not, however, attempt to recover the information when errors have occurred, instead they detect errors and invoke some alternative strategy to deal with them. If a return channel is available, the receiver may call for a retransmission of the message. Alternatively, for data with considerable inherent redundancy it may be possible to reconstitute the corrupted message in a way that minimizes the effects of the loss of information.

There are many reasons why a system designer might opt for an error detection strategy rather than forward error correction. Some of these reasons are bound up with characteristics of an error detection scheme that will emerge in the course of this chapter. One major reason is, however, that error detection can be made many orders of magnitude more reliable than forward error correction and is thus appropriate when a low undetected error rate is essential. It is also often relatively simple to implement an error control strategy based on error detection. Thus if the characteristics are acceptable, error detection strategies, or some hybrid of error detection and forward error correction, is likely to be the most cost-effective solution.

This chapter starts by considering the performance of codes when used for error detection. It then goes on to study techniques based on retransmission, the so-called *automatic retransmission request* (ARQ) or *retransmission error control* (REC) methods. Finally error concealment techniques, in which the effects of information loss are minimized, are briefly discussed. Only a general knowledge of coding, particularly block codes, is required.

9.2   Random error detection performance of block codes

In comparison with error correction, error detection is a relatively straightforward operation, but it is rather more difficult to obtain approximate formulas for the performance because the structure of the code has a much more noticeable effect. It is almost always block codes that are used and, although convolutional codes are possible, we shall look only at the performance of block codes.

If the number of errors in a block is less than the minimum distance, then they will always be detected. If the number is equal to or greater than d_{min}, then we might choose to be pessimistic and assume that error detection will fail. This, however, is far too removed from real performance; only a small proportion of error patterns of weight d_{min} or more will produce another codeword and hence escape detection. Taking the example (7,4) code from Chapter 1 (Table 1.2), we see that there are seven codewords of weight 3, seven of weight 4 and one of weight 7. If, therefore, the all-zero codeword is transmitted, only seven of the 35 possible 3-bit error patterns produce an undetected error, so that 80 percent of 3-bit errors will be detected. The distance properties of the code are the same regardless of which codeword is transmitted, so this result applies to any transmission. Similarly, 80 percent of weight 4 error patterns are detected, 100 percent of weight 5 and 100 percent of weight 6. Only the weight 7 error pattern is sure to evade detection.

Ideally we would wish to know the number A_i of codewords of weight i for the code in use. If we assume that the events causing code failure are essentially independent we can then say

$$P_{ud} = \sum_{i=0}^{n} P(i) \, \frac{A_i}{\left[\begin{array}{c} n \\ i \end{array}\right]} \tag{9.1}$$

where P_{ud} is the probability of undetected error and $P(i)$ is the probability of exactly i symbols in a block being wrong. With a symbol error rate of p_s, we see from equation (1.9) that

$$P_{ud} = \sum_{i=0}^{n} A_i \, p_s^i (1 - p_s)^{n-i} \tag{9.2}$$

Unfortunately the weight structures are not known for all codes. Nevertheless the weight distributions are known for Hamming codes, RS codes and some binary BCH codes. In addition, the weight distribution can be obtained for any code where the weight distribution of its dual code is known.

9.3 **Weight distributions**

Hamming codes

Hamming codes have a *weight enumerator*

$$A(x) = \sum_{i=0}^{n} A_i x^i = \frac{(1 + x)^n + n(1 + x)^{(n-1)/2}(1 - x)^{(n+1)/2}}{n + 1} \tag{9.3}$$

i.e. the coefficient of x^i in $A(x)$ is the number A_i of codewords of weight i. An alternative form is

$$A(x) = \sum_{i=0}^{n} A_i x^i = \frac{(1 + x)^n + n(1 - x)(1 - x^2)^{(n+1)/2}}{n + 1}$$

from which we can obtain expressions for A_i

$$A_i = \begin{cases} \dfrac{\left[\begin{matrix} n \\ i \end{matrix}\right] + n(-1)^{i/2}\left[\begin{matrix} (n-1)/2 \\ i/2 \end{matrix}\right]}{n + 1} & (i \text{ even}) \\[4mm] \dfrac{\left[\begin{matrix} n \\ i \end{matrix}\right] + n(-1)^{(i+1)/2}\left[\begin{matrix} (n-1)/2 \\ (i-1)/2 \end{matrix}\right]}{n + 1} & (i \text{ odd}) \end{cases} \tag{9.4}$$

For the (7,4) Hamming code, $A_0 = 1$, $A_3 = 7$, $A_4 = 7$, $A_7 = 1$ and all the other terms are zero. This corresponds with the results quoted in the above section.

Reed Solomon codes

The weight distribution of a t-error correcting RS code over $GF(q)$ is given by $A_0 = 1$ and

$$A_i = \left[\begin{matrix} q - 1 \\ i \end{matrix}\right](q - 1) \sum_{j=0}^{i-2t-1} (-1)^j \left[\begin{matrix} i - 1 \\ j \end{matrix}\right] q^{i-2t-1-j} \tag{9.5}$$

for $2t + 1 \leq i \leq n$. An alternative (equivalent) form is

$$A_i = \left[\begin{matrix} q - 1 \\ i \end{matrix}\right] \sum_{j=0}^{i-2t-1} (-1)^j \left[\begin{matrix} i \\ j \end{matrix}\right](q^{i-2t-j} - 1) \tag{9.6}$$

For example a double-error correcting RS code over $GF(8)$ has 1 codeword of weight 0, 147 of weight 5, 147 of weight 6 and 217 of weight 7.

Dual code of a code with known weight distribution

For any (n,k) code it is possible to construct the $(n,n-k)$ *dual code* whose generator matrix is the parity check matrix of the original code. If the original code is a cyclic code with a generator $g(X)$, the dual code has generator $(X^n + 1)/g(X)$. The weight enumerator $A(x)$ of a (n,k) linear code over $GF(q)$ is related to the weight enumerator $B(x)$ of its dual by the *MacWilliams Identity*

$$q^k B(x) = [1 + (q-1)x]^n A\left(\frac{1-x}{1+(q-1)x}\right) \tag{9.7}$$

For binary codes this becomes

$$2^k B(x) = (1+x)^n A\left(\frac{1-x}{1+x}\right) \tag{9.8}$$

For a Hamming code with weight distribution given by equation (9.3), the MacWilliams identity gives the following expression for $B(x)$, the weight distribution of the dual code

$$B(x) = 1 + nx^{(n+1)/2}$$

The dual of a Hamming code is in fact a maximal length code or simplex code. That this is indeed the weight distribution of such a code is seen from the discussion of Section 7.4.

If we had only known the numerical values of the coefficients A_i instead of an analytic expression, we could still have obtained the weight distribution of the dual code. For example, if we take the values of A_i for the (7,4) Hamming code we find from equation (9.7)

$$16B(x) = (1+x)^7\left[1 + 7\left(\frac{1-x}{1+x}\right)^3 + 7\left(\frac{1-x}{1+x}\right)^4 + \left(\frac{1-x}{1+x}\right)^7\right]$$

$$16B(x) = (1+x)^7 + 7(1-x)^3(1+x)^4 + 7(1-x)^4(1+x)^3 + (1-x)^7$$

Expanding gives

$$B(x) = 1 + 7x^4$$

The importance of the MacWilliams identity is that for a high rate code it is often much easier to find the weight distribution of the dual code, which will have far fewer codewords. In practice, therefore, the weight distribution of a Hamming code would be obtained from that of a simplex code, rather than vice versa as done here.

9.4 Worst case undetected error rate

Another possibility of interest is to consider as a worst case that the bit error rate approaches 0.5 when using a binary code. The probability of undetected error becomes

$$P_{ud} = \sum_{i=0}^{n} A_i 0.5^i (1 - 0.5)^{n-i}$$

but $\sum_{i=0}^{n} A_i = 2^k$, so

$$P_{ud} = \frac{1}{2^{n-k}}$$

What this means is that if the bits are generated randomly, then there is a chance of 1 in 2^{n-k} of the $n - k$ parity bits being correct. This is true only if the checks can be regarded as independent, and there are some codes where this is not so. Nevertheless the worst case probability of undetected error for well-designed codes can be calculated in this way.

9.5 Burst error detection

As pointed out in Section 6.3, cyclic codes have good burst error detection properties. Any consecutive $n - k$ bits can act as the parity checks on the rest of the codeword and it therefore follows that an error pattern must span more than this number of bits if it is to pass undetected. The only bursts of length $n - k + 1$ that will pass undetected are those that are identical to the generator sequence cyclically shifted to the appropriate position. Thus over any fixed span of $n - k$ bits, there are 2^{n-k-1} error patterns starting and ending in 1, of which only one will pass undetected. Thus the probability of a burst of length $n - k + 1$ being undetected is $2^{-(n-k-1)}$.

This analysis extends fairly easily to longer bursts. For any burst of length $l > n - k + 1$ to pass undetected, it must resemble $g(X)$ multiplied by some polynomial of degree $l - (n - k)$. There are $2^{l-(n-k)-2}$ such polynomials and 2^{l-2} burst patterns of length l. Thus the probability of such a burst being undetected is $2^{-(n-k)}$.

9.6 Examples of error detection codes

There are three cyclic block codes that are fairly standard for use in error detection applications. One is a 12-bit cyclic redundancy check (CRC) and the other two are 16-bit checks.

The generator polynomial for the 12-bit CRC is

$$g(X) = X^{12} + X^{11} + X^3 + X^2 + X + 1$$

or

$$g(X) = (X^{11} + X^2 + 1)(X + 1)$$

The polynomial $X^{11} + X^2 + 1$ is primitive, hence the code is an expurgated Hamming code. The length of the code is 2047 bits ($2^{11} - 1$), of which 2035 are devoted to information and the minimum distance is 4. The code may be shortened to include less information without impairment to the error detection properties.

There are clearly too many codewords to enumerate fully the weight structure. Taking the codewords of weight equal to d_{min} we find that there are 44 434 005 codewords of weight 4 compared with 4.53×10^{10} possible weight 4 sequences. The probability of a weight 4 error sequence being undetected is therefore less than 10^{-3}. The code will detect all errors of weight less than 4, all errors of odd weight, all bursts of length less than 12, 99.9 percent of all bursts of length 12 and 99.5 percent of all bursts of length greater than 12.

The two 16-bit CRCs have generator polynomials

$$g(X) = X^{16} + X^{15} + X^2 + 1$$

and

$$g(X) = X^{16} + X^{12} + X^5 + 1$$

The factor $X + 1$ can be taken out to give

$$g(X) = (X^{15} + X + 1)(X + 1)$$

and

$$g(X) = (X^{15} + X^{14} + X^{13} + X^{12} + X^4 + X^3 + X^2 + X + 1)(X + 1)$$

In both cases the generator is a primitive polynomial multiplied by $X + 1$ to expurgate the code. As a result the codes have $d_{min} = 4$, length up to 32 767, of which all but 16 bits are devoted to information. There are 1.47×10^{12} words of weight 4, giving a probability of undetected error for weight 4 patterns of around 3.05×10^{-5}. The codes will detect all errors of weight 3 or less, all odd weight errors, all bursts of length 16 or less, 99.997 percent of bursts of length 17 and 99.9985 percent of bursts of length 18 or more.

9.7   Synchronization using block codes

Almost all forms of digital communications require some kind of synchronization so that a receiver can determine the important information and code boundaries within the transmitted stream. At the lowest level, the demodulator needs to acquire *bit synchronization* or *symbol synchronization*, i.e. to know where the boundaries between transmitted symbols occur. At a higher level, the receiver must achieve *frame synchronization* or *block synchronization* so that the received sequence is presented correctly to the decoder. One way of achieving this latter objective is to use embedded block codes purely for error detection until synchronization has been achieved. The reception of an apparently error-free block is taken as an indication that the receiver has now synchronized to the block boundaries of the code. Information within that block may then help the receiver to determine any other necessary information about the position that has been reached in the information sequence.

If the receiver already knew the block boundaries, then the problem of confirming that knowledge would be simple. The syndrome would be calculated for one block and a correct value (particularly if repeated in subsequent blocks) would indicate that synchronization had been obtained. The problem faced by the receiver, however, is that of forming syndromes when the block boundaries are not known. One could, of course, employ n parallel decoders (n being the length of the block) to determine which of the possible block start positions was correct. Fortunately, this is not necessary if the code is cyclic because with the arrival of each new symbol we can cancel out the effect of the symbol that arrived n intervals previously, so that the syndrome calculated at each stage is that which applies to the most recent n symbols.

The method for calculating the syndrome is shown in Figure 9.1. The latest n symbols are buffered and as each new symbol arrives it is added to the value received n symbols previously before entering the syndrome computer, which is the usual arrangement of shift registers with feedback.

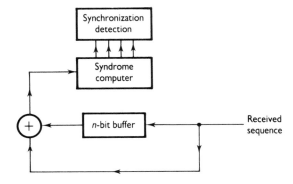

Figure 9.1 Syndrome calculation for synchronization

It is usual to use a shortened cyclic code for this type of application. The reason is that, without shortening, every cyclic shift of a codeword is itself a codeword. Therefore if the symbol before the beginning of the block is identical to the last symbol of the block, synchronization will be declared one symbol early. For example, if the code were an expurgated Hamming code with generator $X^5 + X^4 + X^2 + 1$, the sequence 110011110100001 is a codeword but so is 111001111010000. If the first of those two sequences were transmitted but preceded by 1, then synchronization would be declared 1 bit early.

Problems of this type can be eased if the code is shortened, in which case the way in which the delayed symbol cancels its previous effect has to be amended (see Exercise 6). Clearly with any code there is a probability that synchronization will be declared at the wrong point, either through accident of the sequence transmitted or through the effect of errors. For this reason a single success is not taken as definitive, neither is a single failure to synchronize at an expected position taken as indicating loss of synchronization.

9.8   Automatic retransmission request

If the receiver of information has a return channel available to send messages to the source, then it becomes possible for the receiver to call for the retransmission of messages that contain errors. This type of scheme is known as retransmission error control (REC) or, more commonly, as automatic retransmission request (ARQ). There are many possible protocols for the management of the transmitted and retransmitted packages, the main ones of which are described in the following sections.

The advantage of ARQ over forward error correction is that error detection can be done much more reliably than error correction. The previous sections show that the probability of undetected errors can easily be reduced to whatever figure is required. The disadvantage is that the message repeats use up link capacity and cause variable delays in the system, especially as it is not certain that a retransmission will be successful and several attempts may be required. For real-time applications, ARQ may be completely unsuitable. Nevertheless, the fact that ARQ sacrifices channel capacity rather than error rates when conditions are bad is desirable for many applications.

There are three main ways in which ARQ schemes operate. These are known as stop-and-wait (SW), go-back-N (GBN) and selective repeat (SR) ARQ. The latter two are sometimes grouped together under the heading *continuous ARQ*. It is also possible to create interesting hybrids of ARQ and forward error control.

9.9 Stop-and-wait ARQ

In stop-and-wait ARQ, the transmitter sends a message and waits for acknowledgment of correct reception before sending the next message or repeating the last one as appropriate. The waiting time will depend on the round-trip delay of the link plus processing time for the message and the acknowledgment. If the interval between the start of a message and the start of the next (or the repeat) is enough to contain N messages, the efficiency of the link usage, which is the ratio of correctly received messages to the number on an error-free uncoded link, is

$$\eta_{sw} = \frac{1 - P}{N} \frac{k}{n} \tag{9.9}$$

where P is the probability of message error and a (n,k) code is used for error detection. It is assumed here and subsequently that the probability of an acknowledgment being lost is negligible, but if that is not the case the probability of message error can be increased to include such an event.

In the case where the link delays are long, the best strategy might seem to be long messages to keep down the value of N. Unfortunately the longer the message, the higher the message error rate, which will limit the length that can be used. If the waiting time is A bit periods and message length is n, then $N - 1 = A/n$. If a fixed number of bits, c, is devoted to parity checks, and for random bit error rate p

$$\eta_{sw} = \frac{(1 - p)^{A/(N-1)}}{N} \left[1 - \frac{c(N - 1)}{A} \right]$$

With $c = 20$, $p = 10^{-4}$, $A = 1000$ and assuming N is an integer, the efficiency has its maximum value of 0.44 at the lowest value of N, namely 2. For a longer delay $A = 700\,000$ with $c = 20$, $p = 10^{-5}$, the optimum efficiency is 0.046 for $N = 9$.

Thus SW-ARQ is not viable with long delays and is in any case best suited to the situation where there is time-sharing of the link and the gaps between messages can be assigned to other users.

9.10 Go-back-N ARQ

The transmitter sends messages continuously and, after some delay, starts to receive acknowledgments from the receiver. If any message is not acknowledged or is indicated as being in error, then the transmitter returns to the problem message and restarts the sequence from that point, shown in Figure 9.2 for the case where the transmission goes back by five messages ($N = 5$). The transmission consists of a number of sequences which run for $N - 1$ messages

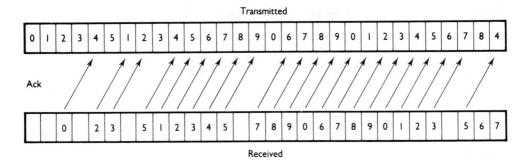

Figure 9.2 Go-back-5 ARQ

beyond the first detected error and then restart from the message in error. Note that the messages need to be numbered in case an acknowledgment is not received and the sequence is repeated when the receiver is not expecting it. Message numbers can be reused, but there must be a cycle of at least N, and $2N$ might be safer.

If a sequence contains n correctly received messages followed by one containing an error, the number of transmitted messages is $n + N$, of which n are accepted by the receiver. Over many sequences, the link efficiency is

$$\eta_{\text{GBN}} = \frac{\bar{n}}{\bar{n} + N} \frac{k}{n}$$

where k/n is the rate of the error detecting code.

Now the probability of correct reception of n messages followed by incorrect reception of the next is

$$P(n) = P(1 - P)^n$$

from which we can calculate

$$\bar{n} = \sum_{n=0}^{\infty} nP(1 - P)^n$$

This sum is found to be equal to $(1 - P)/P$, giving

$$\eta_{\text{GBN}} = \frac{1 - P}{1 + (N - 1)P} \frac{k}{n} \tag{9.10}$$

It is found that relatively short messages give a low message error rate, but that the efficiency of the coding, including the message numbering, means that messages cannot be too short. If we say $N - 1 = A/n$ as for SW ARQ, $k = n - c - \log_2 2N$ and the random bit error rate is p, then

$$\eta_{GBN} = \frac{(1 - p)^{A/(N-1)}}{1 + (N - 1)[1 - (1 - p)^{A/(N-1)}]} \times$$

$$\left[1 - \frac{N - 1}{A}(c + \log_2(A) - \log_2(N - 1) + 1) \right]$$

For $c = 20$, $p = 10^{-4}$ and $A = 1000$, the maximum efficiency is 0.815 at $N = 3$. For $c = 20$, $p = 10^{-5}$ and $A = 700\,000$, the maximum efficiency is 0.122 at $N = 366$. Both are better than for SW-ARQ, but even here the efficiency is low when the delay is long. Even with a well-designed scheme, the efficiency may still be too low to consider for many applications.

9.11   Selective repeat ARQ

This is a form of continuous ARQ in which the transmitter repeats only the message that is in error, as shown in Figure 9.3. This is clearly less wasteful of capacity than the previous forms of ARQ. The efficiency of SR-ARQ is just the probability of message reception multiplied by the rate of the coding, taking into account the overheads for message numbering

$$\eta_{SR} = (1 - P)\frac{k}{n} \qquad (9.11)$$

This gain is not achieved without some loss, and in this case the repeated messages arrive out of sequence. If the messages are self-sufficient and the order is not important, then this is of no concern. In many cases, however, correct

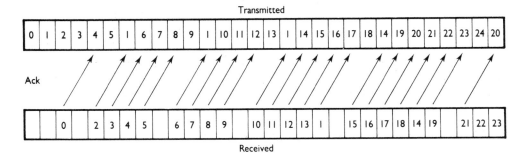

Figure 9.3 Selective repeat ARQ

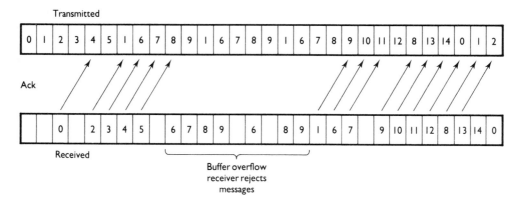

Figure 9.4 Selective repeat ARQ with five-message buffer

ordering is required, in which case the receiver must provide buffering for all the messages correctly received after the one that was in error. It is not possible, however, to guarantee that the messages will be received on the second attempt or within any finite number of attempts. The amount of message buffering required is therefore theoretically infinite unless some amendment to the protocol is introduced.

One common variant of SR-ARQ to allow finite receiver memory operates in conjunction with a buffer of N messages, where N is the number of messages that can be accommodated in the time between the start of a message and the start of its repeat. (N is thus defined the same as for SW-ARQ and GBN-ARQ.) The transmitter sends messages in sequence and receives acknowledgments until a message is not acknowledged. It then inserts the unacknowledged message into the sequence. If the message is not acknowledged the second time, the transmitter goes back in the revised sequence by N messages to prevent the problems that would otherwise arise from overflow of the receiver's buffer. This is illustrated in Figure 9.4.

The limited message buffer also limits the range of numbers used for the messages. If a message number n is lost, its repeat takes the place of message $n + N$. If the second repeat is lost, the reversionary procedure starts at a point where message $n + 2N - 1$ would otherwise have occurred. It is therefore essential that at least $2N$ numbers are provided without repetition. In practice it might be confusing if the original number n is reused shortly after it has finally been received, and so at least $3N$ numbers are generally provided.

9.12   ARQ in communications protocols

A number of standard communications protocols incorporate some form of ARQ. An example is the high-level data link control (HDLC) protocol, which is based on the IBM synchronous data link control (SDLC). The ANSI (American National Standards Institute) advanced data communication control procedure (ADCCP) is closely related and the CCITT X-25 LABP (balanced link access procedure) is a subset.

Messages in HDLC contain synchronization flags at the start and end of each message (8 bits each), an 8-bit address, an 8-bit control, the information packet (if present) and a 16-bit CRC. The control field contains two 3-bit fields for message numbers, one to number the message being sent and one to show the number of the message currently expected from the other end. It is possible to add a further 8 bits to the control field to extend the message numbering to 7 bits. This is commonly done when long delays are expected, e.g. for satellite communication links. Thus message numbers are in the range 0–7 (normal numbering) or 0–127 (extended numbering).

Showing that message number n is expected automatically acknowledges the message before n and all previous messages that have not been acknowledged. A poll/force bit can be set in the control field to force explicit acknowledgment of a particular message. It is also possible to set the control packet to a supervisory format, i.e. without information. Messages may then be acknowledged as before, messages from n onwards may be rejected and the previous messages acknowledged, or a specific message may be rejected. Thus both GBN and SR modes of ARQ can be supported.

Assuming that 3-bit numbers are used, any transmitter can afford to have, at most, seven messages unacknowledged. If eight messages were unacknowledged, the transmitter would not know whether a subsequent acknowledgment showed receipt of all the messages or none of them. Once the maximum number of messages is outstanding, the transmitter must stop.

This is not the place to undertake a detailed explanation or analysis of the possible modes of operation of HDLC. It is worth pointing out, however, that protocols of this type are not necessarily going to provide the best throughput possible for either GBN-ARQ or SR-ARQ. The restricted range of message numbers will limit efficiency for links with long delay times and could mean that selective repeat will not show the expected improvements over GBN.

9.13   Hybrid ARQ/FEC

There are many ways in which ARQ can be combined with forward error correction (FEC) to produce a hybrid showing some of the characteristics of both approaches. The idea is to provide the reliability associated with ARQ without the extremes of capacity loss that are encountered in high error conditions. Some of the ways in which hybrids may be created are explained below.

The obvious way of producing an ARQ/FEC hybrid is to use a code for partial error correction, with detection of more severe errors. This is called a type I hybrid. The code could be a normal error correcting code but using only part of the minimum distance for correction. Alternatively, an error detecting code could be applied and an outer error correcting code added, as described by Kasami *et al.* (1986). The inner code would be intended to detect the decoding errors of the outer code. When errors are detected but not corrected, a retransmission is requested. The error correction is designed to reduce the effective channel error rates encountered by the ARQ. The throughput will be lower than pure ARQ for low bit error rates because of the extra parity checks associated with error correction, but at higher error rates the throughput should be improved. In principle the efficiency can be calculated from the previous formulae after inclusion of the effects of error correction on code rate and message error rates.

A type II hybrid attempts to overcome the disadvantage of type I by restoring the throughput at low error rates. The initial transmission contains parity bits intended for error detection. If a retransmission is needed it consists of parity symbols from an *invertible* code, plus error detecting parity checks. An invertible code is one in which the information may be obtained from the parity, e.g. rate 1/2 RS codes or any cyclic code shortened to rate 1/2. If the second transmission is received without error, the information is decoded from it. If it contains errors, the information from the first and parity from the second transmissions are put together to form an error correcting code.

There are several variations on the type II idea, some of which are somewhere between types I and II in classification. For example, an inner error detecting code plus an outer error correcting code may be used with the outer code punctured for first transmission. On second transmission the missing parity bits may be restored or a different puncturing pattern used. The code could be either a convolutional code or a RS code. Adaptive coding schemes in which the code rate is decreased in response to a high error rate can also be considered to fall into this category.

9.14   Error concealment

Some types of data carry a large amount of inherent redundancy. Examples might be digitized voice or picture information where little use has been made of data compression techniques. The data is usually intended for subjective appreciation, i.e. to be heard or seen. In these circumstances, errors may go unnoticed if they do not exceed certain thresholds. Moreover it may be possible to screen out the errors and use the natural redundancy in the data to reduce the subjective effects, thus allowing a higher channel error rate before there is noticeable degradation. This is called error concealment, and it falls into the realm of digital signal processing. Such processing must be done with a knowledge of the nature of the data and the subjective effects of the concealment technique. The techniques available include substitution of past data, extrapolation from past data, interpolation and replacement with random sequences.

The importance of error concealment as a strategy for error control is that it often works well on data where ARQ is unsuitable. Real-time speech or picture processing could not, for example, tolerate the variable delays imposed by pure ARQ. Using either error concealment or ARQ according to the nature of the data can, however, provide a viable error control strategy based on error detection for a wide range of data types.

It should be realized that when data has high natural redundancy, there will exist, or be under development, techniques for data compression. Compressed data will be more vulnerable to errors, or rather the effects of errors will be subjectively more noticeable. Nevertheless data compression plus forward error correction may be far more efficient in channel usage than uncompressed data with error detection and concealment.

9.15   Further reading

The weight structures of codes and their properties in error detection are very comprehensively covered in most books on coding. Any of the major books of this decade, Clark and Cain (1981), Lin and Costello (1983), Blahut (1983) or Michelson and Levesque (1985), may be consulted.

In contrast, good treatments of ARQ are rare. The best sources are Lin and Costello (1983, 1984) who have full treatment of the throughputs of different schemes, flowcharts for the protocol implementations and many references. Books on computer networks are often good sources for communication protocols incorporating ARQ. One excellent example is Schwartz (1987). Performance analyses of different protocols may be found there and in Kaul (1978, 1979) and Sastry (1982). Easton (1981) shows how standard protocols often degrade the performance of SR-ARQ and how new protocols should be designed.

9.16   Exercises

1   How many codewords of weight 3 and weight 4 are there in a (15,11) Hamming code? If the code were

    (a) expurgated to (15,10) by removal of all odd weight codewords;
    (b) expanded to (16,11) by inclusion of an overall parity check,

how would these values change?

2   For a (15,11) Hamming code, find the probability of undetected error for the following cases:

    (a) Random errors weight 3.
    (b) Random errors weight 4.
    (c) Burst errors length 4.
    (d) Burst errors length 5.
    (e) Burst errors length 6.

3   Find the number of codewords of a (15,11) RS code of weight 5 and 6. Hence find the probabilities that random errors affecting five or six symbols will be undetected.

4   An error detection scheme requires the worst-case probability of undetected errors to be 10^{-6}. How many parity bits are required?

5   A cyclic code generated by $g(X) = X^4 + X^3 + X^2 + 1$ is to be used for synchronization. Find the synchronization point for a received sequence 0110011100111. What would happen if the received sequence were 0010011100111? Comment on the result.

6   The code of Exercise 5 is to be shortened by 1 bit. Find the codewords and, by inspection, the synchronization point for the sequence 10101110110110. Hence compare the robustness of the synchronization process with that of Exercise 5.

     Using the methods for shortened codes discussed in Section 3.16, devise a circuit that will enable the delayed bit to cancel the residual effect from n bits previously.

7   Select possible ARQ schemes for the following data requirements:

    (a) Occasional messages sent over a TDMA link.
    (b) Messages to specific addressees from a source with high transmission requirements but where each addressee receives only occasional messages. Each message is self-contained.
    (c) Image pixels transmitted over satellite channels for non-real-time processing.
    (d) Image pixels passed from one computer to another nearby computer for non-real-time processing.
    (e) Digitized speech.

8   In a GBN-ARQ system, the transmitter starts to send messages number from 0 onwards. Show the message sequence if $N = 5$ and messages 1, 3, 1, 5 and 6 are not acknowledged.

9   Repeat Exercise 8, assuming SR-ARQ with a buffer of five frames and messages 1, 3, 1, 7 and 9 unacknowledged.

10
Selection of a coding scheme

10.1   Introduction

In the previous chapters, similar techniques have been grouped together and their characteristics studied, leading to conclusions about their applicability. Only Chapters 6 and 8 have shown any sort of problem-oriented approach, examining the techniques that are appropriate for a particular problem. The purpose of this chapter is to rectify the imbalance by addressing the subject from the point of view of the engineer with a problem who needs to identify the possible solutions. In particular, the way in which system features shape the final solution will be discussed.

The system factors that affect the choice of a coding scheme are the data, the channel and specific user constraints. That includes virtually everything. The data can have an effect through its structure, the nature of the information and the resulting error-rate requirements, the data rate and any real-time processing requirements. The channel affects the solution through its power and bandwidth constraints and the nature of the noise mechanisms. Specific user constraints often take the form of cost limitations, which may affect not only the codec cost but also the possibility of providing soft-decision demodulation.

One further factor that affects choice of a coding scheme is prejudice or, as it is more kindly known, familiarity. Practitioners of coding tend to divide into two camps, those who favour block codes and those who favour convolutional. Prejudice is inevitable, I must admit to it myself, and familiarity is certainly a valid consideration. Nevertheless I hope to show that the characteristics of the problem may point towards a particular solution that should be considered even if it goes against previous allegiances.

The understanding of this chapter does not require much detailed knowledge of codes. It does, however, require a good general understanding of the benefits and disadvantages of a wide variety of coding schemes, so that these can be put into a system context by the discussions that follow.

10.2   General considerations

The major purpose of incorporating coding into the design of any system is to reduce the costs of the other components. Reliable communications can usually be obtained by simple, yet costly, methods such as increasing power. A well-designed coding scheme should result in a lower overall system cost for an equivalent or better performance. If this objective is to be met, however, the designer needs to make a careful choice and be aware of the whole range of available techniques. Having said that, it can be argued that two major code types, either individually or in combination, can meet a very wide range of system requirements. The codes in question are convolutional codes with soft-decision Viterbi decoding and RS codes. Massey (1984) and Berlekamp *et al.* (1987) give contrasting views on coding philosophy.

Convolutional codes are highly suitable for AWGN channels, where soft decision is relatively straightforward. The coding gains approach the asymptotic value at relatively high bit error rates, so that at bit error rates of 10^{-5}–10^{-7} in Gaussian conditions, convolutional codes are often the best choice. Many types of conditions, however, can give rise to non-Gaussian characteristics where the soft-decision thresholds may need to adapt to the channel conditions and where the channel coherence may mean that Viterbi decoding is no longer maximum likelihood. The complexity of the decoder also increases as the code rate increases above 1/2, so that high code rates are the exception. Even at rate 1/2, the channel speed that can be accommodated is lower than for RS codes, although it is still possible to work at over $100\,\mathrm{Mbits\,s}^{-1}$, which is more than enough for many applications!

Reed Solomon codes have almost exactly complementary characteristics. They do not generally use soft decisions, but their performance is best in those conditions where soft decision is difficult, i.e. non-Gaussian conditions. In Gaussian conditions the performance curves exhibit something of a 'brick wall' characteristic, with the codes working poorly at high bit error rates but showing a sudden transition to extremely effective operation as the bit error rate reduces. Thus they may show very high asymptotic coding gains but need low bit error rates to achieve such gains. Consequently they are often advantageous when bit error rates below 10^{-10} are required. Error rates as low as this are often desirable for machine-oriented data, especially if there is no possibility of calling for a retransmission of corrupted data. The decoding complexity reduces as the code rate increases, and in many cases decoding can be achieved at higher transmitted data rates. They can also, of course, be combined with other codes (including convolutional codes or other RS codes) for concatenated coding.

The above considerations certainly do not mean that other types of codes have no place in error control. Many considerations will lead to the adoption of other solutions, as will be seen from the discussions below. Nevertheless, mainstream interests in future systems are likely to concentrate on Viterbi-decoded convolutional codes and RS codes, and the designer wishing to adopt a standard, 'off-the-shelf' solution is most likely to confine his or her attention to these alternatives.

10.3 Data structure

If information is segmented into blocks, then it will fit naturally with a block coding scheme. If it can be regarded as a continuous flow, then convolutional codes will be most appropriate. For example, protecting the contents of computer memories is usually done by block coding because the system needs to be able to access limited sections of data and decode them independently of other sections. The concept of data ordering applies only over a limited span in such applications. On the other hand, a channel carrying digitized speech or television pictures might choose a convolutional scheme. The information is here considered to be a continuous stream with a definite time order. The effects of errors will be localized, but not in a way that is easy to define.

It is important to separate the structure of the data from the characteristics of the channel. The fact that a channel carries continuous data does not necessarily mean that the data is not segmented into block form. Less obvious, but equally important, a segmented transmission does not necessarily imply segmented data. A time division multiple-access (TDMA) channel, for example, may concentrate several continuous streams of information into short bursts of time, but a convolutional code may still be most appropriate. With adequate buffering, the convolutional code on any stream may be continued across the time-slots imposed by the TDMA transmission.

10.4 Information type

It is conventional to assess the performance of coding schemes in terms that involve bit error rates. This is not really appropriate for many types of information, and the most appropriate measure will often affect the choice of a coding scheme. Indeed it is difficult to think of any application in which the bit error rate is directly important. If discrete messages are being sent, with every bit combination representing a totally different message, then the message error rate is of crucial importance; the number of bit errors in each wrong message is not important at all. Even with information that is subjected to some kind of sensory evaluation (i.e. it is intended for humans, not machines), not all bits are equal. In most cases there are more and less significant bits or some bits whose subjective importance is different from that of others. Digitized speech without any data compression carries a number of samples, each of which has a most and a least significant bit. Only if errors affect all bits equally will bit error rate provide a measure of subjective quality. If the speech is at all compressed, the bits will represent different types of information, such as filter poles or excitation signals, and the subjective effects will vary. Data intended for subjective evaluation may be suitable for error concealment techniques.

Errors on a coded channel can be placed into four categories. There are those that are corrected by the code and allow the information to be passed on to the destination as if those errors had never occurred. There are errors that are detected but that are not corrected and there are errors that are not detected at all. Finally there are errors that are detected but the attempted correction gives the wrong result. Errors are passed on to the destination in the last two cases. For many applications it is important to minimize the probability of unsuspected errors in the decoder output. This will bias the user towards block codes, which often detect errors beyond the planned decoding weight, and away from forward error correction which accepts that undetected decoding errors will occur. The strength of the bias depends on the consequence of errors. If an error could start the next world war it is obviously of more importance than one that causes a momentary crackle on a telephone line.

Acceptable error rates will depend not only on the type of data, but also on whether the data will be processed on- or off-line. If data are to be processed immediately, it may be possible to detect errors and invoke some other strategy such as calling for retransmission. Off-line processing means that errors cannot be detected until it is too late to do anything about it. As a result the error rate specification will commonly be lower.

Note that there must always be some level of errors that is considered acceptable. It is easy to set out with a goal of eliminating all errors. Achieving this goal would require infinite time and an infinite budget.

10.5   Data rate

It is difficult to put figures on the data rates achievable using different codes. This is partly because any figures given can quickly become out of date as technology advances, and partly because greater speeds can usually be achieved by adopting a more complex, and therefore more expensive, solution. Nevertheless, for a fixed complexity, some codes can be processed more rapidly than others.

The codes that can be processed at the highest data rates are essentially simple, not very powerful, codes. Examples are codes used purely for error detection and convolutional codes decoded by majority logic. Concatenated codes using short block inner codes are not far behind because the computations on the RS codes are done at symbol rate, not bit rate, and the block codes used are extremely simple. It follows that RS codes alone are in the highest data rate category. Viterbi-decoded convolutional codes are fast, provided the input constraint length is not too long, say no more than 8. BCH codes and convolutional codes with sequential decoding can also be used at similar rates provided hard decision only is required. Soft-decision sequential decoding, Meggit decoders, block codes with soft decision and the more complex concatenated schemes are capable of only moderate data rates.

Of course the required data rate affects the choice of technology too; the more that can be done in hardware, the faster the decoding. Parallelism can increase decoding speeds, but with higher hardware complexity and therefore cost. A data rate of a few thousand bits per second could allow a general-purpose microprocessor to be used for a wide range of codecs, but obviously that would be uneconomic for volume production. Many of the influences of data rate on system design will be closely bound up with economics.

10.6   Real-time processing

If real-time data processing is required, the decoder must be able to cope with the link data rates. This may be achieved at the expense of delays by, for example, decoding one sequence while the next is being buffered. The decoding delay may in some cases become significant, especially if it is variable.

Forward error correction requires a decoding delay which, in most cases, depends on the exact errors that occur. Nevertheless, there is usually a certain maximum delay that will not be exceeded. Buffering the decoded information until the maximum delay has expired can therefore produce a smooth flow of information to the destination. Two major factors determining the delay will be the data rate and the length of the code. Information theory tells us that long codes are desirable, but for many applications long delays are not. Thus the maximum acceptable delay may limit the length of the codes that can be used.

If no maximum decoding delay can be determined, then the decoded information will come through with variable delays which can cause havoc with real-time information. The main error control strategy that exhibits variable delays is ARQ because one cannot guarantee that any resend will be successful. Sequential decoding of convolutional codes also exhibits variable delays. These problems may be overcome by use of a suitable ARQ/FEC hybrid, or by adopting a time-out on the sequential decoder, accepting the consequent burst of errors.

10.7   Power and bandwidth constraints

These constraints drive the solution in opposite directions. In the absence of bandwidth constraints one would use a low-rate concatenated code to achieve high coding gains or very low error rates. Very tight bandwidth constraints, making binary modulation incompatible with the required data rate and error rates, are rare at present outside the sphere of signalling over telephone lines. When such conditions are encountered, the Ungerboeck codes of Chapter 8 provide the most likely solution. It may be expected, however, that developments will take place in coding techniques for these conditions as the need increases.

Assuming that the major aim of coding is to reduce the power requirement for a given error rate, high coding gains would appear to be desirable. There can be no doubt that the highest gains are achievable using concatenated codes, the only serious rival being relatively long convolutional codes with soft-decision sequential decoding. If the bit error rate requirement is less stringent, convolutional codes with hard-decision sequential decoding or soft-decision Viterbi decoding provide the highest gains on a Gaussian channel. Spectacularly high gains are, in principle, available on bursty or compound channels using RS codes or other appropriate techniques. In practice, however, the transmitter will have to provide sufficient power for reasonably successful demodulation during the worst conditions. As a result the overall system may be overdesigned for the best conditions, providing lower error rates than are strictly necessary in order to cope with the worst-case conditions.

10.8   Channel error mechanisms

Ideally one would design a coding scheme for the precise conditions encountered on the channel. In practice, the channel may not be well characterized and the coding scheme may have to show flexibility to cope with the range of possible conditions. For slowly varying channel conditions that exhibit approximate Gaussian conditions over appreciable periods of time, adaptive coding schemes are a natural choice. These often use punctured convolutional codes, or they may be based around ARQ/FEC hybrids. For slowly varying channels, adaptive coding is preferred, but for uniform noise with occasional bursts of interference a type I hybrid FEC/ARQ scheme is the obvious choice. For channels that may fluctuate rapidly between states, producing mixtures of bursty and random errors, a wide variety of diffuse error correcting schemes, including interleaving, are available. Reed Solomon codes may also be considered to fall into this category; although optimized neither for random errors or general bursts, their low redundancy overhead and erasure-filling capability makes them a good choice for a variety of channel conditions.

10.9   Cost

Any error control scheme is merely a part of a larger system and its costs must be in proportion to its importance within the system. Bearing in mind that error rates may be reduced by the use of higher transmitted power, the aim of coding is to be more cost-effective than other solutions. That, however, is often not the main way in which cost constraints are experienced in a coding system; the major part of the costs of error control are incurred at the decoder, placing the burden of the economics onto the receiving equipment. Since the owners of transmitting and receiving equipment may be different, the economic considerations may not be resolved to optimize overall system costs. Decoder costs must be assessed in terms of what the receiver will be prepared to pay.

A number of fairly straightforward rules may be stated. Firstly as previously indicated, the decoder costs dominate in a forward error correction scheme. Error detection is therefore much cheaper than error correction. High data rates will cost more than low data rates. Complex codes with multiple error correction will cost more than simpler codes. For many applications, however, the main factor affecting cost will be whether there is a codec available commercially or whether it will need to be developed specially. Development costs must be spread across the number of receivers, and if the market is small or particularly cost sensitive it may be impossible to develop a codec for the particular needs of the application. In that case, the choice will be severely limited.

Any very specific advice about commercially available codecs would ensure that this book would quickly be out of date. As with all modern technologies, the product range is expanding and getting cheaper. At the more powerful end of the market, rate 1/2 Viterbi decoders are available and popular, and I would expect to see them incorporate puncturing for higher rates or for adaptable coding schemes (although the latter involve many other system complexities and costs). Certain RS codes are being adopted as standard and codecs are becoming available. Often this will be a spin-off from a particular mass market, such as compact disc players.

Although it seems a shame to sound a negative note, I believe that many interesting ideas in error control will never be implemented simply because their potential market will not make the development costs worthwhile. Similarly, many engineers working on error control techniques will never be allowed to design the best system technically; they will be forced to choose the best of what is available. Those who wish to have a relatively free hand should work on applications where the potential market is large or not very cost sensitive. The same constraints apply, of course, in many other areas. Some would say that is what engineering is all about and error control is, after all, an engineering topic rather than a mathematical one. The mathematics is the servant of the engineer, and the engineering is the most difficult part.

10.10   Applications

Satellite communication channels are often used to carry information that has considerable inherent redundancy, such as television or digitized speech. Relatively high bit error rates are therefore tolerable and convolutional codes are therefore firmly established, especially rate 1/2, $K = 7$. Many satellite channels suffer from slow fades resulting from precipitation and in such circumstances the usual approaches are either to provide sufficient power so that service is still acceptable in the worst case or to provide an adaptive coding scheme in which the code rate (and hence the channel capacity) is reduced as conditions get worse. In the latter case, puncturing is used to provide several higher-rate codes from one low-rate convolutional code. A (127,112) BCH code with $d_{min} = 6$, with the addition of a dummy bit to make the rate exactly 7/8, has been used for TDMA channels. In this case the use of a block code seems to be related to the TDMA operation, although as pointed out in Section 5.12 TDMA does not necessarily preclude the use of convolutional codes. Berlekamp *et al.* (1986) have described a 48 Mbit s^{-1} satellite TDMA system using a (204,192) RS code with 8-bit symbols to achieve bit error rates around 10^{-11}.

Deep space communications provide the closest approximation to an AWGN channel, and here concatenation using a rate 1/2, $K = 7$ convolutional inner code and (255,233) RS outer code with 8-bit symbols is standard. Interleaving to degree 4 is provided between the outer and inner codes. The scheme, described in more detail by Yuen (1983), was used on the NASA *Voyager* mission to Uranus and achieves a bit error rate of 10^{-6} at $E_b/N_0 = 2.53$ dB. Data rates of up to 2 Mbits s^{-1} can be achieved. For higher data rates, up to 300 Mbits s^{-1}, omission of the convolutional code is recommended.

Compact disc players have to operate at a fairly high bit rate (around 2 Mbits s^{-1}) and cope with a wide range of error conditions, all at a low cost. They employ a complex combination of line coding and concatenated RS codes with error concealment. The concatenated scheme is known as a cross-interleaved RS code and consists of two RS codes with 8-bit symbols with convolutional interleaving between the outer and inner codes. It could also be thought of as a product code, but with convolutional rather than block interleaving between the row and column codes. When reading the disc, there is a first stage of interleaving which separates consecutive bytes on the disc into different codewords. The inner code is a (32,28) code and is generally decoded for single errors with other detected error patterns causing erasure. The convolutional interleaving spreads the effect of decoding errors and erasures throughout several words of the outer (28,24) code. Any uncorrectable errors detected at this stage are spread by a final interleaving stage and concealed by interpolation. Sklar (1988) gives more details but reverses the usual terminology of outer and inner codes. One might expect that the requirements of digital audio tape would be the same and that consequently it would employ the same system. In fact it employs two RS codes, (32,26) and (32,28) with 8-bit symbols, as a product code. The main reason for the difference is the requirement to be able to edit tapes; the convolutional interleaving of compact disc would not provide the break points where editing could be achieved. Watkinson (1988) gives more detail.

References

Abramson, N. (1968), 'Cascade decoding of cyclic product codes', *IEEE Transactions on Information Theory*, **IT-14**, pp. 398–402.

Anderson, J.B. and Taylor, D.P. (1978), 'A bandwidth-efficient class of signal-space codes', *IEEE Transactions on Information Theory*, **IT-24**, pp. 703–12.

Anderson, J.B., Sundberg, C.-E.W., Aulin, T. and Rydbeck, N. (1981), 'Power-bandwidth performance of smoothed phase modulation codes', *IEEE Transactions on Communications*, **COM-29**, pp. 187–95.

Aulin, T. and Sundberg, C.-E.W. (1982), 'Minimum Euclidean distance and power spectra for a class of smoothed phase modulation codes', *IEEE Transactions on Communications*, **COM-30**, pp. 1721–9.

Aulin, T., Rydbeck, N. and Sundberg, C.-E.W. (1981), 'Continuous phase modulation', *IEEE Transactions on Communications*, **COM-29**, pp. 187–95.

Berlekamp, E.R., Shifman, J. and Toms, W. (1986), 'An application of Reed Solomon codes to a satellite TDMA system', MILCOM 86, Monterey, Calif.

Berlekamp, E.R., Peile, R.E. and Pope, S.P. (1987), 'The application of error control to communications', *IEEE Communications Magazine*, **25**, no. 4, pp. 44–57.

Bhargava, V.K., Haccoun, D., Matyas, R. and Nuspl, P.P. (1981), *Digital Communications by Satellite*, Wiley, New York.

Blahut, R.E. (1983), *Theory and Practice of Error Control Codes*, Addison Wesley, Reading, Mass.

Blahut, R.E. (1987), *Principles and Practice of Information Theory*, Addison Wesley, Reading, Mass.

Brigham, E.O. (1988), *Fast Fourier Transform and its Applications*, Prentice Hall, Englewood Cliffs, NJ.

Cain, J.B., Clark, G.C. and Geist, J.M. (1979), 'Punctured convolutional codes of rate $(n-1)/n$ and simplified maximum likelihood decoding', *IEEE Transactions on Information Theory*, **IT-25**, pp. 97–100.

Chase, D. (1972), 'A class of algorithms for decoding block codes with channel measurement information', *IEEE Transactions on Information Theory*, **IT-18**, pp. 170–82.

Clark, G.C. Jr. and Cain, J.B. (1981), *Error Correction Coding for Digital Communications*, Plenum, New York.

Easton, M.C. (1981), 'Design choices for selective–repeat retransmission protocols', *IEEE Transactions on Communications*, **COM-29**, no. 7, pp. 944–53.

Farrell, P.G. and Campello de Souza, R.M. (1982), 'An upper bound on the minimum distance of binary cyclic codes, and a conjecture', IEEE International Symposium on Information Theory, Les Arcs, France.

Farrell, P.G. and Daniel, J.S. (1984), 'Metrics for burst error characterisation and correction', IEE Colloquium on Interference and Crosstalk in Cable Systems, London.

Forney, G.D. (1966a), Concatenated Codes, MIT Press, Cambridge, Mass.

Forney, G.D. (1966b), 'Generalised minimum distance decoding', IEEE Transactions on Information Theory, IT-12, pp. 125–31.

Forney, G.D., Gallager, R.G., Lang, G.R., Longstaff, F.M. and Qureshi, S.W. (1984), 'Efficient modulation for band limited channels', IEEE Journal on Selected Areas in Communications, SAC-2, no. 5, pp. 632–47.

Gallager, R.G. (1968), Information Theory and Reliable Communications, Wiley, New York.

Haykin, S. (1988), Digital Communications, Wiley, New York.

Jelinek, F. (1969), 'A fast sequential decoding algorithm using a stack', IBM Journal of Research and Development, 13, pp. 675–85.

Kasami, T., Fujiwara, T. and Lin, S. (1986), 'A concatenated coding scheme for error control', IEEE Transactions on Communications, COM-34, pp. 481–8.

Kaul, A.K. (1978), 'Performance of HDLC in satellite communications', COMSAT Technical Review, 8, no. 1, pp. 41–87.

Kaul, A.K. (1979), 'Performance of data link control protocols over synchronous TDM communication channels', COMSAT Technical Review, 9, no. 1, pp. 203–31.

Kobayashi, H. (1971), 'Correlative level coding and maximum likelihood decoding', IEEE Transactions on Information Theory, IT-17, pp. 586–93.

Lender, A. (1964) 'Correlative digital communication techniques', IEEE Transactions on Communication, COM-12, pp. 128–35.

Lin, S. and Costello, D.J. (1983), Error Control Coding: Fundamentals and applications, Prentice Hall, Englewood Cliffs, NJ.

Lin, S. and Costello, D.J. (1984), 'A survey of various ARQ and hybrid ARQ schemes and error detection using linear block codes', IEEE Communications Magazine, 22, no. 12.

MacWilliams, F.J. and Sloane, N.J.A. (1977), The Theory of Error-correcting Codes, North Holland, New York.

Masamura, T., Samejima, S., Morihiro, Y. and Fuketa, H. (1979) 'Differential detection of MSK with non–redundant error correction', IEEE Transactions on Communications, COM-27, pp. 912–8.

Mason, S. and Zimmerman, P. (1960), Electronic Circuits, Signals and Systems, Wiley, New York.

Massey, J.L. (1984), 'The how and why of channel coding', Proceedings of the International Seminar on Digital Communications, Zurich.

Mazur, B.A. and Taylor, D.P. (1981), 'Demodulation and carrier synchronisation of multi–h phase codes', IEEE Transactions on Communications, COM-29, pp. 257–66.

McEliece, R.J., Rodemich, E.R., Rumsey, H. and Welch, L.R. (1977), 'New upper bounds on the rate of a code via the Delsarte–MacWilliams inequalities', IEEE Transactions on Information Theory, IT-23, pp. 157–66.

Michelson, A.M. and Levesque, A.H. (1985), Error Control Techniques for Digital Communication, Wiley, New York.

Muilwijk, D. (1981), 'Correlative phase shift keying – a class of constant envelope modulation techniques', *IEEE Transactions on Communications*, **COM-29**, pp. 226–36.

Odenwalder, J.P. (1970), 'Optimal decoding of convolutional codes', Ph.D. dissertation, School of Engineering and Applied Science, UCLA.

Oppenheim, A.V. and Schafer, R.W. (1975), *Digital Signal Processing*, Prentice Hall, Englewood Cliffs, NJ.

Proakis, J.G. (1983), *Digital Communications*, McGraw-Hill, Tokyo.

Raveendra, K.R. and Srinivasan, R. (1987) 'Coherent detection of binary multi–h CPM', *IEE Proceedings Part F*, **134**, pp. 416–26.

Sastry, A.R.K. (1982), 'Error control in digital satellite networks using retransmission schemes', *Computer Communications*, **5**, no. 1, pp. 23–8.

Schwartz, M. (1987), *Telecommunication Networks – Protocols, modeling and analysis*, Addison Wesley, Reading, Mass.

Shannon, C.E. (1948), 'A mathematical theory of information', *Bell Systems Technical Journal*, **27**, pp. 379–423 and 623–56.

Shannon, C.E. (1949), 'Communication in the Presence of Noise', *Proceedings IRE*, **37**, p. 10.

Sklar, B. (1988), *Digital Communications – Fundamentals and applications*, Prentice Hall, Englewood Cliffs, NJ.

Ungerboeck, G. (1977), 'Trellis coding with expanded channel signal sets', 1977 IEEE International Symposium on Information Theory, Abstract.

Ungerboeck, G. (1982), 'Channel coding with multilevel phase signals', *IEE Transactions on Information Theory*, **IT-28**, pp. 55–67.

Wainberg, S. and Wolf, J.K. (1972), 'Burst decoding of binary block codes on q–ary output channels', *IEEE Transactions on Information Theory*, **IT-18**, no. 5, pp. 684–6.

Watkinson, J. (1988), *The Art of Digital Audio*, Focal Press, London.

Wei, L.-F. (1984a), 'Rotationally invariant convolutional channel coding with expanded signal space – part I: 180°', *IEEE Journal on Selected Areas in Communications*, **SAC-2**, no. 5, pp. 659–71.

Wei, L.-F. (1984b), 'Rotationally invariant convolutional channel coding with expanded signal space – part II: nonlinear codes', *IEEE Journal on Selected Areas in Communications*, **SAC-2**, no. 5, pp. 672–86.

Yuen, J.H. (ed.), (1983), *Deep Space Telecommunications Systems Engineering* Plenum, New York.

Index

adaptive coding 127, 182, 190
ADCCP 181
additive inverse 71, 72, 74
additive white Gaussian noise channel 4, 15–20, 186
algebraic decoding 82
ARQ 169, 176–83
  hybrids with FEC 181–2
  incorporation into protocols 180–1
associative law 71
asymptomatic coding gain 17–19
asymptotic coding gain, of Ungerboeck codes 166
AWGN channel 4, 15–20, 186

bandwidth 20, 159–61, 168, 189
BCH code 16, 67–8, 81–4, 86–9, 95–6, 104–5, 108, 188, 192
Berlekamp–Massey algorithm 97, 99–101, 107
Berlekamp–Preparata codes 140
bi-orthogonal code 152, 153
binary arithmetic 23–4
binary symmetric channel 4
bit error rate 13–18, 95, 126
bit synchronization 175
block code 3, 9–15, 23–44, 46–68, 70–108, 134, 135–8, 139–42, 144–8, 150–5, 156–7
block interleaving 141–2
block synchronization 175
bound
  Elias 44
  Gallager 138, 140, 141
  Gilbert–Varsharmov 42–3
  Griesmer 39, 41–2
  Hamming 34, 39, 40
  McEliece 44
  Plotkin 39, 40–1

Reiger 135
Singleton 39, 42
branch metric 119, 120–2
burst
  distance 148
  end-around 135
  length 134, 148
bursty channel 4, 18, 133–4, 190
Burton codes 139

catastrophic error propagation 117–18, 130
channel capacity 1, 19–20
chase algorithm 108, 152, 154–5
code
  rate 3, 113, 191–2
  trellis 118–19
codec 31–3, 34–6
coding gain 15–18, 134, 166, 186, 190
commutative law 71
compact disc 192
complementary error function 8
complexity, of decoder 35, 124, 186
compound channel 5, 133–4, 140–1
concatenation 19, 150–2, 155–7, 186, 188, 189, 192
conjugate roots 78, 86
constraint length 113, 124, 128, 191–2
continuous ARQ 176
convolution 48–9, 87, 89
convolutional
  code 3, 17, 18, 110–31, 134, 138–9, 140, 141, 142–3, 150, 151, 155–6, 160, 164, 182, 185, 186, 187, 188–92
  interleaving 143–4, 192
Cooley–Tukey algorithm 107–8
correlative decoding 152, 154
coset 34

cost, effects of   190–1
CRC   173–4
cross-interleaved Reed Solomon code   192
cyclic
    code   46–68, 80–108, 135–8, 139–41, 145–8,
        152, 173–6, 182
    redundancy check   173–4

data
    rate   188–9
    structure   187
decision boundary   160
decoder
    Meggit   57–65, 66–7, 135
    Viterbi   110, 119–24, 126–8, 150, 186, 188,
        190, 191
    complexity   35, 124, 186
decoding
    delay   35, 189
    incomplete   34
    window   123
deep space communications   192
degree of polynomial   49
differential phase shift keying   4
diffuse
    channel   5, 133–4, 140–1
    codes   141
digital audio tape   192
dimension of block code   29
discrete Fourier transform   70, 84–5, 88, 90–6,
    101–4, 106–8
distance   5, 6–7, 9–11
    structure of convolutional codes   114–17
distributive law   71
division of binary polynomials   51, 53, 54
DPSK   4
dual code   152, 172

Eb/No   15–16, 19–20, 134, 160–1
edge
    frequencies   101–4
    symbols   102–4
efficiency of
    GBN-ARQ   178–9
    SR-ARQ   179
    SW-ARQ   177
Elias bound   44
encoder state diagram   113–14
end-around burst   135
energy per bit   15
equivalence of codes   26, 27, 43, 111
erasure   22, 104–7, 140, 141
    locator polynomial   105–7

error
    concealment   182–3, 192
    detection   31–2, 95, 169–83
    evaluator polynomial   97
    exponent   19, 156
    locator polynomial   68, 87–9
    propagation   124, 130
    rate
        bit   13–18, 95, 126
        message   14, 18
    trapping   135–6
Euclid's algorithm   89, 97–9, 107
Euclidean distance   159, 163–4, 166
even parity   26–7
exclusive-OR   24, 36
expanded code   37
expurgated code   65–7, 174
extended Reed Solomon code   101–4
extension field   73–4, 77–9

factorization of polynomial   79
Fano
    algorithm   127–8
    metric   127
feedback decoding   130, 138
finite field   23–4, 70–9
fire code   136–8, 139, 141
Fourier transform   70, 84–5, 88, 90–6, 101–4,
    106–8
frame synchronization   175
free distance   17, 115–17, 127
frequency domain decoding   88–96
    effect on bit error rate   95
frequency shift keying   19, 153
FSK   19, 153

Gallager
    bound   138, 140, 141
    code   139
Galois Field   70–9
generalised minimum distance decoding   157
generating function of convolutional code
    117, 125
generator
    matrix   28–9, 41, 153–4
    polynomial   48–51, 53–4, 56–7, 61–2, 64–7,
        80, 83, 108
    polynomials, for convolutional codes   112,
        114, 115–16, 118, 126–7
Gilbert–Varsharmov bound   42–3
go–back–N ARQ   176, 177–9
Golay code   34, 61
Good–Thomas algorithm   108

Griesmer bound   39, 41–2
group codes   43
guard space   138–9, 141

Hamming
    bound   34, 39, 40
    code   31, 34, 47–8, 51, 66, 81, 171, 172
    distance   9, 164
hard decisions   5
hardware complexity   35
HDLC   180
Hsaio codes   39
hybrid ARQ/FEC   181–2, 189, 190

incomplete decoding   34
inner code   151–7
input
    constraint length   113
    frame   112, 114, 155
interference   4, 133, 141
interleaving   4, 140, 141–4, 147, 151, 155–6,
        190, 192
invertible code   182
irreducible polynomial   78, 108
Iwadare–Massey codes   138

Justesen code   157

key equation   89, 91, 92, 93, 96–7, 104, 106

length of
    block code   29
    concatenated code   151
    cyclic code   50–1
linear
    code   24–7, 111
    independence   28

M–ary phase shift keying   160–1, 166, 167
MacWilliams identity   172
majority logic decoding   130, 154, 188
maximal length code   152–3, 172
maximum likelihood decoding   5, 9–11, 104,
        110, 118–23, 155
McEliece bound   44
Meggit decoder   57–65, 66–7, 135
memory
    constraint length   113
    order   112–13, 114
memoryless channel   4, 118
message error rate   14, 18
metric
    branch   119, 120–2

path   119–22, 127–8
metrics   6–8
MFSK   153
minimum
    distance   5, 12–13, 14, 17–18, 28, 51, 64–6,
        68, 87–8, 115, 129, 140
    polynomial   78, 80
    shift keying   168
    weight codeword   28, 88
modulation   4, 15–16, 159–61
modulo–2 arithmetic   23–4, 26–7
MPSK   160–1, 163, 166, 167
MSK   168
multilevel BCH code   86, 97
multipath   133
multiplicative inverse   71, 72–3

nesting of codes   150
noise power spectral density   7, 15–16, 19–20,
        134, 160–1
non-systematic code   26, 27, 111

odd parity   26–7
orthogonal
    code   152, 153, 157, 159
    signalling   19, 153, 157, 159
outer code   150–2, 155–7
output
    constraint length   113
    frame   112, 114, 142–3

parity
    check matrix   29–33, 37–9, 42, 80–3
    checks   26–7, 28–33
    even   26–7
    odd   26–7
path metric   119–22, 127–8
perfect code   34, 61
performance curves   15–18
phase shift keying   15–16
Plotkin bound   39, 40–1
polynomial
    irreducible   78, 108
    primitive   51–2, 73–4, 78
    roots of   78–81, 86, 87, 96
premultiplying of syndrome   59–60, 64–5
primitive element   72, 73–4, 78
product code   141, 144–8, 192
protocols, effect on ARQ operation   180–1
PSK   15–16
punctured code   126–7, 141, 182, 190

QAM   161–2, 163–5, 166, 167

QPSK 166
quadrature amplitude modulation 161–2, 163–5, 166, 167
quaternary phase shift keying 166

rate 3, 113, 191–2
read-only memory 29, 35–6
real time requirements 128, 176, 189
REC 169
recursive extension 89, 91–2, 93, 94–5, 96, 99, 104, 106–7
Reed Muller code 152, 153–4
Reed Solomon code 24, 85, 86–7, 88–95, 101–4, 105–8, 139–40, 150–2, 155–7, 171, 182, 186, 188, 190–2
Reiger bound 135
retransmission error control 169
ROM 29, 35–6
root of unity 84

satellite communications 191–2
SDLC 181
SECDED codes 37, 38–9, 65–7, 174
selective repeat ARQ 176, 179–80
sequential decoding 127–8, 189–90
set partitioning 162–7
shadowing 133
Shannon 1, 19, 21
Shannon–Hartley theorem 20
shortened codes 37–9, 64–5, 176, 182
simplex code 152–3, 172
Singleton bound 39, 42
soft decision 5, 7–8, 17, 104, 108, 110, 124, 125, 128, 152, 154–5, 157
spectral zeros 86–96, 101–3
squared Euclidean distance 159, 163, 164, 166
stack algorithm for sequential decoding 127, 128
standard array 33–4
state diagram 113–17
stop–and–wait ARQ 176, 177
structure of data 187
superchannel 151
symbol 3, 13–15, 23–4, 86

synchronization 175
symmetric channel 4
synchronization
    bit 175
    block 175
    frame 175
    of demodulator 16
    properties of convolutional codes 124
    symbol 175
syndrome 31–4, 40, 54, 57–67, 82, 83, 89, 93, 97, 99, 101, 103, 106, 129–30, 142, 175
    decoding 129–30, 142
systematic code 9, 27, 29, 31, 52–3, 111, 129, 141

table look-up decoding 129
TDMA 187, 192
threshold decoding 129, 130
time division multiple access 187, 192
transfer function of convolutional code 117
tree code 3, 113
trellis
    code 113
    for convolutional code 118–19
type I hybrid 181–2
type II hybrid 182

Ungerboeck
    code 160, 162–8
    set partitioning 162–7

Viterbi decoding 110, 119–24, 126–8, 150, 186, 188, 190, 191

weight distribution 116–17, 170–2
Winograd algorithm 108

X–25 LABP 181

Zech logarithm 75, 76–7